Early Civilizations in the Americas
Biographies and Primary Sources

Early Civilizations in the Americas
Biographies and Primary Sources

Sonia Benson

Deborah J. Baker, Project Editor

U·X·L
An imprint of Thomson Gale, a part of The Thomson Corporation

Detroit • New York • San Francisco • San Diego • New Haven, Conn. • Waterville, Maine • London • Munich

THOMSON

GALE

Early Civilizations in the Americas: Biographies and Primary Sources

Sonia Benson

Project Editor
Deborah J. Baker

Editorial
Michael D. Lesniak, Sarah Hermsen, Allison McNeill

Rights Acquisitions and Management
Shalice Shah-Caldwell, William Sampson

Imaging and Multimedia
Kelly A. Quin, Lezlie Light, Dan Newell

Product Design
Jennifer Wahi, Pamela Galbreath

Composition and Electronic Prepress
Evi Seoud

Manufacturing
Rita Wimberley

Cover photograph: Montezuma, photo-graph by Archivo Iconografico, S.A. Cor-bis. Reproduced by permission.

While every effort has been made to ensure the reliability of the information presented in this publication, Thomson Gale does not guarantee the accuracy of data contained herein. Thomson Gale accepts no payment for listing; and inclusion in the publication of any organization, agency, institution, publi-cation, service, or individual does not imply endorsement by the editors or publisher. Errors brought to the atten-tion of the publisher and verified to the satisfaction of the publisher will be cor-rected in future editions.

LIBRARY OF CONGRESS CATALOGING-IN-PUBLICATION DATA

Benson, Sonia.

Early civilizations in the Americas. Biographies and primary sources / Sonia G. Benson; Deborah J. Baker, pro-ject editor.

p. cm. – (Early civilizations in the Americas reference library)

Includes bibliographical references and index.

ISBN 0-7876-7680-2 (hardcover : alk. paper) – ISBN 0-7876-9395-2 (ebook)

1. Aztecs–Biography. 2. Mayas–Biography. 3. Incas–Biography. 4. Indians of South—America–Biography. I. Baker, Deborah J. II. Title. III. Series.

F1219.74.B46 2005

972–dc22

2004020337

This title is also available as an e-book.
ISBN 0-7876-9395-2 (set).
Contact your Thomson Gale representative for ordering information.

Printed in the United States of America
10 9 8 7 6 5 4 3 2 1

Contents

Reader's Guide

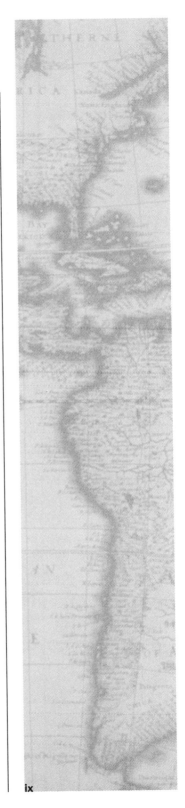

Many American history books begin with the year 1492 and the discovery of the Caribbean Islands by Spanish explorer Christopher Columbus (1451–1506). For the great civilizations of Mesoamerica and South America, though, 1492 proved to be the beginning of the end of their civilization. The products of thousands of years of history—the cities, the architecture, markets, governments, economic systems, legal systems, schools, books, holy shrines—even the daily prayers of the people—were about to be willfully eliminated by the conquering European nations. The rupture would prove so deep that many aspects of pre-Hispanic American culture and tradition were forever deleted from the human memory. Fortunately, some of the important history of the early civilizations has survived and more is being recovered every day.

The three-volume Early Civilizations in the Americas Reference Library provides a comprehensive overview of the history of the two regions of the American continents in which two of the world's first civilizations developed: Mesoamerica (the name for the lands in which ancient civilizations arose in Central America and Mexico) and the Andes Mountains region of South America (in present-day Peru and parts of Bolivia, northern Argentina, and Ecuador). In both cases, the history of civilization goes back thousands of years. Recent studies show that the first cities in the Americas may have arisen as early as 2600 B.C.E. in the river valleys of present-day Peru. The earliest evidence of civilization in Mesoamerica dates back to about 2000 B.C.E.

The year 1492 has traditionally been used to mark the division in the American past between history and prehistory. The historic times came after the Spanish arrived in 1492 with their writing systems and began to record events. Prehistory is defined as the time before there was writing to record history. We now know that it is incorrect to use the word "prehistory" for some of the ancient civilizations of Mesoamerica, which developed writing systems long before the Spanish arrived. But the written records left behind by the early civilizations are scarce and often difficult to decipher. Most historians also rely on evidence from the field of archaeology, the scientific recovery and study of artifacts, or objects made or used by humans of earlier times. By examining artifacts, archaeologists have been able to reconstruct parts of the daily lives of the people of early cultures. Analyzed in laboratories, artifacts can be accurately dated and provide a useful timeline for early civilizations.

Historians have accumulated many more details about the Incas, the Aztecs, and the Mayas, groups who were still around in large numbers when the Spaniards arrived, than they have for groups who lived in earlier times. We have many accounts from the conquistadores, the soldiers who overthrew the native civilizations, describing the people and their habits. We also have accounts written by indigenous (native) survivors of the Spanish conquest of the Inca empire in 1531 and the Spanish conquest of the Aztec empire in 1521. Many accounts by these survivors were narrated to Spanish missionaries who wrote them down. Some survivors, or their children in the next generation, were able to write or collect their own histories of the ancient civilizations.

The twenty-three biographical and primary source entries in *Early Civilizations in the Americas: Biographies and Primary Sources* are based on sources from all of the categories mentioned above: the early writing systems, archaeological artifacts, Spanish accounts, and the accounts of native people who told their experiences to the Spaniards or wrote in the Spanish language.

The biographical information about people who existed before the Spanish arrived usually comes from oral traditions, the memorized stories handed down generation to generation. The story of Pachacutec, the remarkable founder of the Inca empire, for example, comes to us through hundreds of years of spoken transmission. Some of the biographies may arise from archaeological discovery, such as the biography of Pacal, the Maya king who went to great lengths to leave behind his story on an elaborate, inscribed tomb that reveals much to experts about his rule.

Primary sources from the early American civilizations are a combination of artifact and text. Included in this volume are many photographs of artifacts: from *quipus,* the knotted cord counting devices used to keep track of the vast holdings of the Inca empire, to the Maya stelae, the inscribed and sculpted stone pillars with their written histories, to the Aztec Sun Stone, a monument or time piece with hundreds of symbols, glyphs, and pictorial representations on its thirteen-foot face. To help the reader understand the writing systems of Mesoamerica, the volume includes diagrams and illustrations of glyphs, calendars, and numbering systems, and selections from the codices (painted books). The volume's textual documents are the writings of witnesses to the Spanish conquest of the American civilizations or people in direct communication with people who were there. Each primary source entry is accompanied by a detailed introduction to the source and many points for consideration or research.

A note about the use of the word "civilization" in these volumes. The word "civilization" is used here to convey the type of organization and the size of a society, and certainly not to make a quality judgment about whether the society was sophisticated or refined. Besides the civilizations that arose in Mesoamerica and the Andean region, there were thousands of indigenous societies throughout the two American continents with varying levels of the kind of organization experts call "civilization." The civilizations featured in Early Civilizations of the Americas Reference Library are the New

World civilizations that developed around the same time and with some patterns similar to those of the Old World: Mesopotamia, Egypt, the Indus Valley, and China. Their history has been little known until the last century; indeed, only recent studies have included the Americas in the list of the world's first civilizations.

Features

Early Civilizations in the Americas: Biographies and Primary Sources is divided into three chapters: the Incas, the Mayas and their Ancestors, and the Aztec Empire. Each chapter contains both biography and primary source sections and is arranged loosely by topic and chronology. In addition, a timeline for each specific civilization is included in each chapter. Sidebar boxes that highlight people and events of special interest are sprinkled throughout the text, and each entry offers a list of additional sources that students can consult for more information. The material is illustrated by 63 black-and-white photographs and illustrations. The volume begins with a "Words to Know" section that introduces students to difficult or unfamiliar terms, and concludes with a general bibliography and a subject index so students can easily find the people, places, and events discussed throughout *Early Civilizations in the Americas: Biographies and Primary Sources*.

Early Civilizations in the Americas Reference Library

Early Civilizations in the Americas: Biographies and Primary Sources is one of two components of the three-volume U•X•L Early Civilizations in the Americas Reference Library. The other title in the set is:

- *Early Civilizations in the Americas: Almanac* (two volumes) presents the story of the development of early American civilizations from the earliest known societies to the Spanish conquest—the dates, locations, sites, history, arts and sciences, religions, economies, governments, and eventual declines of the great ancient American civilizations. Volume 1 features an overview of ancient civilization in general and a brief summary of modern theories about the earliest immigrants and early life in the Americas. The remainder of the volume focuses on the rise of the Andean civilization from the early urban centers to the Inca empire, including the societies of the Chavín, the Moche, the Nazca, the Wari, the Tiwanaku, and the Chimú. Volume Two focuses on the rise of the Mesoamerican civilizations, including the Olmecs and Zapotecs, the people of the great city of Teotihuacán, the Toltecs, and the Aztecs.

- A cumulative index of both titles in the U•X•L Early Civilizations in the Americas Reference Library is also available.

Comments and Suggestions

We welcome your comments on *Early Civilizations in the Americas: Biographies and Primary Sources* as well as suggestions for other topics to consider. Please write to: Editor, *Early Civilizations in the Americas: Almanac*, U•X•L, 27500 Drake Road, Farmington Hills, Michigan, 48331-3535; call toll-free: 800-877-4253; fax to 248-699-8097; or send e-mail via http://www.gale.com.

Words to Know

A

aboriginal: Native to the land; having existed in a region from the earliest times.

aclla: A young woman chosen by the Incas to live in isolation from daily Inca life while learning how to weave and how to make *chicha* and foods for festivals; some *acllas* were eventually married to nobles, and others became religious workers.

acllahuaci: A house where young women chosen by the Incas were isolated from daily Inca life; these women were trained in the arts of weaving fine cloth and making *chicha* and foods for festivals, and some went on to become religious workers.

administration: The management and work (rather than the policy making or public relations) of running a public, religious, or business operation.

administrative center: The place in a region or state in which the day-to-day operations of business, government, and religion are carried out.

administrator: A person who manages or supervises the day-to-day operations of business, government, and religious organizations.

adobe: Sun-dried earthen brick used for building.

agriculture: The science, art, and business of cultivating the soil, producing useful crops, and raising livestock; farming.

alliances: Connections between states or other political units based on mutual interests, intermarriage of families, or other relations.

alpaca: A member of the camelid family; a domesticated mammal related to the llama that originated in Peru and is probably descended from the guanaco. The Andeans used the long silky wool of the alpaca in their textiles.

altiplano: A high plateau; also referred to as a puna. In the central Andes Mountains of South America, where early Andean civilizations arose, the altiplano is about 12,000 to 16,500 feet (3,658 to 5,029 meters) high.

Amerindian: An indigenous, or native, person from North or South America.

anthropology: The study of human beings in terms of their social structures, culture, populations, origins, race, and physical characteristics.

aqueducts: Human-made channels that deliver water from a remote source, usually relying on the pull of gravity to transport the water.

archaeological excavation: The scientific process of digging up and examining artifacts, remains, and monuments of past human life by experts in the field.

archaeology: The scientific study of digging up and examining artifacts, remains, and monuments of past human life.

architecture: The art or practice of designing and constructing buildings or other large structures.

Arctic: The areas centered on the North Pole consisting of the Arctic Ocean and the lands in and around it.

artifact: Any item made or used by humans, such as a tool or weapon, that may be found by archaeologists or others who seek clues to the past.

astronomer: A person who studies the planets, sun, moon, and stars and all other celestial bodies.

astronomical observatory: A place designed to help people observe the stars and planets and all celestial phenomena.

astronomy: The science that deals with the study of the planets, sun, moon, and stars and all other celestial bodies.

atlantes: Large stone statues of warriors, often used as columns to support the roofs of Toltec buildings.

atlatls: Spearthrowers.

authoritarian government: Strict rule by the elite; in this type of government, leaders are not constitutionally responsible to the people, and the people have little or no power.

ayllu: A group of extended families who live in the same area, share their land and work, and arrange for marriages and religious rituals as a group; the basic social unit of the Andean peoples.

B

bajo: The Spanish word for "under," referring to lowlands or swampy depressions in the earth's surface. In a rain forest, *bajos* are generally wetlands from July to November and dry the rest of the year.

baptism: A Christian ritual celebrating an individual joining a church, in which sprinkling holy water or dunking signifies his or her spiritual cleansing and rebirth.

barbarian: A word used to describe people from another land; it often has a negative meaning, however, suggesting the people described are inferior to others.

basalt: A fine-grained, dark gray rock used for building.

bas-relief: A carved, three-dimensional picture, usually in stone, wood, or plaster, in which the image is raised above the background.

bioglyph: A symbolic animal or plant figure etched into the earth.

burial offerings: Gifts to the gods that are placed with the body of a deceased person.

C

cacao beans: Beans that grow on an evergreen tree from which cocoa, chocolate, and cocoa butter are made.

callanca: An Inca word meaning "great hall"; a place where people gathered for ceremonies and other events.

calpulli: (The word means "big house"; the plural form is *calpultin.*) Social units consisting of groups of families who were either related in some way or had lived among each other over the generations. *Calpultin* formed the basic social unit for farmers, craftspeople, and merchants. The precise way they worked is not known.

camelid: A family of mammals that, in the Americas, includes the llama, the alpaca, the vicuña, and the guanaco.

cenote: Underground reservoirs or rivers that become accessible from above ground when cave ceilings collapse or erode.

ceque: A Quechua word meaning "border"; *ceques* were imaginary lines that divided Cuzco into sections, creating distinct districts that determined a person's social, economic, and religious duties.

ceremonial centers: Citylike centers usually run by priests and rulers, in which people from surrounding areas gather to practice the ceremonies of their religion, often at large temples and plazas built specifically for this purpose.

chacmool: A stone statue of a man in a reclining position, leaning to one side with his head up in a slightly awkward position; the statue's stomach area forms a kind of platform on which the Toltecs placed a bowl or plate for offerings to the gods—sometimes incense or small animals, but often human hearts.

chasqui: A messenger who was trained to memorize and relay messages. *Chasqui* posts stood about a mile apart along the road system of the Inca empire. When a message was given to a *chasqui,* he would run to the next post and convey the message to the *chasqui* there, who would then run to the next post, and so on.

chicha: A kind of beer that Andean peoples made from maize or other grains.

chiefdom: A social unit larger and more structured than a tribe but smaller and less structured than a state, which is mainly governed by one powerful ruler. Though there are not distinct classes in a chiefdom, people are ranked by how closely they are related to the chief; the closer one is to the chief, the more prestige, wealth, and power one is likely to have.

chinampa: A floating garden in a farming system in which large reed rafts floating on a lake or marshes are covered in mud and used for planting crops.

chronicler: A person who writes down a record of historical events, arranged in order of occurrence.

city-state: An independent self-governing community consisting of a single city and the surrounding area.

codex: (plural: codices) A handmade book written on a long strip of bark paper and folded into accordion-like pages.

colca: Storehouse for food and goods.

colony: A group of people living as a community in a land away from their home that is ruled by their distant home government.

conquistador: (plural: conquistadores) The Spanish word for "conqueror"; in English, the word usually refers to the leaders of the Spanish conquests of Mesoamerica and Peru in the sixteenth century.

controversial: Tending to evoke opposing views; not accepted by everyone.

coya: The Sapa Inca's sister/wife, also known as his principal wife, and queen of the Inca empire.

creole: A person of European descent who is born in the Americas; in this book, a Spaniard who is born in Mexico.

cult: A group that follows a living religious leader (or leaders) who promote new doctrines and practices.

cultural group: A group of people who share customs, history, beliefs, and other traits, such as a racial, ethnic, religious, or social group.

culture: The arts, language, beliefs, customs, institutions and other products of human work and thought shared by a group of people at a particular time.

curaca: A local leader of a region conquered by the Incas; after the conquest, *curacas* were trained to serve their regions as representatives of the Inca government.

D

decipher: To figure out the meaning of something in code or in an ancient language.

deify: Place in a godlike position; treat as a god.

deity: A god or goddess, or a supreme being.

drought: A long period of little or no rainfall.

E

egalitarian: A society or government in which everyone has an equal say in political, social, and economic decisions and no individual or group is considered the leader.

El Niño: An occasional phenomenon in which the waters of the Pacific Ocean along the coast of Ecuador and Peru warm up, usually around late December, sometimes bringing about drastic weather changes like flooding or drought.

elite: A group of people within a society who are in a socially superior position and have more power and privileges than others.

empire: A vast, complex political unit extending across political boundaries and dominated by one central power, which generally takes control of the economy, government, and culture in communities throughout its territory.

encomienda: A grant to Spanish conquistadores giving them privilege to collect tribute from Amerindians in a particular region. The *encomendero* (grant holder) had the responsibility to train Amerindians in Christianity and Spanish, and to protect them from invasion.

Most *encomenderos,* however, treated the Amerindians under their grants like slaves, forcing them into inhuman labor conditions often resulting in the collapse or death of the workers.

epidemic: A sudden spreading of a contagious disease among a population, a community, or a region.

evolution: A process of gradual change, from a simple or earlier state to a more complex or more developed state.

excavation: The process of carefully digging out or uncovering artifacts or human remains left behind by past human societies so that they can be viewed and studied.

export: To send or transport goods produced or grown in one's home region to another region in order to trade or sell them there.

F

feline: A member of the cat family; or resembling a member of the cat family.

fertility: The capacity of land to produce crops or, among people, the capacity to reproduce or bear children.

frieze: A band of decoration running around the top part of a wall, often a temple wall.

G

geoglyph: A symbolic figure or character etched into the earth.

glyph: A figure (often carved into stone or wood) used as a symbol to represent words, ideas, or sounds.

government: A political organization, usually consisting of a body of people who exercise authority over a political unit as a whole and carry out many of its social functions, such as law enforcement, collection of taxes, and public affairs.

guanaco: A member of the camelid family; a South American mammal with a soft, thick, fawn-colored coat, related to and resembling the llama.

H

hallucinogenic drug: A mind- and sense-altering drug that may create visions of things not physically present.

heartland: The central region of a cultural group where their traditional values and customs are practiced.

hierarchy: The ranking of a group of people according to their social, economic, or political position.

highlands: A region at high elevation.

huaca: A sacred place, usually used for a temple, pyramid, or shrine.

human sacrifice: Killing a person as an offering to the gods.

I

iconography: A method of relaying meaning through pictures and symbols.

idol: A likeness or image of an object of worship.

import: To bring goods from another region into one's home region, where they can be acquired by trade or purchase.

Inca: The word Inca originally meant "ruler" and referred to the king or leader. It is also used to mean the original group of Inca family clans that arose to prominence in the city of Cuzco. As the empire arose, the supreme ruler was called the "Sapa Inca" and members of the noble class were called "Incas."

indigenous: Native to an area.

L

legend: A legend is a story handed down from earlier times, often believed to be historically true.

llama: A member of the camelid family; a South American mammal that originated in Peru and probably descended from the guanaco. Llamas were used for their soft, fleecy wool, for their meat, and for carrying loads.

logogram: A glyph expressing a whole word or concept.

logosyllabic: A mixed system of writing in which some symbols represent whole words or ideas, while other symbols represent the syllables or units of sound which make up words.

lowlands: An area of land that is low in relation to the surrounding country.

M

mammoth: An extinct massive elephant-like mammal with thick, long hair and long curved tusks.

mass human sacrifices: Large-scale killing of people—or many people being killed at one time—as offerings to the gods.

mercenary soldiers: Warriors who fight wars for another state or nation's army for pay.

Mesoamerica: A term used for the area in the northern part of Central America, including Guatemala, Honduras, El Salvador, and Belize, and the southern and central parts of present-day Mexico, where many ancient civilizations arose.

mestizo: A person having mixed ancestry, specifically European and Amerindian.

missionary: A person, usually working for a religious organization, who tries to convert people, usually in a foreign land, to his or her religion.

mit'a: A tax imposed on the common people by the Inca government; the tax was a labor requirement rather than a monetary sum—the head of every household was obliged to work on public projects (building monuments, repairing roads or bridges, transporting goods) for a set period each year.

mitima: An Inca resettlement policy that required potential rebels in newly conquered regions to leave their villages and settle in distant regions where the majority of people were loyal to the Inca empire; this policy helped the Incas prevent many uprisings.

monogamy: Marriage to one partner only.

monumental architecture: Buildings, usually very large, such as pyramids or temple mounds, that are used for religious or political ceremonies.

mummification: Preservation of a body through a complex procedure that involves taking out the organs, filling the body cavity with preservative substances, and then drying out the body to prevent decay; mummification can also occur naturally when environmental conditions, such as extreme cold or dryness preserve the body.

mummy: A body that has been preserved, either by human technique or unusual environmental conditions, such as extreme cold or dryness.

myth: A traditional, often imaginary story dealing with ancestors, heroes, or supernatural beings, and usually making an attempt to explain a belief, practice, or natural phenomenon.

N

Nahuatl: The language spoken by the Aztecs and many other groups in the Valley of Mexico.

New World: The Western Hemisphere, including North and South America.

nomadic: Roaming from place to place without a fixed home.

O

observatory: A building created for the purpose of observing the stars and planets.

obsidian: Dark, solid glass formed by volcanoes used to make blades, knives, and other tools.

offerings: Gifts for the gods.

oral tradition: History and legend passed from generation to generation through spoken accounts.

outpost: A remote settlement or headquarters through which a central government manages outlying areas.

P

Paleoamerican: A member of a theoretical first population group in the Americas; scholars use this term to make a distinction between this group and the Paleo-Indians, a later group, who are generally considered to be the ancestors of modern Amerindians.

Paleo-Indian: A member of the group of people who migrated to the United States from Asia during the last part of the Great Ice Age, which ended about ten thousand years ago; Paleo-Indians are thought to be the ancestors of modern Amerindians.

pampa: The partly grassy, partly arid plains in the Andean region.

pantheon: All of the gods that a particular group of people worship.

Patagonia: A vast barren flat-land spreading through Argentina and into Chile between the Andes Mountains and the Atlantic Ocean.

Peninsulares: People living in Mexico who were born in Spain.

pilgrim: A person who travels to a holy place to show reverence.

pilgrimage: A journey to a holy place to show faith and reverence.

plateau: A large, elevated level area of land.

polygamy: Marriage in which spouses can have more than one partner; in Inca society, some men had multiple wives, but women could not take multiple husbands.

pre-Columbian American: A person living in the Americas before the arrival of Spanish explorer Christopher Columbus in 1492.

prehistory: The period of time in any given region, beginning with the appearance of the first human beings there and ending with the occurrence of the first written records. All human history that occurred before there was writing to record it is considered prehistoric.

primogeniture: A system in which the oldest son inherits his father's position or possessions.

Q

Quechua: The Inca language, still spoken by Andean people today.

quetzal: A Central American bird with bright green feathers.

quinoa: A high-protein grain grown in the Andes.

quipu: Also *khipu.* A set of multicolored cotton cords knotted at intervals, used for counting and record keeping.

R

radiocarbon dating: A method of testing organic (once living) material to see how old it is. Radiocarbon dating measures the amount of carbon 14 found in a sample. All plant and animal matter has a set amount of carbon 14. When an organism dies, the carbon 14 begins to decay at a specific rate. After measuring the extent of the decay, scientists can apply a series of mathematical formulas to determine the date of the organism's death—and consequently the age of the organic matter that remains.

rain forest: Dense, tropical woodlands that receive a great quantity of rain throughout the year.

religious rites: Established ceremonial practices.

remains: Ancient ruins or fossils, or human corpses or bones.

ritual: A formal act performed the same way each time, usually used as a means of religious worship by a particular group.

S

sacrifice: To make an offering to the gods, through personal possessions like cloth or jewels, or by killing an animal or human as the ultimate gift.

sacrifice rituals: Ceremonies during which something precious is offered to the gods; in early civilizations, sacrifice rituals often involved killing an animal or sometimes even a human being—the life that was taken was offered as a gift to the gods.

Sapa Inca: Supreme ruler of the Incas.

sarcophagus: A stone box used for burial, containing the coffin and body of the deceased, or sometimes only the body.

scribe: Someone hired to write down the language, to copy a manuscript, or record a spoken passage.

script: Writing.

sedentary: Settled; living in one place.

shaman: A religious leader or priest who communicates with the spirit world to influence events on earth.

smallpox: A severe contagious viral disease spread by particles emitted from the mouth when an infected person speaks, coughs, or sneezes.

stela: (plural: stelea) A stone pillar carved with images or writing, often used to provide historical details or for religious or political purposes.

stonemasonry: The work of a skilled builder who expertly lays cut or otherwise fitted units of stone in construction.

subordinate: Subject to someone of greater power; lower in rank.

succession: The system of passing power within the ruling class, usually upon the death of the current ruler.

surplus: The excess above what is needed; the amount remaining after all members of a group have received their share.

syllabograms: Symbols that represent the sounds of a language (usually a combination of a vowel sound and consonants).

T

terrace: One of a series of large horizontal ridges, like stairs, made on a mountain or hillside to create a level space for farming.

theorize: Create an explanation based on scientific evidence or historical analysis that has not yet been proven.

tlatoani: A Nahuatl word meaning "speaker" or "spokesperson" used by the Aztecs to refer to their rulers, or "they who speak for others." The Aztec emperor was often called *huey tlatoani,* or "great speaker."

trance: An altered mental state.

transformation: Changing into something else.

tribute: A payment to a nation or its ruler, usually made by people from a conquered territory as a sign that they surrender to the imposed rule; payment could be made in goods or labor or both.

trophy head: The head of an enemy, carried as a token of victory in combat.

U

urbanization: The process of becoming a city.

ushnu: A large platform in a central part of a city plaza, where the king or noblemen stood to address the public or view public festivities.

V

Valley of Mexico: A huge, oval basin at about 7,500 feet (2,286 meters) above sea level in north central Mexico, covering an area of about 3,000 square miles (7,770 square kilometers) and consisting of some of the most fertile land of Mexico.

vicuña: A South American mammal related to the llama and having a fine silky fleece, often used by the Andeans for making textiles. The early Andeans hunted vicuña for skins and meat.

vigesimal: Based on the number twenty (as a numeric system).

Villac Umu: Inca term for chief priest.

W

welfare state: A state or government that assumes responsibility for the welfare of its citizens.

Y

yanacona: A commoner who was selected and trained in childhood to serve the Inca nobility, priests, or the empire in general; the position was a form of slavery.

Yucatán: A peninsula separating the Caribbean Sea from the Gulf of Mexico, which includes the nation of Belize, the Petén territory of northern Guatemala, and the southeastern Mexican states of Campeche, Quintana Roo, and Yucatán. Yucatán is also the name of a state of Mexico, in the northern portion of the Yucatán peninsula.

Z

ziggurat: A platform or terrace with a tall temple tower or pyramid atop it in ancient Mesopotamia.

Text Credits

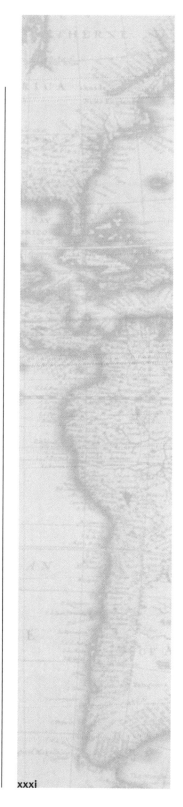

The following is a list of the copyright holders who have granted us permission to reproduce excerpts from primary source documents in *Early Civilizations in the Americas: Biographies and Primary Sources*. Every effort has been made to trace copyright; if omissions have been made, please contact us.

Copyrighted excerpts were reproduced from the following books:

Betanzos, Juan de. From "Chapters XI and XII," in *Narrative of the Incas*. Edited by Roland Hamilton and Dana Buchanan. Translated by Roland Hamilton and Dana Buchanan. University of Texas Press, 1996. Copyright © 1996. All rights reserved. Reproduced by permission of the University of Texas Press.

de la Vega, Garcilaso. From "Chapters I-III," in *Royal Commentaries of the Incas and General History of Peru*. Translated by Harold V. Livermore. University of Texas Press, 1966. Copyright © 1966. Reproduced by permission of the University of Texas Press.

The Incas

The Inca chapter of this volume is loosely arranged by topic and chronology. The entries cover the relatively short duration of the Inca empire—from 1438 to 1533—as well as the era surrounding its demise. (An empire is a vast political unit extending across political boundaries and dominated by one central power.) The opening entry is a biography of the first Inca emperor, **Pachacutec** (d. 1471), who extended Inca rule over an immense part of the central Andes Mountain region in South America and its millions of diverse peoples. Rightly or not, Pachacutec has been credited with most of the accomplishments of the Inca empire, including rebuilding the capital city of Cuzco, reforming the Inca religion, and creating a sophisticated government and economic system that held the empire together.

Pachacutec lived long before there were writing systems in the Andean region to record his life and works. His biography is correctly called legend (a story handed down from earlier times, often believed to be historically true). It has been formed over many centuries, beginning with Pachacutec's instructions for the Inca storytellers, dictating what

1

Quick Facts about the Incas

- The ancient Andean civilizations arose in the central portion of the Andes and along the coastal plains to the west; this area included almost all of present-day Peru, and parts of Bolivia, northern Argentina, and Ecuador.

- The Incas were a group of family clans that arrived in 1200 in the already-existing town of Cuzco, a city in the highlands of southeast Peru. The group had risen to prominence in the city by 1438, when the emperor Pachacutec began to expand the empire.

- The word *Inca* originally meant "ruler" and referred to the king or leader. The term *Incas* referred to the original group of Inca family clans that rose to prominence in the city of Cuzco. After the Incas gained power and developed a large empire, their supreme ruler was called the "Sapa Inca" and members of the noble class throughout the empire were called "Incas."

- The Incas called their empire Tawantinsuyu (also Tahuantinsuyu), which means "land of four quarters."

- The Inca empire existed from 1438 to 1533.

- At its peak, around 1525, the Inca empire included most of the Andean region; its population was somewhere between 9 million and 16 million people.

- Quechua was the Inca language and is still spoken by many Andean people today.

he wanted them to pass on to others about Inca history. After his death, Pachacutec was remembered almost universally as a great hero and the founder of the empire. The Incas told and retold his story and recited poems about his life, and members of each new generation memorized what they heard so that Pachacutec and his accomplishments would never be forgotten. When the Spanish arrived in 1531—bringing with them their writing system—a variety of people, Spanish and native, began to write down the life story of Pachacutec. Many different versions of his life were recorded at that time, but certain significant events and accomplishments prevail in most of them. Modern biographies of Pachacutec are constructed from bits and pieces of these early writings.

The Spanish-born writer **Juan de Betanzos** was one of the first to write down a version of Pachacutec's life. He included Pachacutec's story in *Narrative of the Incas,* a history of the Incas that he wrote in 1557. Betanzos was an interpreter who arrived in Cuzco not long after the Spanish conquest in 1533. His most vital connection to Inca history was his wife, Doña Angelina Yupanqui (also spelled Yupanque), who was the niece of Sapa Inca Huayna Capac; (ruled 1493–1525), the principal wife of Sapa Inca **Atahuallpa** (c. 1502–1533) and, after Atahuallpa's death, mistress to Spanish conquistador (Spanish word for "conqueror") Francisco Pizarro (c. 1475–1541). Betanzos viewed himself not as a writer but as a translator of the stories his wife and her family related to him. In the excerpt featured in this chapter, he depicts Pachacutec setting in motion the complex, empire-wide economic system that sustained the Incas.

Map showing important sites in the Inca empire.
Map by XNR Productions. The Gale Group.

Like other historians, Betanzos portrays Pachacutec as a precise leader who had an unusual amount of control over every aspect of the huge Inca empire. To maintain this control, Pachacutec and his representatives relied heavily on the *quipu* (or *khipu*), a set of dyed and knotted cords used to record numbers—of crops, populations, labor obligations, soldiers, and many other things that were important to the economic success of the empire. *Quipus* were also used to record nonnumerical information, though experts do not know what the knotted, colored cords signified in these cases. Some modern scholars theorize that, over time, *quipus* may have come to form a writing system as well as a numerical record-keeping system. Their theories, along with photos of *quipu* artifacts and illustrations of the Incas working with *quipus,* are presented in the third entry of this chapter.

This chapter also presents an excerpt from *Royal Commentaries of the Incas and General History of Peru* (two parts, 1609 and 1617) by the Peruvian writer and historian **Garcila-**

so de la Vega, who was known as "El Inca" (1539–1616). In this passage, Garcilaso, the son of a Spanish conquistador and an Inca princess, attempts to make some connections between Christian traditions and those of the Incas, comparing the members of the Inca *acllahuaci*—"house of the chosen women"—to a Catholic nunnery. Garcilaso hoped that this comparison would help the Spanish conquistadores appreciate Inca civilization as he did. He also hoped that his writing would be a tribute to the Inca empire and its past grandeur. His book is considered one of the first truly literary works of the Americas, meaning that his story of the Incas was expressed in a manner that was artistically satisfying.

A biography of Atahuallpa, the Sapa Inca at the time of the conquest, brings the focus to the last days of the empire. In his short life, Atahuallpa was involved in the principal events that destroyed the Inca civilization: a vicious civil war against his half brother that caused thousands of deaths, a smallpox epidemic that decimated the Inca population, and the fatal meeting with Spanish conquistador Francisco Pizarro and his army at Cajamarca.

The final entry in this chapter features illustrations of Atahuallpa's meeting with Pizarro and his capture by the Spanish. The illustrations were drawn by **Felipe Huaman Poma de Ayala** (c. 1535–c. 1615) for his massive work *La primer nueva corónica y buen gobierno* (*The First New Chronicle and Good Government,* written and illustrated 1587–1615). This twelve-hundred-page account of Inca history and life before and after the Spanish conquest included nearly four hundred drawings. Poma, a native Andean with royal Inca blood on his mother's side, wanted to present a history of native Andeans from an Andean perspective, an alternative to the prevailing Spanish accounts. After trying to work with the Spanish colonial government for many years, Poma felt betrayed by the Spanish. He thought that the Spanish ought to restore native Andeans as the rulers of the region. Poma's drawings are familiar to students of the Inca civilization; they appear throughout this chapter and in most modern histories of the Inca empire. They provide an informative visual record that brings the lost empire to life.

Each of the entries in this chapter presents different aspects of Inca civilization so that readers can consider the

Incas from a variety of angles. Along with the stories and traditions of Inca life, the chapter examines some of the sources that scholars use to develop histories of ancient civilizations, including text documents, artifacts, and drawings. The entries in the chapter are intricately linked to one another. While reading them and learning about the Incas, it is important to keep in mind that there is no true or final version of Inca history, only hundreds of stories, pictures, and artifacts—clues that offer insight into a lost civilization.

Timeline: The Incas

c. 7000–3000 B.C.E. Formerly nomadic people in the Andes Mountain region of South America begin to settle into rough homes and gradually form tiny villages.

3000 B.C.E. The Andean people in a number of different areas begin building very large ceremonial complexes and making advances in art, religion, politics, and trade.

c. 2600 B.C.E. The city of Caral arises in the Supe Valley of Peru, with thousands of permanent residents, complex architecture, trade, and smaller urban centers surrounding it. It may have been the first city of the Americas.

c. 7000 B.C.E.
The first human settlements were developed in Mesopotamia

c. 2680–2526 B.C.E.
Building of the Great Pyramids near Giza, Egypt

7000 B.C.E.   3000 B.C.E.

1800 B.C.E. Andean societies begin to organize themselves by the river valleys in which they live. Several large, advanced cities and some empires rise and collapse over the next centuries.

600 C.E. In the Andes Mountain region of South America *quipus* are being used by the Wari people and others for record-keeping and counting.

1200 The Incas rise to prominence in Cuzco, in the highlands of southeast Peru.

c. 1350 The Incas begin a series of military campaigns, conquering the communities surrounding Cuzco.

1438 Inca noble **Pachacutec** successfully fights the invading Chanca army at Cuzco and becomes Sapa Inca, or supreme Inca leader; this event marks the beginning of the one hundred-year Inca empire.

1471–1493 Pachacutec dies and his son Tupac Inca takes over as Sapa Inca of an ever-expanding Inca empire.

1493–1525 Huayna Capac rules the Inca empire, but takes up residence in Quito (Ecuador), dividing the Incas.

1525 Huáscar takes over the rule of the Inca empire, but his brother **Atahuallpa** continues to rule the armies in Quito.

1525 A deadly smallpox epidemic strikes the Inca empire. It will eventually kill an estimated 75 percent of the population of the Inca empire.

1529 Civil war breaks out among the Incas, with the forces of Huáscar fighting the forces of Atahuallpa.

1532 Atahuallpa captures Huáscar and becomes Sapa Inca.

1532 Spanish conquistador Francisco Pizarro and his expedition arrive at Atahuallpa's camp at Cajamarca. The

776 B.C.E.
Greece's first recorded Olympic games are held at Olympia

1200
Famine ravages England and Ireland throughout this century

1421
Mohammed I dies

1502
First slaves are shipped to the New World

800 B.C.E.   1200 C.E.   1400 C.E.   1500 C.E.

next day, at an agreed-upon meeting on the plaza, the Spanish slaughter about six thousand unarmed Incas and take Atahuallpa prisoner.

1533   Spaniards kill Atahuallpa and take over the rule of Cuzco and the Inca empire.

1536–1572   The Incas operate a rebel capital in Vilcabamba, a mountainous region northwest of Cuzco.

1540s   Spanish interpreter **Juan de Betanzos** marries the Inca princess Doña Angelina Yupanqui in Cuzco, Peru. She helps him write *Narrative of the Incas,* a history of the Inca empire, completed in 1557.

1572   **Garcilaso de la Vega, "El Inca,"** the son of a Spanish conquistador and an Inca noblewoman, begins to write his masterwork, *Royal Commentaries of the Incas and General History of Peru* (two parts, 1609 and 1617), a chronicle of the Inca civilization, from its origins to the arrival of the Spaniards.

1615   **Felipe Huaman de Poma de Ayala**, an Andean writer, completes his massive book *La primer nueva corónica y buen gobierno* (*The First New Chronicle and Good Government*) a 1,200-page history of the Andean peoples illustrated by nearly 400 drawings.

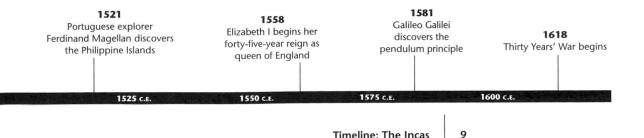

1521
Portuguese explorer
Ferdinand Magellan discovers
the Philippine Islands

1558
Elizabeth I begins her
forty-five-year reign as
queen of England

1581
Galileo Galilei
discovers the
pendulum principle

1618
Thirty Years' War begins

1525 C.E.   1550 C.E.   1575 C.E.   1600 C.E.

Pachacutec, or Pachacuti, Inca Yupanqui

Birth date unknown
Cuzco, Andean region, present-day Peru
Died 1471
Cuzco

Sapa Inca, or supreme ruler of the Inca empire

Pachacutec (pronounced pah-chah-KOO-teck) came to power within the small community of Incas in Cuzco (pronounced KOO-sko) in 1438; this marked the beginning of one of the world's greatest early civilizations. As Sapa Inca, or supreme ruler, Pachacutec greatly expanded Inca territory and at the same time devised a structured government, economy, and way of life that could sustain the many diverse peoples who would fall under Inca rule. Even though some of the accomplishments attributed to Pachacutec may be mythical and others may have been carried out by his son, Tupac Inca Yupanqui (ruled 1471–1493), or grandson, Huayna Capac (pronounced WHY-nah CAH-pahk; ruled 1493–1525), many historians consider Pachacutec one of the most remarkable leaders of all time.

"When he became Inca [ruler] his people were only an unimportant village community. At his death they ruled over the mightiest empire of South America."

Friedrich Katz, The Ancient American Civilizations.

A heroic rise to power

In the early fifteenth century the eighth Inca leader, Viracocha Inca, ruled over the town of Cuzco and a surrounding area of about 25 square miles (64.8 square kilometers). At that time there were several groups of people living peaceful-

Pachacutec Inca Yupanqui.
The Art Archive/Museo Pedro de Osma Lima/Mireille Vautier.

11

ly with one another in the area of Cuzco. However, sometime around 1438 the Chancas, a powerful and warlike group who lived northwest of Cuzco, prepared to attack the city. Viracocha fled the city with his chosen heir, Urco. He also took with him the noblemen of the city and all except one of his many sons. Viracocha's youngest son, Inca Yupanqui (also spelled Yupanque; later Pachacutec), was ashamed of his father and the nobles for running away and decided to stay and defend Cuzco against the Chancas.

After the nobles had left the city, Inca Yupanqui and a few loyal friends sent word to the rulers of neighboring towns that Cuzco needed help in defending itself against the Chancas. The neighboring rulers, aware that Inca Yupanqui had no forces of his own to assist in the battle, refused to commit themselves to the fight. Most said they would come only if Inca Yupanqui could build an army to back them up. This left Inca Yupanqui with only a few of his closest companions to defend the city. The young Inca began to spend his nights praying. Not long before the Chancas attacked, Inca Yupanqui is said to have received a vision from the sun god; this vision made Inca Yupanqui believe that he would receive help in the battle. On the day the Chanca army was due to strike Cuzco, Inca Yupanqui and the few men he could muster marched out of town to meet the Chancas in battle. According to the legends, a large army of men suddenly joined him as he approached the Chancas. Inca Yupanqui had never seen any of them before. Some accounts say this army was made up of stones that came to life to help Inca Yupanqui. By most accounts, Inca Yupanqui won his battle through the intervention of the gods.

After the battle, the noblemen who had fled with Viracocha Inca returned to Cuzco and pledged their loyalty to Inca Yupanqui. Neighboring cities sent their armies to Cuzco when they saw that he now had the forces to win the fight. Soon Inca Yupanqui had a massive army of a hundred thousand men from areas near and far. They knew a large force of Chancas and their allies would return to fight again. When the Chancas launched their second attack, Inca Yupanqui's army was ready for them. Many were killed on both sides, but the Inca army won, vanquishing the Chancas forever. Inca Yupanqui hanged the leaders of the Chanca army and then demanded that thousands of Chanca soldiers join his army

Enough Great Deeds for Two Sapa Incas

The legends of Pachacutec credit him with many great deeds, and most historians believe that he was a great emperor whose military feats and visions of empire changed the ancient world. However, the legends often seem to exaggerate the proportions of Pachacutec's achievements. One possible explanation for the great size and scale of his accomplishments is that they were in fact the work of two men: Pachacutec and his son Tupac Yupanqui. Tupac succeeded his father in 1471, becoming the tenth Sapa Inca. Tupac expanded the empire greatly, until its northern boundary reached present-day Quito, Ecuador, and its southern boundary extended to present-day Santiago, Chile.

According to Peruvian writer and historian Garcilaso de la Vega (1539–1616) in *Royal Commentaries of the Incas and General History of Peru* (1609), chroniclers sometimes confused Pachacutec (also called Inca Yupanqui) and his son Tupac Yupanqui. Garcilaso explains that this confu-

sion stemmed from a failure to understand the Inca naming system:

> The Spanish historians confuse these two Kings, father and son, giving the names of both to one. The father was named Pachacutec. The name Ynca [Inca] was common to all.... The word Yupanqui ... was also the name of this King [Pachacutec], and combining the two names, they [the Incas] formed Ynca Yupanqui, which title was applied to all the King Yncas, so that Yupanqui ceased to be a special name. These two names [Ynca Yupanqui] are equivalent to the names Caesar Augustus, given to all the [Roman] Emperors. Thus the Indians, [Incas or native Andeans] in recounting the deeds of their Kings, and calling them by their names, would say, Pachacutec Ynca Yupanqui. The Spaniards understood that this was one King, and they do not admit [recognize the existence of] the son and successor [one who takes over the throne from another ruler, usually upon his death] of Pachacutec, who was called Ynca Yupanqui, taking the two titles as his special name, and giving the same name to his own eldest son. But the Indians [native Andeans], to distinguish him from his father, called the latter Tupac (which means "He who shines") Ynca Yupanqui.

and fight for the Inca state. With an unbeatable new army, he was ready for more conquests.

Building the empire

After the defeat of the Chancas in 1438, Viracocha Inca gave up his position as king to his son, Inca Yupanqui, who took the name Pachacutec (or Pachacuti; the name means "he who changed the world" or "earthquake"). Pachacutec became the ninth Sapa Inca, or supreme ruler. Soon after taking power, he led an army south, into the Colloa area near Lake Titicaca and quickly conquered the region. In battle after battle, he forced the surrender of regional armies and added important new territory to his empire, extending Inca control over the central and southern highlands of present-day Peru. During these military campaigns, he organized the fighting himself, using strategy as well as brute force to conquer any resistance. Few armies could stop the Incas, and many communities did not bother to mount a defense.

The new regions Pachacutec added to the empire were usually allowed to govern themselves and retain their customs as long as they could produce goods or food for the empire and provide the labor demanded by the Incas. In governing the empire, Pachacutec did not force people to immediately adopt the Inca culture. Conquered peoples were allowed to practice their own religions and keep their own local governors; this may be the reason that there were not more rebellions within the Inca empire. As a ruler, though, Pachacutec was not always lenient (easygoing). He demanded absolute loyalty, and penalties for disobedience were severe. Pachacutec would not bend the rules, even for his own brother, who held a position as one of his military commanders. When this brother saw an opportunity to conquer Cajamarca, he ignored Pachacutec's orders to return home. His conquest was highly successful and brought a desirable new territory to the empire, but Pachacutec ordered that his brother be hanged for disobeying his orders.

Pachacutec focused on empire-building and military campaigns for more than twenty years of his long reign. In 1463, after large military campaigns in the north, the Sapa Inca turned military affairs over to his son Tupac (also called Tupa or Topa) Inca. Tupac would go on to greatly expand the Inca empire.

Rebuilding Cuzco

Freed from his military command, Pachacutec turned his attention to the capital city of Cuzco, which he decided to rebuild in splendor, reorganizing it from top to bottom. The tremendous amount of labor it took to build Cuzco's huge stone structures indicates the extent of Pachacutec's power. He began by ordering the evacuation of the city—that is, he forced everyone to leave—and then he had parts of it demolished. Then the massive labor projects began. Spanish chronicler Pedro de Cieza de León, quoted by Brian Fagan in *Kingdoms of Gold, Kingdoms of Jade* (1991), describes the building process: "[Pachacutec] ordered twenty thousand men in from the provinces, and that the villages supply them with food.... Four thousand of them quarried and cut the stones; six thousand hauled them with great cables of leather and hemp; the others dug the ditch and laid the foundations, while still others cut poles and beams for the timbers." Carrying out Pachacutec's commands, the Incas replaced small, thatched-roof houses with impressive stone structures. They transformed the village of Cuzco into a great city, worthy of its role as the capital of the Inca empire.

Pachacutec is said to have redesigned Cuzco in the shape of the sacred puma (a large wild cat resembling a lion). A magnificent fortress just north of the city, called Sacsahuaman (pronounced sox-ah-wah-MAHN), formed the head of the puma, and the two rivers that flowed through the city were diverted to form the tail. Within the city Pachacutec designed a huge central plaza for festivals and ceremonies; he also directed builders to construct a walled-in area off to the side for palaces and temples. He had the Coricancha, or Temple of the Sun, built to the south of the plaza at the heart of the city. Like other structures in the city center, the stone walls of the Coricancha were covered in gold. Pachacutec ordered that temples similar to the Coricancha be built in urban centers throughout the empire. Although he allowed the people he conquered to worship their own gods, Pachacutec demanded that they worship Inti, the sun god, as the supreme god.

Pachacutec ordered the construction of many other buildings in the city's core. There were *huacas* (sacred monuments), *callancas* (great halls), temples, and *colcas* (storehouses for food and goods). There was also a large complex called the *acllahuaci,* or "house of the chosen women," where carefully selected girls and women lived in isolation from the public. These girls and women played a special role in the religious ceremonies of the Incas. (See **Garcilaso de la Vega, El Inca** entry for more information on *acllahuaci*.)

The public buildings in Cuzco were made from large, precisely cut stones. The stonemasonry (cutting and fitting of

the stones) that went into these buildings was an architectural feat. The massive stone blocks that formed the walls were cut and sculpted so perfectly that they fit together like pieces of a jigsaw puzzle. Not even a piece of paper could fit between them. It is estimated that hundreds of thousands of people worked on these building projects over many decades. The city's plumbing was also remarkable. Stone-lined channels in the middle of the city's paved streets carried away waste in flowing water. At its peak before the Spanish conquest of 1533, Cuzco was home to a large number of people; population estimates range from forty thousand to one hundred thousand residents. Nearly five centuries later, Cuzco still stands. It is the oldest continuously inhabited city of the Americas.

Creating Inca institutions

During his reign, Pachacutec thoroughly reformed the Inca religion. Spanish chronicler and missionary (a person, usually working for a religious organization, who tries to convert people to his or her religion) Father Bernabé Cobo (1580–1657) describes Pachacutec's impact on the Inca religion in *Historia del Nuevo Mundo* (*History of the New World*, 1653). "He injected order and reason into everything; eliminated and added rites and ceremonies ... established the sacrifices and the solemnity with which the gods were to be venerated [worshiped], enlarged and embellished the temples with magnificent structures, income, and a great number of priests and ministers."

Pachacutec made it clear that he and all Sapa Incas were direct descendants of Inti, the sun god. He taught the empire's storytellers his own version of history and forbade them to repeat or create other versions. According to Pachacutec, there was no civilizing force in the world before the Inca kings came to power; Inti created the Incas to bring people out of chaos and to create a great civilization. This "history" served to unite Pachacutec's diverse empire beneath him, providing conquered peoples with a compelling story and explanation of Inca dominance. Pachacutec seems to have deliberately shaped history for his own political purposes. This is one reason why histories of the Incas that have been passed down through the ages cannot always be taken as literal fact.

Pachacutec was responsible for many other significant changes in the Inca culture. He required that everyone in his empire learn the Quechua (pronounced KECH-wah) language for the sake of efficient communication. (In the twenty-first century, about thirteen million people in the Andean region still speak this language.) Pachacutec ordered the building or rebuilding of roads and bridges, creating a highly efficient network for transportation and communication within the vast empire. He created a legal system that assigned specific punishments for crimes; he also introduced new laws that regulated the way people in the empire lived. Pachacutec's laws dictated how clean Inca homes had to be, when children should begin to work, and how unwanted children would be cared for. Pachacutec created thousands of official positions for police agents and inspectors to make sure the people of the empire were living by his rules.

Through military conquest and his many cultural achievements, Pachacutec lived up to his name: "he who changed the world." Utilizing advances developed by preceding Andean civilizations, Pachacutec devised a remarkable administrative system. Before this time central control over such a vast territory had never been carried out on such a large scale in the Andes. Pachacutec set up an efficient network of governors and administrators throughout the empire—guided by the Inca nobility but run by the local leaders—so that his vision could be carried out to the smallest detail even in the most remote regions. One of the principal instruments of organization he used was the *quipu,* a counting and record-keeping device invented and used by prior Andean cultures. The *quipu* (pronounced KEE-poo) consisted of a rope with many knotted cords attached to it; the knots signified the items being counted. With the help of the *quipu,* Inca representatives could account for every hour of human labor and every grain of food throughout the empire without any written records. (See **Juan de Betanzos** and *Quipu* entries for more information on the administration—the management and work of running a public operation—and record-keeping systems of Pachacutec.)

The death of Pachacutec

Well before his final days, Pachacutec arranged for his own funeral and even planned the mourning ceremonies for his subjects to observe. Like most Andean rulers, he believed his authority over his people extended beyond his life, and he expected his family and subjects to continue to honor him and serve him after his death. In making arrangements for his handling after death, he paid careful attention to symbols and rituals (formal acts performed the same way each time) surrounding the office of Sapa Inca. Pachacutec probably set the standard for the extreme ceremonial reverence with which Inca rulers were treated from his time onward.

When Pachacutec died of disease as a very old man (Pedro Sarmiento de Gamboa, in *History of the Incas,* claims that Pachacutec was 125 years old when he died), his relatives had the body mummified. That is, they removed the organs and then preserved the body by treating it with herbs and drying it out so that it would not decay. Thereafter, Pachacutec's mummified body was treated as if it were still alive. All of Pachacutec's relatives except for his son Tupac, the successor to the throne, continued to live in his *panaca* (the household of the dead Inca), where they could serve his mummified body and prepare it for appearances at public festivals and ceremonies. Tupac left the house and established a new kingdom and his own palace and property.

Tupac Inca's career (ruled 1471–1493) as ruler was nearly as remarkable as his father's, and he made even more territorial additions to the empire than his father did. Tupac Inca's son, Huayna Capac (ruled 1493–1525) succeeded him in 1493. When Huayna Capac died in 1525, the Inca empire had been in existence for almost ninety years. Thanks to Pachacutec's vision and leadership, this empire gave birth to one of the world's most remarkable civilizations.

For More Information

Books

Betanzos, Juan de. *Narrative of the Incas.* Translated and edited by Roland Hamilton and Dana Buchanan from the Palma de Mallorca manuscript. Austin: University of Texas Press, 1996.

Fagan, Brian M. *Kingdoms of Gold, Kingdoms of Jade: The Americas before Columbus.* London and New York: Thames and Hudson, 1991.

Katz, Friedrich. *The Ancient American Civilizations.* London: Phoenix Press, 2000.

Sarmiento de Gamboa, Pedro. *History of the Incas.* Translated by Clements Markham. Cambridge, England: The Hakluyt Society, 1907.

Von Hagen, Adriana, and Craig Morris. *The Cities of the Ancient Andes.* London and New York: Thames and Hudson, 1998.

Web Sites

Rostworowski, Maria. "The Incas." http://incas.perucultural.org.pe (accessed on December 14, 2004).

Juan de Betanzos

Excerpt from Narrative of the Incas
Originally titled *Suma y narración de los Yngas;* written in 1557

**Translated and edited by Roland Hamilton and Dana Buchanan
from the Palma de Mallorca manuscript, 1996**

The details known about the life of Juan de Betanzos, the author of *Narrative of the Incas,* are sketchy at best. His birth and death dates are unknown. Betanzos was born in Spain but traveled to the Americas as a young man. By the beginning of the 1540s he was living in Cuzco (pronounced KOO-sko), a Spanish colony (a group of people living as a community in a land away from their home that is ruled by their distant home government), and had already spent several years learning Quechua (pronounced KECH-wah), the language of the Inca people. He was one of the first to translate Quechua into Spanish and quickly earned a reputation among the Spaniards as the best interpreter in Cuzco. The Spanish colonial government in Peru hired him around 1544 to help write a bilingual (two-language) manual for Spanish missionary priests. The manual was designed to help these priests communicate with the Incas. It was a large project that involved translating basic Christian beliefs and prayers from Spanish to Quechua. The Spanish government hoped that speaking the native language would help the priests convert the Incas to Christianity more quickly.

Narrative of the Incas is believed to be one of the most authentic sources ever written about the Inca empire.

In the 1540s Betanzos married an Inca noblewoman named Doña Angelina Yupanqui (also spelled Yupanque; born c. 1522). Doña Angelina herself has a remarkable background. Her original name was Cuxirimay Ocllo. She was the niece of the eleventh Sapa Inca, or supreme ruler of the Incas, Huayna Capac (pronounced WHY-nah CAH-pahk; ruled 1493–1525). When Doña Angelina was only an infant, Huayna Capac chose her to become the principal wife (the main and legitimate spouse) of his son Atahuallpa (pronounced ah-tah-WAHL-pah; c. 1502–1533; ruled 1532–1533). In 1532, the ten-year-old Cuxirimay was brought to the Quito kingdom in the north, where she married Atahuallpa just before he became Sapa Inca. Shortly after the marriage took place, Atahuallpa was taken prisoner by the Spanish at Cajamarca. Cuxirimay stayed with him in prison until his death at the hands of the Spanish in 1533. In the years that followed, Cuxirimay probably converted to Christianity. She took the name Doña Angelina, and at some point she became the mistress of the Spanish conqueror Francisco Pizarro (c. 1475–1541); they produced two sons. After Pizarro's death in 1541, Doña Angelina married Juan de Betanzos. She then worked with Betanzos to record the story of the Incas.

In 1551 Betanzos received a commission (an order or job) from the Spanish viceroy (regional governor who represents the king of the ruling country) of Peru to write the history and traditions of the Incas. He worked on the project until 1557, when he stopped to take on a very different kind of project. At that time, there was still an Inca stronghold in the mountainous region of Vilcabamba, northwest of Cuzco; this rebel government had been in place since the first years of the Spanish takeover. The Vilcabamba government-in-exile was led by a series of Sapa Incas from the royal family. The Spanish had made many unsuccessful attempts to bring the rebel government back to Cuzco to live under Spanish rule. Betanzos asked for, and received, the post of interpreter with these Spanish ambassadors (diplomatic officials who represent a government or a society). Because he stopped writing his book to take this mission, the *Narrative of the Incas* ends in the year 1557, well before the end of the rebel government.

Narrative of the Incas is believed to be one of the most authentic sources ever written about the Inca empire. Because of his connections to the Incas through his wife, Betanzos was able to interview and record the testimony of Incas who were directly related to the Sapa Incas. According to Roland Hamilton and Dana Buchanan, who translated and edited the English version of the book in 1996, Betanzos had access to many members of Atahuallpa's family. Though these family members had little knowledge of the Sapa Incas who reigned before Pachacutec, they were well educated in Inca history that occurred after Pachacutec came to power in 1438. Hamilton and Buchanan make note of this fact: "Evidently, Doña Angelina and her family were taught epic poems detailing the life and times of their lineage from Pachacuti to Huayna Capac.... These poems included speeches or statements by the main characters in the account."

Scholars who have studied Betanzos's work believe he had little formal education, because there are few if any Latin influences on his writing. (Latin influence was evident in the writing of most educated Spanish writers of the time.) *Narrative of the Incas* is instead written in an informal, conversational style. Indeed, in a 1551 letter to the viceroy, which served as a prologue to the first part of the book, Betanzos describes his role in the book as that of a translator rather than a writer. The people he interviewed told their stories in their native Quechua language, and he merely wrote down a literal translation of their words. Besides providing a chronological history of the Incas, the book sets out many otherwise unknown details of the culture, such as the rituals (formal acts performed the same way each time) performed for important life events such as births, deaths, puberty, religious festivals, and so on. It describes legal, military, and government administration and many other aspects of Inca life.

Things to remember while reading the excerpt from *Narrative of the Incas:*

- In 1438 Pachacutec (pronounced pah-chah-KOO-teck; also called Inca Yupanque or Inca Yupanqui; ruled 1438–1471) became the ninth Inca king and the first Inca emperor, or Sapa Inca. Among the many challenges he faced was the task of putting together economic and government systems that could sustain the expanding empire. The ingenious systems he devised brought the Inca empire into its greatest period and maintained the strength of the empire for almost a hundred years. Many historians consider Pachacutec one of the most remarkable leaders of all time, and Betanzos is no exception. He portrays Pachacutec as a cultural hero—a man who changed the world through his own inventions—and as the true founder of the Inca culture.

- In the passage that follows, Pachacutec is in the process of creating some of the economic and governmental systems of his empire. Note the chain of command as he gives the top Inca lords their orders: They command the *orejones* (pronounced oh-ray-HOE-nays; Inca lords or nobles; *orejones* is a Spanish word meaning "big ears," a reference to the large earplugs that Inca nobility wore in their earlobes) to call the *caciques* (the leaders of the outlying cities and provinces) to a meeting. The *caciques,* or *curacas,* were local rulers whose city or region had been conquered by the Incas. Pachacutec allowed them to continue to rule as long as they pledged their loyalty to the Incas. In order to maintain control over the vast area of the empire and over millions of people, Pachacutec created a hierarchy, or ranking of the leaders. This system ensured that every person under his rule—top lords, *orejones,* local leaders, and common working people—would fulfill a specific role to support the empire.

- When the Incas conquered a region, they took ownership of all the land. When Pachacutec instructed the *caciques* to distribute the land among the people of their region, they distributed it in parcels to the *ayllus* (pronounced EYE-yoos) for farming. *Ayllus* were groups of extended families who lived close together in villages, towns, or farming settlements. They worked together and shared their land and animals as well as the goods they produced by farming. Along with supporting themselves, the members of the *ayllus* were required to use the lands that had been distributed to them to produce food and goods for the use of the central administration of the empire and the Inca religious institutions.

- The Inca economy was not based on a money system, and there were no merchants to trade goods. Instead, the Inca government determined what crops were to be grown and how they were to be exchanged between different cities and regions. The government promised to take care of the old and the sick. To do this, the Incas put away huge amounts of goods in storehouses. They reserved surplus food and goods and distributed them when and where they were needed. In the excerpt below, Pachacutec arranges to have many storehouses built so that he can feed the tens of thousands of laborers who will rebuild the city of Cuzco.

- At the end of the passage, Betanzos describes the way Pachacutec cements his relationship with the *caciques* by giving them precious jewels and fine clothing. Pachacutec also gave each *cacique* a principal wife with Inca bloodlines. However the wives were a gift with a purpose: when the children of a *cacique* succeeded to their father's position, they would have family ties through their mothers to the Incas in Cuzco and were therefore more likely to be loyal to the Inca empire. In exchange for these favors, Pachacutec demanded crops and labor. The Incas always tried to obtain the loyalty of the conquered territories in their empire through a system of give and take.

- Note that Betanzos, whose wife came from the royal family, focuses strictly on the nobles; little is said about the experiences of the common working people. Farmers were by far the largest and most important group of people in the Inca empire. Most farmers were poor and uneducated, but everything in the Inca empire depended on them. They provided the tremendous surplus of goods that kept the empire and the state religion operating. They worked very hard and were well organized for maximum production.

Excerpt from Narrative of the Incas

Part One: Chapter XII

Wherein Inca Yupanque [another name for Pachacutec] brought together the lords of all the land who were under his dominion, and how he improved the lands around the city of Cuzco, made the first storehouses of food, and took other measures that were necessary for the good of the republic in Cuzco....

Inca Yupanque ordered in the city of Cuzco that all the important cacique lords who had pledged obedience to him and were living in the provinces and neighboring lands around the city of Cuzco attend a meeting on a certain designated day because he had certain things to communicate to them. Once the major lords of Cuzco heard the order, they sent their lord orejones to the provinces and neighboring places.... With them was sent the order that the [Sapa] Inca had made, and on that designated day they were all to come to the city. As soon as these lords found out about Inca Yupanque's order, they came to the city of Cuzco as soon as possible. When they were all together, Inca Yupanque told them that they could see that **the Sun** was on his side and that it was not fair that they be satisfied with little. It seemed to him that as time went by war would not allow them to care for their lands and conserve them ... [and] that once and for all he wanted the lands to be improved so that **perpetually** they and their descendants could farm and be supported. It seemed to him that each one of them should have designated and recognized lands to be farmed and maintained for each one by the people of their house and their friends. He said all of this to the lords and inhabitants of the city of Cuzco. And thus all together, having received this great favor that he did for them by giving them lands that would be recognized **in perpetuity** for each one of them, all together they gave him many thanks, giving him the title of Yndichuri, which means child of the Sun.

Then from there Inca Yupanque ordered them all to go to a certain place where the lands were painted. He gave to each one of them the land that he thought adequate for them. After doing this, he ordered that **his friends the three lords** distribute the lands to all the lords of the city just as Inca Yupanque had ordered. Afterward, they were all to appear again before him. Thus the lords went and distributed the lands, giving possession to those whom the [Sapa] Inca had favored. On their return, the [Sapa] Inca ordered the caciques and lords who were there to bring to him the number of **Indians** that each one had there with him. Soon the cacique lords counting with **quipos**, which means numerical record, brought him the total number of Indians they had. After the [Sapa] Inca found out how many Indians there were, he ordered the lords to distribute them by houses. This was done the next day and he ordered each one of those of Cuzco who had been lucky enough to get lands to go out and work and improve them, making canals for irrigation, all of

The Sun: The sun was generally considered a deity or a symbol of a deity in Inca times.

Perpetually: Forever.

In Perpetuity: Forever.

His friends the three lords: Three caciques.

Indians: Betanzos uses the term Indians to refer to the commoners who worked for the Incas.

Quipos: Referring to quipu (also spelled khipu); a counting and record-keeping device consisting of a rope with many knotted cords attached to it used to record important numbers, such as population counts and amounts of stored food and goods.

which was repaired and made from building stones so that the construction would last forever. He ordered them to put their boundary stones high in such a way as never to get lost. Under each of these boundary stones he ordered that there be placed a certain amount of **carbon**, saying that, if at some time the boundary stone fell, the carbon would mark the boundaries of the lands. After this was arranged, while the lands were being improved, Inca Yupanque spent some days relaxing and watching how each one worked and improved the land he had been given. He gave help to those whom he noticed having some difficulty. He saw that the construction and improvements on those lands was taking a long time, considering the way the work was going, and since this construction could not be finished so easily, he ordered the lords and caciques who were there to come to a meeting in his house one day. They met just as he ordered. With them there in his house he told

them that it was urgent that in the city of Cuzco there be storehouses for all foods such as **maize**, … beans, **choclo**, **chuño**, **quinua**, dried meat, and all the other dried provisions and foods that they have. For that, it was necessary that they have it sent from their lands. Then the lord caciques said that they would be very pleased to have it brought, for him to send from the city of Cuzco some noble orejones to accompany the Indians that they were sending so that in their lands they could tell those who were there that it was the [Sapa] Inca's will to provide such supplies to the city of Cuzco because that was the first time. They were very pleased to do this service for the city and for their lord Inca Yupanque. The [Sapa] Inca thanked them for all of this and then ordered those lords of Cuzco to make the arrangements there in their lodgings, along with those cacique lords, for the orejones who for their part were to go to the towns and provinces to gather and bring the food and provisions mentioned. Thus the lords went to their lodgings and had their meeting there with the caciques. The lords designated what each province had to bring and contribute. The caciques there were as-

Incas worked to improve the land by planting crops such as maize. *The Art Archive/Archaeological Museum Lima/Dagli Orti.*

Carbon: A natural element; sometimes carbon produces black markings.

Maize: Corn.

Choclo: Maize cobs.

Chuño: Freeze-dried potatoes.

Quinua: Alternate spelling of quinoa, a kind of grain.

TRAVAXA

3ARACARPAIIACOMVC

Inca irrigating a field of crops. *The Art Archive/Archaeological Museum Lima/Dagli Orti.*

Sierras: Rugged range of mountains.

signed the storehouses that were to be made. The order was given and the time designated that every so many years they were perpetually to fill them, unless some other order was given by the [Sapa] Inca. All of this the caciques agreed to do because they understood that Inca Yupanque was a lord who knew well how to honor any service that might be done for him.

Next there in the meeting, the lords designated the noble orejones *who were to go and also the* caciques, leaders, *with whom they were to go. Thus these noble* orejones *and leaders left to bring the foods and provisions mentioned. The lords and* caciques *left the meeting and went to where Inca Yupanque was. They told him what they had done and arranged, as he had suggested. They asked him to indicate the places where the storehouses were to be built. The ones which each one was to make had already been assigned. Then Inca Yupanque pointed out certain hillsides of the* sierras *in view which surrounded the city of Cuzco, and he ordered that the storehouses be built there right away so that when the provisions mentioned were brought, there would be a place to put them. Then the lords went to the places that the [Sapa] Inca had pointed out to them. They had the work started to build the storehouses. Making these storehouses and preparing the land for them took five years because they made a great many storehouses. Inca Yupanque ordered so many because he had a very large amount of food, enough so that he would not run out. This food he had there was also for those whom he wanted to make stone structures in the city of Cuzco and repair the rivers that run through it. He thought that, by itself having such a large amount of provisions, none would be lacking to feed the men he wanted to have construct the buildings and houses he wanted rebuilt.*

After the storehouses were made and supplied, the lands improved, and all this work done, Inca Yupanque ordered the caciques *and lords to come to a meeting. In all that has been stated they had complied. It seemed to Inca Yupanque that it was proper for him to do them some favors and do something to please them. In the as-*

*sembly he gave them many jewels of gold and silver that he had made while they were doing their work. He also gave each one two sets of the garments he wore, and to each one he also gave a lady born in Cuzco and of Inca lineage. Each of these women was to be the **principal wife** of the* cacique *to whom she was given. The children of these unions would inherit the **domain** of their father. Because of these family ties, they would never rebel. There would be perpetual friendship and **confederation** between them and those of the city of Cuzco.*

After all this was done and the caciques *saw the great favors he was doing for them, they were all inclined to kiss his feet and thank him very much. Then Inca Yupanque told them to go to their lands to rest and return to the city of Cuzco in one year. During this time, each of them should have a great many fields sown with all of their foods. The [Sapa] Inca believed it [storing large amounts of food] would be necessary some day. He recommended that in their lands the young men and women not be idle so that such idleness would not cause their people to imitate bad habits. They should keep their people busy all the time in farming, preparing for war, and similar pursuits such as practicing with slings, shooting arrows, [and] handling arms. All of this the young men were to do in their lands, putting an equal number on each side. On hearing all this, the* caciques *said that they would do it as ordered and that what he told them was good. Thus the [Sapa] Inca bade them farewell and, making their **gestures of obeisance**, they left and returned to their lands.*

What happened next ...

After Betanzos and his wife Doña Angelina wrote *Narrative of the Incas*, they disappeared from historical records. Their manuscript was lost for centuries. No one knows how it ultimately arrived in Spain, but an incomplete version was found in a library there and was published in Madrid in 1880. This first-published edition, which consisted of an introductory letter and eighteen chapters of Part One, was dated 1551. Later, the complete manuscript, dated 1557, was found in a library in Palma de Mallorca. It was published in Spanish in

Quipu

Photograph and illustrations of the Inca quipu, *a knotted string recording device from the Inca culture*

Date of origination: c. 600 C.E. (Andean region); fifteenth century (Incas)

Writing systems generally have been deemed necessary achievements in the development of the world's early civilizations. Without writing, it would be impossible to keep track of the people, goods, debts, taxes and tributes, and laws of a vast empire; without records of these things, there could be no order or unity among large, diverse populations. The Incas have always stood out as the exception to this rule; they had no known writing system, and yet their civilization was extremely orderly and advanced. For the Incas, a record-keeping device called the *quipu* (pronounced KEE-poo; often spelled *khipu*) served some of the same purposes that writing served for other developing civilizations. Made of dyed, multicolored cotton cords that are knotted together, *quipus* look like old, tangled mops or Hawaiian grass skirts. The knots and other variables were used to keep track of numerical information. Most likely *quipus* were used to record nonnumerical information as well. In fact, some experts have recently suggested that the Incas may have used *quipus* as a system for writing language, but these theories remain controversial.

The Incas used *quipus* to record inventory, such as how much grain was in a storehouse. They also used them to count the number of people in a given area, to keep track of labor obligations owed by the provinces, and to plot their military strategies.

Quipus arose long before the Incas appeared in Cuzco. They were probably first used around 600 C.E. among Andean civilizations, such as the Wari empire, which was located in the central Andes Mountain region of Peru. When the Incas began using *quipus* in the fifteenth century, the instruments quickly became vital to the maintenance of the government and economic system throughout the Andean region. The Incas used *quipus* to record inventory, such as how much grain was in a storehouse. They also used them to count the number of people in a given area, to keep track of labor obligations owed by the provinces, and to plot their military strategies. Along the excellent Inca road system, runners could carry *quipus* from faraway places to nobles in the urban centers of the empire. In this way, up-to-date information was rapidly transmitted, so the Inca nobles could keep track of their vast territory down to the smallest details.

Professionals with extensive training, called *quipu camayocs,* were the record keepers. *Quipu camayocs* had access to information that was vital to the empire and often unknown to anyone else, and scholars believe the *camayocs* kept their *quipu* coding system secret. It was crucial that these *camayocs* be honest and attentive to detail. The penalties for errors among *quipu camayocs* were harsh, but, in general, these officials had very high status within the empire.

The Spanish conquistadores (Spanish word for "conquerors") and missionaries (people usually working for a religious organization who try to convert people, usually in a foreign land, to their religion) who arrived in the Andes region in the sixteenth century had the opportunity to watch the *quipu camayocs* at work. The work usually involved recording the stock held in a particular storehouse or taking a census, a count of the population of a region. According to the Spanish reports, the *camayocs* read the *quipus* by examining the knots, first with their eyes and then with their hands.

Some of the Spanish eyewitnesses report that *quipus* also held nonnumerical data; sometimes they witnessed *camayocs* using the *quipu* to retrieve language information: poems, songs, stories, and Inca history. Modern scholars have theorized that these *quipu camayocs* memorized long passages of history, legends, speeches, or poems that had been passed down orally through the generations; then, when they were called on to present a story or poem, the *camayocs* used the variations of knots on their *quipus* to help jog their memories. Most scholars believe that these *camayocs* retrieved the words from memory, not directly from the knots.

Things to remember while examining the photograph and illustrations of Inca *quipus:*

- A *quipu* generally consisted of many dyed cotton cords (occasionally the wool of the alpaca was used). There was a horizontal main cord with a set of pendant cords (those hanging down from it). There were also cords directed upward from the main cord (if lying on a table they would extend up from the rope, while the pendants would extend down), called top cords, and there were cords called subsidiary cords attached to the pendant cords. The pendant and top cords were knotted at intervals along their lengths. These cords were dyed—some were one color and others multicolored—and they were tied with single knots, long knots, and figure eights (knots shaped like the number eight).

- Most *quipus* were used to record numbers. Historian L. Leland Locke (1875–1943) discovered their decimal (base-ten) system of numeration in the 1920s, so numerical *quipus* can now be deciphered. These *quipus* work like an abacus (a bead counter), using knots rather than beads. The lowest knot on the pendant cord represents the ones column, and the next knot up the cord represents the tens column, and so on, similar to a decimal place system. For example, a pendant cord with three knots at the lowest (ones) position, two at the next (tens) level, and four knots at the top (hundreds) position would represent the number 423.

- About six hundred known *quipus* have survived into modern times. Locke studied about one hundred of them and showed conclusively that they were all used to record numbers. However, mathematician Marcia Ascher (1935–) and her husband, archaeologist Robert Ascher (1931–), estimate that 20 percent of the surviving *quipus* cannot be deciphered (made sense of) using Locke's decimal system. In 1970 the Aschers began to examine as many of the sur-

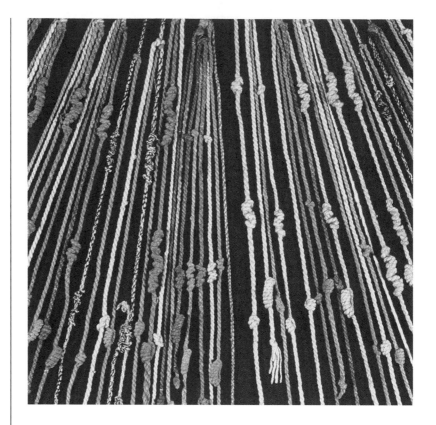

viving *quipus* as they could find. They cataloged the size, colors, shapes, and knot types of each *quipu* in "databooks" and then published their findings, hoping that if enough people had access to all available *quipu* constructions, perhaps someone would crack the code. To date, the Aschers have described more than two hundred *quipus* and made their descriptions available to the public on the Internet. Though no one has yet cracked the code, the Aschers's work has stimulated new interest in *quipus*.

• In the late 1990s, scholars were studying the many different details of surviving *quipus:* cord colors, cord twists, knot types, and how pendant cords hang from the main cord. Anthropologist Gary Urton (1946–) viewed these variations in the makeup of *quipus* as a set of binary "either/or" choices. He theorized that the Incas were working in a code similar to modern computer code, which represents all numerals and words by sequences of zeros and ones. By investigating the entire

COTADOR MAIOR I TEZORERO
TAVANTIN SVIO QVIPO
CVRACA CON DOR CHAVA

con tador ytezorero   con tador

sequence of choices made in the construction of a *quipu*—calculating the material used, the type of weave, the type of knot, and a number of other factors—Urton concluded that each knot had a seven-bit sequence (seven either/or choices). He estimated that *quipu ca-mayocs* had about 1,536 possible units of information in their coding system, noting that this exceeds the number of signs that existed in the early writing systems of

Incas used *quipus* to record the number of supplies and goods in their storehouses. Illustration by Felipe Huaman Poma de Ayala, from *La primer nueva corónica y buen gobierno.* *The Art Archive/Archaeological Museum Lima/Dagli Orti.*

Mesopotamia or Egypt. Urton believes the Incas may have expanded the record-keeping function of the *quipu* into a three-dimensional writing system. In 2004 Urton and Carrie Brezine, a mathematician, software developer, and weaver, finished work on a database cataloging the details of all known *quipus*. They hope this database will lead to the cracking of the *quipu* code. However, many Inca scholars doubt Urton's theories.

What happened next ...

Quipus were made from highly perishable cotton or wool. They would decompose unless preserved in an extremely dry climate. Most Inca *quipus* that survived the Spanish conquest rotted or turned to dust long ago.

In the years after the Spanish conquest of 1533, Spanish conquistadores and missionaries destroyed all the Inca *quipus* they could find. The Spaniards believed the *quipus* contained "evil" information: the non-Christian and, from the Spanish point of view, uncivilized lore of Inca religion and history. They burned the *quipus* so that their efforts to convert the Andean people to Christianity would be easier.

Before the Spaniards burned the *quipus,* some officials called in *quipu camayocs* to "read" their *quipus* to them. They had these readings transcribed (written down). To date, thirty-two of these transcripts have been found in Peru. Urton and other scholars are hoping they can match a *quipu* to one of the transcripts in order to crack the code of the *quipus.*

Did you know ...

- Twenty-first-century shepherds in the Andes Mountains use a form of *quipu* to record information about their flocks.

- Scholars used to think that the Maya glyphs (written or drawn symbols used to represent words or sounds) were limited to numbers, dates, and names. In recent decades, scholars cracked the Maya code—discovering that the glyphs actually represent every part of the spoken language—and can now read Maya history as the Maya wrote it. It is possible that archaeologists and mathematicians will someday decipher the *quipu* codes of the Incas. If, as Urton and other scholars believe, *quipus* were used by the Incas to record some aspects of their spoken language, the surviving *quipus* might relate the story of the Inca people in their own words.

Consider the following ...

- Make your own version of a *quipu*. You will need a length of rope about 3-feet (1-meter) long, scissors, and yarn or string, preferably in several colors. Tie knots at both ends of the rope and lay it across a flat surface. Cut the yarn or string into fifteen 2-foot (0.6-meter) lengths. Tie the 2-foot pieces of string or yarn onto the rope. Make sure that they all hang down from the rope in the same direction. Then begin recording information. You can use the decimal number system described in this chapter or, by attaching meaning (numbers, letters, sounds, or words) to different size knots and different positions of the knots, you can make up your own code and pass information to a friend or classmate. Imagine the complexity of the Inca *quipus* that could record all of the empire's most important figures, and possibly some of their language as well.

- Why would the Spanish conquistadores and missionaries want to destroy *quipus* in the first decades after the conquest? What harm might they have believed a *quipu* could cause? Of what do you think they may have been afraid?

For More Information

Books

Ascher, Marcia, and Robert Ascher. *Code of the Quipu: Databook* I & II. Ann Arbor: University of Michigan Press, 1978 and 1988.

Ascher, Marcia, and Robert Ascher. *Code of the Quipu: A Study in Media, Mathematics, and Culture.* New York: Dover Publications, 1997.

Urton, Gary. *Signs of the Inka Khipu: Binary Coding in the Andean Knotted-String Records.* Austin: University of Texas Press, 2003.

Periodicals

Mann, Charles C. "Anthropology: Cracking the Khipu Code." *Science Magazine* (June 13, 2003). This article can also be found online at http://209.157.64.200/focus/f-news/928058/posts (accessed on November 5, 2004).

Potier, Beth. "String Theorist: Anthropologist Gary Urton Untangles the Mystery of Inkan Khipus." *Harvard University Gazette* (May 22, 2003). This article can also be found online at http://www.news.harvard.edu/gazette/2003/05.22/03-urton.html (accessed on November 5, 2004).

Wilford, John Noble. "The Khipu: String, and Knot, Theory of Inca Writing." *The New York Times* (August 12, 2003). This article can also be found online at http://www.ee.ryerson.ca:8080/~elf/abacus/ inca-khipu.html (accessed on November 5, 2004).

Garcilaso de la Vega, El Inca

Excerpts from **Royal Commentaries of the Incas and General History of Peru**

Reprinted from edition translated by Harold V. Livermore, 1966

Originally published in two parts as *Comentarios reales de los Incas*, Part One (1609); and *Historia general del Perú*, Part Two (1617)

Garcilaso de la Vega (1539–1616), known as "El Inca," has been called the first classic author of the Americas. The Peruvian writer and historian's master work, *Royal Commentaries of the Incas and General History of Peru* (two parts, 1609 and 1617), presents a vivid chronicle of the personalities, events, customs, rites, and royal lineage from the Inca civilization's beginnings to the arrival of the Spaniards. The book is noted as great literature as well as useful—though somewhat romanticized—history.

Born in 1539 in Cuzco, Peru, shortly after the Spanish conquest of Peru (1533), Garcilaso's family background connected him with both Inca and Spanish traditions. His father, Sebastian Garcilaso de la Vega, was a Spanish conquistador (Spanish word for "conqueror") and military captain from a distinguished Spanish family. Garcilaso's mother, Isabel Suarez Chimpu Ocllo, was the niece of the last great Inca emperor, Huayna Capac (pronounced WHY-nah CAH-pahk), who ruled from 1493 to 1525.

After Garcilaso's birth, his father married a Spanish woman and arranged for Isabel to marry a commoner, despite

> "The Incas never made laws to frighten their subjects or to be mocked by them, but always with the intention of applying them to anyone who dared to break them."

41

Garcilaso de la Vega, "El Inca." *The Library of Congress.*

her rank as a royal Inca. Both parents wanted Garcilaso to know the traditions of their respective cultures. From his mother, who reared him, Garcilaso learned Quechua (pronounced KECH-wah), the language of the Incas, as well as Inca customs, myths, and legends—stories handed down from earlier times, often believed to be historically true. His father made sure he was educated as a nobleman in the classical traditions of Spain. Along with Quechua and Spanish, Garcilaso learned Latin and the histories of ancient Rome and Greece. He was raised in the Catholic religion.

When Garcilaso was twenty-one years old his father died, leaving Garcilaso money for his education. The young man made his way to Spain where he got a chilly reception from his father's family and acquaintances who were suspicious of the half-Inca, half-conquistador *mestizo* (person of mixed European and Amerindian ancestry). Garcilaso eventually settled near Cordova in 1571, where he remained for the rest of his life.

In 1572 Garcilaso learned his mother had died. He also heard grim reports of the stern measures Spanish authorities in Peru had taken to suppress the Inca people. The Spanish had sacked the Inca rebel stronghold in Vilcabamba in 1572 and beheaded the Sapa Inca (supreme ruler of the Inca empire), Tupac Amarú (1544–1572; ruled 1571–1572). Garcilaso decided to write about the Inca civilization and defend its vanished greatness. Tireless and diligent, he assembled information on all aspects of Inca history and culture. In order to persuade the Spanish to change their policies, Garcilaso wanted to write in a language that would be accepted by the elite (people in socially superior positions who have more power and privileges than others). He therefore taught himself Castilian, the dominant Spanish dialect in Spain.

To write about the origins and rise of the Inca empire in *Royal Commentaries of the Incas*, Garcilaso relied on his memory of the stories his Inca relatives told him in his youth. He also received helpful information from Inca friends who wrote to him from Peru. His background as a bilingual (speaking two languages) child trained in both the Inca and the Spanish worlds is evident in the book; Garcilaso often seems to attempt to fit the glories of the Inca empire into the realm of European literary tradition. His outlook was quite romantic; his account of the Incas casts them as wise rulers who were similar to the ancient, pre-Christian Romans. Garcilaso believed the Incas' major shortcoming, like that of the ancient Romans, was that they were ignorant of Christianity before the Spanish arrived. Though Garcilaso approved of Spanish attempts to convert the native Andean people to Catholicism, he did not approve of the abuses the Spanish were inflicting on them. His book was, in part, an attempt to change the Spanish policies.

Things to remember while reading the excerpts from *Royal Commentaries of the Incas and the General History of Peru:*

- In the following excerpts, Garcilaso describes the *acllahuaci* (pronounced ahk-lah-WAH-see) or "house of the chosen women" in Cuzco. His comparison of the Inca *acllahuaci* to a Roman Catholic convent, and particularly his focus on the purity and virginity of the *aclla,* or chosen women, seems to be an attempt to prove the worthiness and civility of the Inca people to a skeptical readership in Spain. According to historians, his description paints only a portion of the picture of the institution. He leaves out facts that may provide a less-idealized (making the subjects more perfect than they were) view. For example, when the young girls who had been trained in *acllahuacis* throughout the empire turned fourteen, they were sent to a festival in Cuzco. There, the Sapa Inca would select wives for himself from among them. He chose others to be given as gifts to noblemen he wished to reward. At various times of the year, young women trained at the *acllahuaci* were chosen to be sacrificed (killed as an offering) to the gods. A relatively small portion of the young women were married symbolically to the Inca sun god, Inti, or to other gods.

- If Garcilaso's writings seem idealized, many of the Spanish chroniclers writing about the Incas erred gravely in the other direction. Most of the missionaries (people who try to convert others, usually in a foreign land, to their religion) and soldiers were not sympathetic in their descriptions of the Incas or open to learning about their culture. For example, conquistador Hernando Pizarro (d. 1560; brother of expedition leader Francisco Pizarro) described the "chosen women" of the *acllahuaci* as "women of the devil." In the second paragraph of the first excerpt below, Garcilaso, however, counters the claims of Spanish historians that the "chosen women" mingled with males regularly and participated in human sacrifice rites in the Temple of the Sun.

- Garcilaso refers to the Incas burning the city of Cuzco. After the Spanish had occupied Cuzco, Inca leader Manco Inca (ruled 1533–1545) fled the city and set up camp. In 1536 he sent word throughout the empire that he would lead a rebellion against the Spanish, asking for help in the fight. Andean men rushed to the Cuzco area by the thousands to fight the hated Spanish. A force of about forty thousand Andean warriors joined together against the Spanish-held Cuzco. They began their attack on the Spanish by shooting red-hot stones from their slings, setting the capital on fire. In the siege, the Spanish were trapped for nearly a year in Sacsahuaman (pronounced sox-ah-wah-MAHN), the stone fortress perched on a hill just north of Cuzco. As Garcilaso mentions, out of respect the Andean warriors spared only a few buildings from the flames: the *acllahuaci* and the Temple of the Sun.

Excerpts from Royal Commentaries of the Incas and the General History of Peru

Chapter I: The House of the Virgins Dedicated to the Sun

*The Inca kings had in their vain and **heathen** religion some great things worthy of much consideration. One of these was the*

Heathen: Relating to people who do not accept the God of the Christian, Jewish, or Muslim religions.

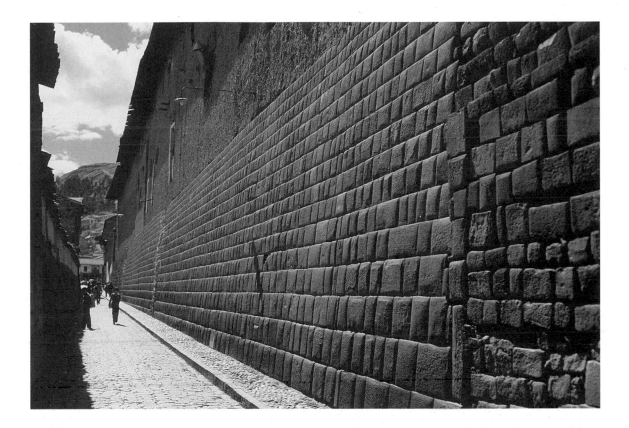

*profession of **perpetual** virginity observed by women in many **conventual** houses built for them in various parts of the empire.*

*A **quarter** of the city of Cuzco was called Acllahuaci, "house of the chosen women." The quarter is between two streets that run from the main square to the convent of St. Dominic, which used to be the house of the Sun.... Between it and the temple of the Sun there was a large block of houses and a big square which is in front of the temple. This shows how far off the mark were these historians who say that the virgins were in the temple of the Sun, that they were priestesses and that they aided the priests in the sacrifices. In fact the house and the temple are a great distance apart, and the chief object of the Inca kings was that men should not enter the nunnery, or women the temple of the Sun. They called it "the house of the chosen" because the nuns were chosen for their rank or beauty; they must be virgins, and to ensure this, they were set apart at the age of eight years or under.*

As the virgins of the house of Cuzco were dedicated to the Sun, they had to be of his own blood, or daughters of Incas, either of the king or of

This wall in Cuzco was once part of an *acllahuaci*, or "house of the chosen women." *The Art Archive/Dagli Orti.*

Perpetual: Lasting forever.

Conventual: Relating to convents—the houses of Catholic nuns.

Quarter: District of a town.

members of his family, and legitimate and free from all foreign blood.... They reasoned that the Sun would have children and that they must not be bastards with a mixture of human with their divine blood. The women devoted to the Sun must therefore be of the legitimate royal blood, which was that of the Sun himself. They were usually more than fifteen hundred nuns, but there was no established limit of number.

Within the house there were senior women who had grown old in their vocation. If they had entered it long ago they were called mamacuna *because of their age and of the office they performed. Superficially this word means "matron," but its real significance is a woman entrusted with the duties of a mother: it is composed of* mama, *"mother," and the particle* cuna, *with no fixed meaning....*

Chapter II: Rules and Duties of the Chosen Virgins

*They lived in perpetual **seclusion** to the end of their days and preserved their virginity. They had no **locutory** or hatch or any other place where they could see or speak to men or women except one another. As women of the Sun they were not to be made common by being seen by anyone. Their seclusion was so absolute that even the [Sapa] Inca never used the privilege he might have had as king of seeing or speaking to them, lest anyone else should have ventured to seek the same privilege. Only the* coya, *or queen, and her daughters had **leave** to enter the house and converse with the nuns, both young and old.*

*The [Sapa] Inca sent the queen and her daughters to visit them and ask how they were and what they needed. I saw this house intact, for only its quarter and that of the temple of the Sun, and four other buildings that had been royal palaces of the Incas were respected by the **Indians** in their general rebellion against the Spaniards. Because they [these buildings] had been the house of the Sun, their god, and of his women, and of their kings, they did not burn them down as they burnt the rest of the city. Among other notable features of this building there was a narrow passage wide enough for two persons that ran the whole length of the building. The passage had many cells on either side, which were used as offices where women worked. At each door were trusted **portresses**, and in the last apartment at the end of the passage where no one entered were the women of the Sun. The house had a main door as convents do in Spain, but it was only opened to admit the queen or to receive women who were going to be nuns.*

*At the beginning of the passage which was the service-door for the whole house, there were a score of **porters** to fetch and carry things needed in the house as far as the second door. The porters*

Seclusion: Isolation.

Locutory: A room, usually in a monastery or convent, where conversation is permitted.

Leave: Permission.

Indians: The native Andeans.

Portresses: Female doorkeepers.

Porters: Male doorkeepers.

Early Civilizations in the Americas: Biographies and Primary Sources

could not pass this second door under pain of death, even if they were called from within, and no one was allowed to call them in under the same penalty. The nuns and their house were served by five hundred girls, all maidens and daughters of **Incas by privilege**, those whom the first [Sapa] Incas had reduced to [their] service and not those of the royal blood. They did not enter the house as women of the Sun, but only as servants. Daughters of foreigners were not admitted for this service, but only those of Incas by privilege....

The various duties of the women of the Sun were spinning, weaving, and making all the clothes and headwear the [Sapa] Inca and the coya, his legitimate wife, wore on their persons. They also made the fine garments that were offered as sacrifices to the Sun. The [Sapa] Inca wore on his head a band, the llautu, which was as broad as the little finger and very thick, so as to be almost square, being passed four or five times around the head, and the scarlet fringe which stretched across his temples. His dress was a tunic falling to the knees, the uncu. The Spaniards call it cusma, but this is not in the general language but a word from some provincial dialect. He wore also a blanket two **piernas** square instead of a cloak, the yacolla. The nuns also made for the [Sapa] Inca a kind of pouch, about a quarter of a **vara** square. These pouches are carried under the arm on a highly embroidered band, two fingers in width and passed like a **bandolier** from the left shoulder to the right side. They are called chuspa....

Chapter III: The Veneration They Had for Things Made by the Virgins and the Law Against Those Who Might Violate Them

All these things were made by the nuns in great quantities for their bridegroom the Sun. As the Sun could not wear these garments, they were sent to the [Sapa] Inca as his legitimate son and legal heir that he might wear them. He received them as sacred things, and he and his whole empire held them in greater **veneration** than the Greeks and Romans would have done if the goddesses Juno, Venus, and Pallas had made them. For these **gentiles** of the New World, being simpler than those of antiquity, worshiped with extreme veneration and heartfelt affection everything they held sacred and divine in their false faith.... The [Sapa] Inca likewise could not give them to anyone not of his own blood and kin, for they held that divine things could not be put to human purposes without **sacrilege,** and it was therefore prohibited even to the king to offer them to **curacas** and captains, however well they had served him, unless they were of his blood....

In addition the nuns occupied themselves in due season in making the bread called cancu for the sacrifices they offered to the Sun at

Incas by privilege: A group of Inca nobility who were not Inca by birth, but who spoke the Quechua language and had lived in the Cuzco area for many generations; though they were given some of the powers and privileges of the elite, they were considered inferior to Incas by birth.

Piernas: Old Spanish units of measure.

Vara: A Spanish word for a measure of length of about one yard.

Bandolier: A military belt that has small pockets or loops for carrying cartridges and is worn over the shoulders and across the chest.

Veneration: Profound respect.

Gentiles: People of a tribe or clan.

Sacrilege: A violation of something sacred.

Curacas: Locals rulers of a conquered people who after the conquest continued to serve as officials of the Inca government in their regions.

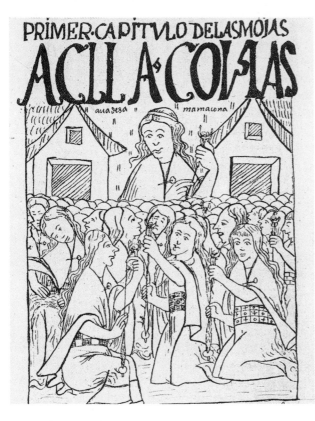

PRIMER·CAPITVLO DELASMOIAS ACLLACOIAS

the great festivals of Raimi and Citua. They also brewed the drink the Inca and his kinsfolk drank on the festivals, called in their language aca.... All the vessels of the house, even pots, pitchers, and vats, were of silver and gold, as in the house of the Sun, for they were his wives and were worthy of it by their rank. There was also a garden of trees and plants, herbs and flowers, birds and animals, done in gold and silver like those in temple of the Sun.

The things we have mentioned were the main occupations of the nuns of Cuzco. Otherwise they lived and conversed like women dedicated to perpetual seclusion and perpetual virginity. There was a law that a nun who forfeited her virginity should be buried alive and her accomplice hanged. As they thought it was a small punishment merely to kill a man for so grave an offence as venturing to violate a woman dedicated to the Sun, their god and father of their kings, the law provided that the guilty man's wife, children, and servants should be slain too, together with his kinsmen, his neighbors, and fellow townsmen, and all his flocks, without leaving a babe or suckling, as the saying is. His village was destroyed and strewn with rocks, and the home and birthplace of so wicked a son left forsaken and desolate and the place accursed, to remain **untrodden** by the foot of man or beast, if possible.

This was the law. But it was never applied, for no one ever **transgressed** it. As we have said, the Peruvian Indians were very fearful of breaking the laws and extremely observant of them, especially those relating to their religion or their king. But if anyone did transgress, the law was applied literally without any **remission**, as if it were merely a matter of killing a puppy. The Incas never made laws to frighten their subjects or to be mocked by them, but always with the intention of applying them to anyone who dared to break them.

Illustration by Felipe Huaman Poma de Ayala, from *La primer nueva corónica y buen gobierno.* **The Inca "chosen women,"pictured in this illustration, spent many days weaving textiles for the Sapa Inca.** *The Art Archive/Archaeological Museum Lima/Dagli Orti.*

Untrodden: Not walked upon.

Transgressed: Disobeyed.

Remission: Reduction in intensity.

What happened next ...

Garcilaso went on to write a second volume of the *General History of Peru,* published a year after his death in 1616. The second volume depicts the Spanish reign as bloody and chaotic, a vivid contrast to the much more rational Inca authority he had described in the first volume. Garcilaso's book conveyed an unpopular position in Spain at the time: in order to rule the Andean people, the Spanish should learn the language and customs of this vastly different culture. The second volume of his book was ignored.

Between ill-treatment by the Spanish, disease, and lack of food and resources, the native population of the Andean region was reduced by as much as 75 to 90 percent during the century after the Spanish conquest. In 1780 Tupac Amarú II (c. 1740–1781), an Andean leader who claimed to be a grandson of the last Inca king, demanded the Spanish return the rule of the Andean highlands to its people. His call rallied tens of thousands of native and *mestizo* descendents to join him in an uprising. The Spanish, however, put down the rebellion, killing thousands.

Tupac Amarú II was captured and tortured to death in 1781. A few months later, the Spanish king sent a message to his viceroy (regional governor who represents the king of the ruling country) in Lima, the new capital of Peru, urgently requiring that he collect all existing volumes of Garcilaso's history of Peru. The viceroy felt that the book, with its noble vision of the ancient civilization, might incite the native Andean people against the Spanish. As requested, Peruvian officials confiscated all known copies of Garcilaso's books, which were then not read in Peru or Spain for many years.

Did you know ...

• After the siege of Cuzco, the Spanish built their own city on top of the remaining Inca buildings. A Roman Catholic convent was built on top of the Inca *acllahuaci's* foundation. Tourists in Cuzco today are still able to view the bottom of the sturdy cut-stone walls of the Inca house of chosen women.

Consider the following ...

- Describe the life of a woman who lives in the "house of chosen women" as Garcilaso portrays it in these excerpts. If you were an Inca parent, would you want your daughter to be chosen for such a life? Why or why not?

- How do you think Garcilaso's background—half Spanish, half Inca—might have affected his writing? Who do you think he was writing this book for? What was his purpose for writing it?

- Why does Garcilaso compare the women of the Inca *acllahuaci* to Catholic nuns?

For More Information

Books

Davies, Nigel. *The Ancient Kingdoms of Peru.* London and New York: Penguin Books, 1997.

Garcilaso de la Vega, El Inca. *Royal Commentaries of the Incas and General History of Peru: Part One.* Translated by Harold V. Livermore. Austin and London: University of Texas Press, 1966.

Von Hagen, Adriana, and Craig Morris. *The Cities of the Ancient Andes.* London and New York: Thames and Hudson, 1998.

Web Sites

"Garcilaso Inca de la Vega." *Selections from the Library of José Durand: University of Notre Dame Rare Books and Special Collections.* http://www.rarebooks.nd.edu/exhibits/durand/biographies/garcilaso.html (accessed on November 4, 2004).

Other Sources

Pizarro, Hernando. Letter to the Royal Audience of Santo Domingo, November, 1533. *Reports on the Discovery of Peru.* Edited and translated by Clements R. Markham. London: Hakluyt Society, 1872. This letter can also be found online at http://www.shsu.edu/~his_ncp Pizarro.html (accessed on November 4, 2004).

Atahuallpa

Born c. 1502
Cuzco, Andean region, present-day Peru
Died July 26, 1533
Cuzco

Sapa Inca, or supreme ruler of the Inca empire

A tahuallpa (pronounced ah-tah-WAHL-pah; also spelled Atahualpa, Atagualpa, or Atabalipa) was the thirteenth Inca ruler and the last to preside over the Inca empire before the Spanish conquest of South America in 1533. Prior to the death of Atahuallpa's father, Huayna Capac (pronounced WHY-nah CAH-pahk; ruled 1493–1525), in 1525, the Inca empire had been prosperous and strong, the home of the largest civilization in the Americas. Its territory extended 2,500 miles (4,023 kilometers) from north to south in the Andes Mountain region: from the southern part of present-day Ecuador down through present-day Peru and Bolivia and into the northern half of present-day Chile. Yet within ten years of Huayna Capac's death, the empire had collapsed. In a six-year span of time, a smallpox epidemic (sudden spread of a contagious disease) decimated the population, civil war divided the empire, and Spaniards destroyed the Inca cities and temples and took over as rulers of the land.

Atahuallpa survived the epidemic and won the civil war. In November 1532, he prepared for his trip to Cuzco (pronounced KOO-sko) to claim his position as Sapa Inca. It was a

"When Atahuallpa died, all the Indians gathered there in Cajamarca returned to their lands, and the roads were full of them as if they were rows of ants."

Juan de Betanzos, Narrative of the Incas

Atahuallpa. © *Hulton-Deutsch Collection/Corbis.*

precarious time in the history of the Incas: Atahuallpa's brother, the recently ruling Sapa Inca, had been captured in battle and Atahuallpa was not yet on the throne. It was Atahuallpa's bad fortune that, just at that time, a small but determined expedition of Spanish conquerors was on its way to his camp. In the surprising events that followed, Atahuallpa was captured and the powerful Inca empire was doomed to collapse.

The son of a Sapa Inca and a Quito princess

Sapa Incas, supreme rulers of the Inca empire, were required to select a principal wife, or *coya*, from among their sisters in order to keep the Inca bloodlines pure (however, experts believe that many Sapa Incas chose cousins as their principal wives). Usually the heir to the Sapa Inca was chosen only from the offspring of the Sapa Inca and his *coya*. Besides their *coyas*, though, the Sapa Incas usually had many secondary wives. There were often hundreds of children from these matches.

Atahuallpa's father, Huayna Capac, married his principal wife at a fairly young age, but during his lifetime he is said to have had about six hundred secondary wives. While still a young man, Huayna Capac traveled north to the kingdom of Quito in present-day Ecuador. While he was there, he took a Quito princess as one of his secondary wives. Many historians believe she was a particular favorite of Huayna Capac's. He brought her back to Cuzco where she gave birth to their son, Atahuallpa. Though illegitimate (at least in terms of inheriting the Inca throne), Atahuallpa, like his mother, was a special favorite of the Sapa Inca.

Sometime around the age of twelve, Atahuallpa was given his *huarachicoy*, an Inca ceremony marking a boy's passage through puberty and into adulthood. The ritual involved long endurance ordeals and tests of Atahuallpa's military prowess. It was during this ceremony that he actually received the name Atahuallpa, which means "fortunate warrior" (translating more literally as "sweet and virile"). Shortly after the completion of Atahuallpa's *huarachicoy* ceremony, major uprisings broke out in the northern part of the empire. Setting out to crush this rebellion, the Sapa Inca brought thirteen-year-old Atahuallpa along with him on a military campaign in the Quito kingdom, which happened to be the home of Atahuallpa's mother. For several years the Sapa Inca and Atahuallpa led large Inca armies in heavy battles in the north. They succeeded in defeating the rebel Quito armies and went on to extend the borders of the Inca empire.

After the battles were won, Huayna Capac chose to continue living in the area of present-day Ecuador rather than returning to his home in Cuzco. He built a magnificent new city in Quito, beginning what was meant to become a second Inca capital. Atahuallpa and large numbers of Inca troops remained in the area with him.

By about 1524 the Incas in Quito began hearing of strange, bearded, white-skinned visitors who had arrived in huge ships on the coast to the north of the empire. Soon a terrible epidemic began. The Europeans had brought small-pox with them to the shores of the Americas, and infected native people probably carried it down the coast. People throughout the empire fell ill and began dying in great num-bers—eventually the dead numbered into the tens of thou-sands. Sapa Inca Huayna Capac died of the disease in 1525. According to many accounts, Huayna Capac's chosen succes-sor, a son named Ninancuyoci, died of the disease around the same time as his father.

The divided succession

There are several different accounts of the selection of the new Sapa Inca after Huayna Capac's death. According to some histories, Huayna Capac had requested that the empire be divided between two of his sons: Huáscar (d. 1532), the son of Huayna Capac's principal wife, was to rule over Cuzco and the southern half of the empire, and Atahuallpa was to rule over Quito and the northern part of the empire. Other historians say that the Inca nobility chose Huáscar to rule the entire empire from Cuzco but that Atahuallpa simply held on to his power and his father's army in the north. Either way, the result was the same: a divided empire.

As a rival to his brother, Atahuallpa knew he was like-ly to be killed if he returned to Cuzco. Therefore, he decided not to accompany his father's body back to the Inca capital. Instead, he prepared the body for burial and sent a group of

Good Brother/Bad Brother?

Many of the people who recorded Inca history take sides as they describe the battle between Atahuallpa and Huáscar, half brothers who were both determined to take the throne after their father's death. Some believe that Huáscar was a great reformer who justly inherited his position as king; they think that he was victimized by the ambitious Atahuallpa. Other historians describe Huáscar as a poor leader and an evil and vicious person; they tend to portray Atahuallpa as a strong and able leader who was justified in fighting for his life as the jealous Huáscar repeatedly tried to kill him. Since there are no known written documents from the time of the half brothers' wars, the truth may never be known.

Certainly both of them committed horrific, brutal acts and were responsible for much death and suffering. But all Sapa Incas exercised life-and-death power over their people and were guilty of violent acts. Huáscar and Atahuallpa's actions seem to stand out as worse than those of earlier rulers, but history can be misleading. Both Huáscar and Atahuallpa were killed early in their rule; therefore, unlike other Sapa Incas, they never had a chance to revise the history that Inca storytellers narrated about their lives. If they had lived longer, Huáscar and Atahuallpa probably would have made certain that their ugly and violent acts did not remain as part of the historic record.

nobles from Quito to escort the body to Cuzco. Remaining in Quito, Atahuallpa maintained command of his father's fifty thousand troops. When Huayna Capac's body arrived in Cuzco and Atahuallpa was not in the procession, Huáscar seized the nobles who had accompanied the body, torturing them for information about Atahuallpa's plans and eventually murdering all of them.

Following the ceremonies for the deceased Sapa Inca, the Inca nobility in Cuzco staged the royal enthronement of Huáscar. Forty of his brothers attended, but Atahuallpa was not among them. Atahuallpa remained in Quito with his army for several years, despite Huáscar's constant requests that he return to Cuzco. Finally, Atahuallpa sent two army generals to speak to Huáscar on his behalf. Huáscar responded by torturing and killing the generals and sending his own army up to Quito in pursuit of Atahuallpa. Atahuallpa then gathered his own forces, and the two Inca armies met in battle. It was the start of a violent civil war in the Inca empire.

For three years terrible warfare raged between the armies of the two half brothers. Tens of thousands died, and the people of the empire became divided in their loyalties. Finally, Atahuallpa's troops captured Huáscar. Atahuallpa showed his brother no mercy. Huáscar was tied up and forced to watch the brutal slaughter of his wives, children, friends, and relatives. Then Atahuallpa put Huáscar in prison and proclaimed himself Sapa Inca. But he never made it to Cuzco to take the throne. He was still resting with his soldiers after battle, camped out at the hot springs of the northern city of Cajamarca, when he learned that nearly two hundred Spaniards were marching toward the site.

The Spaniards arrive

Spanish conquistador (Spanish word for "conqueror") Francisco Pizarro (c. 1475–1541) had set out from Panama in January 1531, accompanied by his four half brothers, his partner Diego de Almagro (1475–1538), 180 other men, and twenty-seven horses. Pizarro had received permission from the Spanish king to conquer and govern the territory of Birú (Peru). He and his men began their expedition in search of the "cities of gold" they had heard existed within the Inca empire. When they arrived in the city of Tumbes in the north, however, they found it in ruins, destroyed by a recent battle in the Inca civil war that had taken place there. The local people told the Spaniards that the winning army and its leader, the new Sapa Inca Atahuallpa, were camped out at Cajamarca. Sensing that the recent war might have weakened the Inca armies, providing them unforeseen opportunities to invade, they sent presents to Atahuallpa and immediately headed for his encampment. After a difficult journey across cold and mountainous terrain, they arrived in Cajamarca in November 1532.

Atahuallpa heard reports that the Spanish were approaching, but his messengers told him these strange foreigners were not warriors; besides, there were less than two hundred of them. Since the Inca troops stationed at Cajamarca numbered about forty thousand, Atahuallpa probably felt secure. Nonetheless, there was tension on both sides as Pizarro and his men marched into the city of Cajamarca. The

Spaniards were surrounded by warriors on all sides as far as the eye could see. Witnesses of the event write of the Spaniards' terrible fear as they gazed upon the massive Inca army. Though they outnumbered the Spaniards, the Inca soldiers had reason to fear as well. The Spaniards rode in on horses, and none of the Inca soldiers had ever seen a horse before. The Spaniards also had cannons and other advanced weapons.

The Spaniards marched into the city's main square and remained there. Pizarro sent his half brother Hernando (c. 1475–1578), Spanish explorer Hernando de Soto (1500–1542), and a native interpreter named Felipillo to ask for a meeting with Atahuallpa. (On an earlier expedition, the Spaniards had kidnapped Felipillo and taught him Spanish so he could interpret for them.)

The arranged meeting

Atahuallpa's attendants brought Pizarro's messengers to see him. One of the emperor's wives held a screen in front of Atahuallpa's face so the visitors could not look upon the Inca leader. This was a customary practice for the Incas when addressing the Sapa Inca. De Soto, though, was unhappy at being treated as an inferior. He rushed his horse at Atahuallpa in an effort to scare him, but the Sapa Inca did not flinch. After discussion, Atahuallpa agreed to meet with Pizarro in the Cajamarca plaza the next day.

The next day, November 16, 1532, the Spaniards stationed themselves in groups within the buildings surrounding the Cajamarca plaza. While they were preparing to attack the Incas, Atahuallpa was busy putting together an elaborate ceremonial procession for the meeting. Most historians believe that Atahuallpa did not suspect the outnumbered strangers would attack and therefore did not prepare for warfare at that first meeting. However, some historians believe Atahuallpa's plans for the Spanish were probably not friendly. Some accounts indicate that the Inca leader sent thousands of his troops to surround the city in order to capture the Spanish after the meeting. According to some, Atahuallpa planned to offer the Spaniards as human sacrifices (human killings offered as gifts to the gods) and keep their horses for breeding.

The Spaniards waited for Atahuallpa, who did not arrive until late in the afternoon. According to **Juan de Betanzos** (see entry) in *Narrative of the Incas,* a book written in 1557, the Sapa Inca stopped to share a glass of *chicha* (a kind of beer made from maize or other grains) with quite a few of his subjects while he was on the way to the plaza and was drunk by the time he reached it. Other sources make no mention of this. Whatever Atahuallpa's condition, after much delay he arrived in the plaza in his royal splendor. He was seated on a litter (an enclosed platform, usually borne on the shoulders of servants) carried by eighty Inca lords dressed in blue tunics. Atahuallpa was adorned in gold, emeralds, silver, and parrot feathers. Bright feathers were strewn about the litter around him. The Incas accompanying him numbered in the thousands, but they were unarmed.

Atahuallpa in his royal splendor. *The Art Archive/Biblioteca Nazionale Marciana Venice/Dagli Orti.*

Upon reaching the plaza, the Sapa Inca found no one there to meet him. The Spaniards were all stationed inside the buildings, waiting for the signal to attack. After a few moments, Spanish missionary Vicente de Valverde (1490–1543) strode out onto the plaza with a Bible in hand and Felipillo the interpreter accompanying him. (A missionary is a person, usually working for a religious organization, who tries to convert people, usually in a foreign land, to his or her religion.) It was Spanish custom to give native peoples a chance to convert to Catholicism before attacking them. Valverde attempted to explain to Atahuallpa that, with the approval of the pope (the head of the Catholic Church), the Spanish were going to take over the area. He asked Atahuallpa to accept the Christian religion and the rule of the Spanish as well. According to many accounts of this exchange, when Atahuallpa understood that he was being asked to accept the god of the Spaniards, he pointed to the sky and said that his god, the sun, was still very much alive and that the god the missionary described, Jesus Christ, was dead. Atahuallpa asked to see the Bible. Apparently the book did not impress him as a sacred object, and he threw it contemptuously to the ground.

When Atahuallpa rejected the Bible, the Spanish took it as their signal to attack. They began by shooting cannons at the unsuspecting crowd. Though they were instructed not to kill Atahuallpa, Pizarro's troops began to mercilessly slaughter everyone else. In *Narrative of the Incas*, Betanzos describes the chaotic scene:

> Then everybody came out at once and fell upon [attacked] the [Sapa] Inca's men. The horsemen lanced them and the foot soldiers cut with their swords without the [Sapa] Inca's men putting up any resistance. Given the suddenness of the attack and never having seen a similar thing in all their days, the Indians [native Andeans] were so shocked that … they tried to flee…. [The fleeing Inca soldiers were held in by a wall that collapsed upon them; hundreds were trampled or crushed.] Some horsemen reached where the [Sapa] Inca was and with their swords cut off the arms and hands of the lords and leaders who were carrying the litter on their shoulders in order to bring down the litter and force the [Sapa] Inca to get out. Even though they cut off their hands and arms, the lords and leaders continued to support the litter with the stubs that remained to them until some of them were killed and the litter was partially knocked down.

The small group of Spaniards killed an estimated six thousand unarmed Inca troops on the plaza that day. By most reports, no Spaniards died in the attack. Atahuallpa was taken prisoner. The Inca troops posted on the outskirts of Cajamarca fled when they learned what had happened.

The Sapa Inca in captivity

Most descriptions of Atahuallpa written by Spanish eyewitnesses depict the Sapa Inca in his days of captivity. While he was in prison, Atahuallpa was allowed to receive visitors from among his people. He was attended by his wives and servants. His subjects treated him with the utmost respect, carrying out elaborate routines for ceremony and for his comfort. Most of his Spanish captors were very impressed with Atahuallpa's dignity, intelligence, and courage. They observed that he learned to speak Spanish quickly and even learned to play chess and to read a little. In his book *Verdadera relación de la conquista del Perú* (*The True Story of the Conquest of Peru*, c. 1534), eyewitness Francisco de Xerez describes his general impression of Atahuallpa:

> Atahuallpa was a man of thirty years of age, of good appearance and manner, although somewhat thick-set. He had a large face, handsome and fierce, his eyes reddened with blood. He spoke with much gravity, as a great ruler. He made very lively arguments; when the Spaniards understood it they realized that he was a wise man. He was a cheerful man, although unsubtle. When he spoke to his own people he was incisive [insightful] and showed no pleasure.

Atahuallpa's ransom

With Atahuallpa in prison, the Spaniards looted the surrounding cities, taking large quantities of the gold and silver that adorned the temples and other architecture. Atahuallpa soon realized that the Spaniards were obsessed with obtaining gold and silver, so he decided to try to pay them for his freedom. He was being held prisoner in a room that measured 23 feet (7 meters) by 16 feet (5 meters). He offered to fill the room up to a certain height with gold. In addition, he promised to give them twice as much silver. Pizarro enthusiastically agreed, creating a signed document that promised Atahuallpa would be released as soon as the Spanish received the promised goods.

Atahuallpa set his nobles and generals to work. They began collecting gold and silver, mainly from Cuzco. Load after load of gold and silver streamed into Cajamarca from cities in the south. In Cuzco, the Spaniards wanted the gold that covered the face of the sacred Temple of the Sun; they also wanted the gold and silver from some of the Incas' religious shrines and sacred objects. No Inca was willing to touch these, so the Spanish soldiers took it upon themselves to pry gold off the face of the temple and to dismantle sacred monuments. Back at Cajamarca, Pizarro had already begun the process of melting down massive quantities of the exquisite gold artwork of the Incas. In the end, Atahuallpa's ransom was more than fully paid.

Atahuallpa's ransom produced about 6 tons (5.4 metric tons) of melted gold and 12 tons (10.9 metric tons) of silver. Pizarro was required to send the king of Spain one-fifth of those amounts as a royal tax. The flood of gold and silver sent back to Spain was the equivalent of about fifty years of normal Spanish production of the precious metals at that time. The massive quantities of gold and silver overwhelmed the Spanish economy, instantly causing inflation (a continuing rise in prices caused by an abnormal increase in the amount of money or credit that is available) throughout Europe.

While the gold was being collected and melted down, Atahuallpa apparently grew nervous about what his brother Huáscar was up to. He probably feared that Huáscar would bribe the Spaniards with gold and silver and enlist their help in a war against Atahuallpa. From prison, Atahuallpa ordered his generals to murder Huáscar, and they dutifully obeyed his command.

Death of the emperor

Atahuallpa's attempts to save himself were of no use. The Spaniards did not keep their end of the bargain. They had heard rumors that despite his captivity, Atahuallpa was organizing his armies. Some of Pizarro's men claimed that a large army of Incas was on its way to the city, although this was not true. Under pressure, Pizarro charged that Atahuallpa had plotted against the Spanish crown. He also brought criminal charges against Atahuallpa for arranging the murder of Huáscar. Atahuallpa was then sentenced to death without a fair trial.

Observers noted that Atahuallpa quickly accepted his captors' intention to kill him. When he realized that they were planning to burn him alive, though, he became visibly upset for the first time. The Incas believed that eternal life could be achieved only if the body was left intact after death, so being burned to death was far worse than being executed in some other way. Thus, at the last minute, Atahuallpa agreed to convert to the Christian religion if the Spaniards would agree not to burn him. He asked that they give his body to his people to be mummified (treated with preservative herbs so that it would not decay). The Spanish agreed, and on August 29, 1533, they killed him by strangulation. Cruelly, after his death they burned part of his body and then buried him.

With Atahuallpa and Huáscar gone, the Spaniards moved on to occupy the Inca capital of Cuzco. They brought with them a brother of the two deceased Sapa Incas and installed him as a puppet ruler—someone whom the Incas would accept as their leader but whose actions could be easily controlled. At first the Inca nobles in Cuzco welcomed the Spanish and the new Sapa Inca. Many had distrusted Atahuallpa and his Inca settlement at Quito. They hoped that, with the civil war over, they could resume their old routines. Soon after arriving, though, the Spaniards exerted harsh and repressive control over their new colony in the Andes. It was not long before the Incas understood that the age of their great empire was gone forever.

Illustration by Felipe Huaman Poma de Ayala, from *La primer nueva corónica y buen gobierno*. The Spaniards strangled Atahuallpa, then burned his body. *The Art Archive/Archaeological Museum Lima/Dagli Orti.*

For More Information

Books

Betanzos, Juan de. *Narrative of the Incas.* Translated and edited by Roland Hamilton and Dana Buchanan from the Palma de Mallorca manuscript. Austin: University of Texas Press, 1996.

Davies, Nigel. *The Ancient Kingdoms of Peru*. London and New York: Penguin, 1997.

Web Sites

Bailey, David. *Incas and Conquistadors*. http://www.hc09.dial.pipex.com/incas/home.shtml#top (accessed on November 4, 2004).

"The Conquest of the Inca Empire: Francisco Pizarro." *The Applied History Research Group/The University of Calgary*. http://www.acs.ucalgary.ca/applied_history/tutor/eurvoya/inca.html (accessed on November 4, 2004).

Rostworowski, Maria. "Ambush at Cajamarca." *The Incas*. http://incas.perucultural.org.pe/english/hissurg10a.htm (accessed on November 4, 2004).

Felipe Huaman Poma de Ayala

Illustrations from La primer nueva corónica y buen gobierno
Also referred to as *Nueva corónica y buen gobierno;* translated as
The First New Chronicle and Good Government

Written and illustrated 1587–1615

For illustrations of life in the Inca empire, many modern history books include the drawings of Felipe Huaman (often spelled Guaman) Poma de Ayala (c. 1535–c. 1615). Poma was the author and artist responsible for *La primer nueva corónica y buen gobierno* (*The First New Chronicle and Good Government*) a 1,200-page account of the history and life of the Andean peoples who lived in the Inca empire before and after the Spanish conquest. The work was completed in 1615 and included 398 drawings. Poma's manuscript, though lost to historians for centuries, is now known as one of the most unusual and remarkable documents to be written about the Inca empire and its aftermath.

Poma was born around 1535, soon after the Spanish conquest of the Inca empire in 1533. Though there are no records, historians speculate that he was born in the town of Huamanga in the present-day department (state) of Ayacucho in southern Peru. Poma was a full-blooded Andean native, a person from the Andes Mountain region of South America. In Quechua (pronounced KECH-wah), the language of the Incas, his name, *Huaman,* means "falcon," and *Poma* means "leop-

La primer nueva corónica y buen gobierno is one of the few accounts of the Incas written by a native Andean. In Peru and other South American countries in which Quechua is spoken by a large portion of the population, Poma has become a hero and a symbol of native pride.

ard." Poma's father was a *curaca,* a non-Inca official in a conquered territory. He worked for the Inca government in the conquered territory around Huamanga. Poma's mother was the daughter of the Sapa Inca (supreme ruler of the Inca empire) Tupac Inca Yupanqui (ruled 1471–1493).

In the early years of the Spanish rule, Inca nobles were accorded the preferential treatment due to royalty, living in better homes and receiving education, land, and higher status in society from the ruling Spaniards. As the son of Inca nobility, Poma was raised in two worlds: the native Andean culture he shared with his family and friends in Huamanga, and the Spanish culture he shared with friends from among the families of Spanish colonial officials (people living in South America who represented the Spanish government). Poma received much of his education from Spanish missionaries (people who try to convert others, usually in a foreign land, to their religion) and priests, and was a devout Christian from an early age. As a child he learned to read and write in Spanish and Quechua, as well as other native languages.

As a young man Poma's skills in interpreting native languages for the Spanish helped him secure work in the local colonial government's administration. Some of his work over the next few decades, however, involved suppressing native Andean culture and basic rights. In one of his early jobs, he translated the words of the missionaries as they spread the Christian religion and tried to eliminate the religious beliefs of the native people. Poma also participated enthusiastically in the efforts of the Spanish colonial leaders to crush a native resistance movement called Taki Unquy, which urged the native Andeans to reject the Europeans and their religion. He later participated in the Spanish colonial government's removal of native communities from their traditional homelands. Many of these relocated people were sent to forced labor sites, such as silver mines, where Spanish colonials often mistreated them. Many died from overwork and abuse.

In these years Poma began to question Spanish policies. While working with the colonial government, he witnessed the suffering brought about by the Spaniards' rigorous attempts to destroy all non-Christian practices. Though he had strongly supported the Spanish as a young man, Poma began to fear that their abuses of the Andean people, as well as the intermarriage of Andean natives and Spanish, would cause Andean culture to disappear altogether.

Poma began trying to help the people of his community. Many Andean natives were losing their land through unfair legal processes. Poma taught them how to read and write in Spanish so they could take their land claims to court. During the late sixteenth century, Poma defended his own family's right to their land near Huamanga. After a long legal battle, Poma lost his lawsuit and the land. In the end the Spanish colonial court charged him with criminal offenses for his part in the lawsuit. Sentenced to exile and frustrated with the broken promises of the Spanish, Poma moved to another part of Peru and devoted himself to writing the massive chronicle of the Inca empire. (A chronicle is a continuous historical account of events arranged in order of time without analysis or interpretation.)

The chronicle

The entire text of *La primer nueva corónica y buen gobierno* was written in the form of a letter to King Philip III of Spain (1578–1621) as an attempt to persuade him to restore land and self-rule to the Andean people. The division of the title suggests the book's unusual two-part structure. The first part is the "nueva corónica," or "new chronicle," the history of the Andean peoples and a detailed account of their daily life and practices. It was called "new" because it greatly differs from accounts Spanish writers had produced about the people of the Andes by presenting it from the Andean people's viewpoint. The second part begins with the Spanish conquest of 1533 and chronicles the abuses of the native people under the Spanish colonial government. The "buen gobierno," or "good government," Poma describes was to be achieved through a series of his own proposed reforms: a combination of the best of European culture—in Poma's view, its advanced technology and Christian religion—and the Inca style of government and economic system. Ultimately, Poma sought self-rule for the native Andeans.

Poma grew up among the Spanish. He thus faced a difficult challenge trying to convey the history and traditions of the conquered Andeans to their conquerors. He chose to write his chronicles mostly in Spanish, but he wrote some sections in Quechua. Along with his text he included 398 full-page pen-and-ink drawings. The pictures add a visual dimension to his work. Although at first glance they appear simple or even cartoonlike, they are skillfully crafted and present an amazing range of subjects. Though the drawings are presented with the text, they can easily be viewed independently from the text, presenting their own visual story of the Andean people.

Huaman Poma was born after the Spanish conquest. He was not present to observe the Inca empire in pre-Hispanic times (before the Spanish conquest) nor at the time of the conquest itself. But he lived in close contact with people who lived during that time. Poma's historical descriptions of the Incas rely on oral traditions (history and stories passed by spoken word from generation to generation) he had learned from family and friends. He also relied strongly on accounts written by the Spanish conquistadores (Spanish word for "conquerors") and missionaries. His manner of putting factual, legendary, and purely fanciful stories and ideas together creates a compelling, though not always accurate, portrait of the Inca empire and its aftermath. His pictures, on the other hand, relate information in a more clear and direct manner.

Things to remember while examining the illustrations from *La primer nueva corónica y buen gobierno:*

- The first drawing depicts the historic meeting at Cajamarca on November 16, 1532, between the Sapa Inca **Atahuallpa** (pronounced ah-tah-WAHL-pah; c. 1502–1533; see entry) and Spanish conquistador Francisco Pizarro (c. 1475–1541). The massive Inca army stands behind Atahuallpa. Also present before him are Pizarro's partner, Diego de Almagro (died 1538), Catholic missionary Vicente de Valverde (1490–1543), and an interpreter named Felipillo. Note the labels for the Spaniards, showing who each one is, within the picture. In the section of his manuscript associated with the drawing, Poma describes the scene:

  > Fray Vicente entered … carrying a cross in his right hand and a breviary [book of prayers] in his left. And he told the Inca Atagualpa [Atahuallpa] that he was also an ambassador and a messenger from another lord, a very great one, a friend of God, and

COIQVISTA ESTA·EN LA
ATAGVALPAINGACIVDAD
DE CAXAMARCA·EN SV TRONO·VSNO

ciudad de caxa mar ca sca sienta
ata gual pa ynga ensu truno —

First meeting between Atahuallpa and Spanish conquistador Francisco Pizarro at Cajamarca, November 16, 1532. *The Art Archive/Archaeological Museum Lima/Dagli Orti.*

that he should be his friend and that he should adore the cross and believe in the Gospel of God and not worship any thing, that all the rest was mere mockery. The Inca Atagualpa responded, saying that he had to worship no one but the Sun, who never dies.

- The second drawing depicts Atahuallpa in manacles (handcuffs) after the Spaniards have taken him captive. The armored Spaniard with him in the prison cell is labeled *guarda* (Spanish for guard). In the text associated

with this picture, Poma observed: "[Atahuallpa] was left very sad and disconsolate [miserable] and dispossessed [no longer in possession] of his majesty, sitting on the ground, his throne and kingdom gone." Other writers who described Atahuallpa in captivity reported that he was treated well and attended by his own servants and wives. The two drawings featured here—one showing the majesty of the Sapa Inca and the strength of his army and the next showing a downcast Atahuallpa in manacles—reflect Poma's deep respect for the Inca government and his sadness at its demise.

- By the time he wrote his chronicles, Poma viewed the Spanish conquest as a greedy and brutal act. Describing the Pizarro expedition, Poma said: "And they did not wish to rest a single day in any port. Each day they did nothing but think of the gold and silver and riches of the Indies of Peru. They were like a desperate man, foolish, crazy, out of their minds with their greed for gold and silver. At times they could not eat for thinking about gold and silver."

What happened next ...

Upon finishing the 1,200-page chronicle in 1615, Poma wrote a short letter to King Phillip III asking if he would like to see the manuscript. It is not known if the manuscript ever made it into the king's hands. Poma died at the age of eighty, shortly after finishing it. Sadly, he spent nearly three decades writing a work that was unlikely read during his lifetime.

The manuscript of *La primer nueva corónica y buen gobierno* was lost for nearly three centuries. In 1908 a professor researching the ancient history of Peru discovered it in the Royal Library of Copenhagen in Denmark. Even then, most historians were not very interested in Huaman Poma's rough and often fanciful storytelling.

In the 1970s modern readers began to recognize the merits of Poma's text. Poma's attempt to tell the story of the Andean people from their point of view—giving them back their history—was a welcome perspective. *La primer nueva corónica y buen gobierno* is one of the few accounts of the Incas written by a native Andean. In Peru and other South American countries in which Quechua is spoken by a large portion of the population, Poma has become a hero and a symbol of native pride.

Did you know ...

- After the execution of Atahuallpa at Cajamarca in 1533, the Spanish took over the rule of Cuzco, the capital of the Inca empire in Peru. They brought one of Atahuallpa's many brothers, Manco Inca (d. 1545), to serve as the new Sapa Inca, believing they could control his actions. Manco Inca, though, saw that the Spaniards were destroying the Inca culture. He fled Cuzco and established a stronghold in a remote, mountainous region called Vilcabamba. There he led a powerful revolt against the Spanish at Cuzco, which ultimately failed. Manco Inca died in 1545. After his death a series of Sapa Incas succeeded to the throne, though still in exile at Vilcabamba. They continued to defy the orders of the Spanish to return to Cuzco and acknowledge Spanish leadership and the Christian religion.

• In 1569 Spanish noble Francisco de Toledo (1515–1582) became the viceroy (regional governor who represents the king of the ruling country) of Peru. In 1572 he declared war on the rebel Incas, sending a group of Spanish soldiers to destroy their stronghold. The soldiers captured the new Sapa Inca, Tupac Amarú (1544–1572). They brought him back to Cuzco, gave him a brief and unfair trial, and tried to convert him to Christianity. Though many Spanish priests and officials pleaded for Tupac Amarú's life, he was sentenced to death. At a huge gathering of more than ten thousand people, including the mourning Incas, Tupac Amarú was beheaded. The Spanish rounded up other Inca royalty and banished them to faraway places. Any remaining hope for a renewed Inca empire was lost.

Consider the following ...

• Page through the Inca chapter of this volume and find all the Poma illustrations. Create a list and briefly describe what you see in each illustration.

• Historians have observed that Poma's illustrations, though simple in style, tell the Inca story almost as well, or perhaps even better, than the written chronicles from his times. Describe one of the Poma illustrations in this book, discussing how the picture conveys the Inca culture and/or history.

For More Information

Books

Adorno, Rolena. *Guaman Poma: Writing and Resistance in Colonial Peru.* Austin: University of Texas Press, 1994.

Davies, Nigel. *The Ancient Kingdoms of Peru.* London and New York: Penguin, 1997.

Guaman Poma de Ayala, Felipe. *La primer nueva corónica y buen gobierno.* 1615. Available online at *The Guaman Poma Web site.* http://www.kb.dk/elib/mss/poma/ (accessed on November 5, 2004).

Time-Life Books. *Incas: Lords of Gold and Glory.* Alexandria, VA: Time-Life Books, 1992.

Periodicals

Adorno, Rolena. "Early Peruvian Recorded Daily Life Under the Rule of Spanish Conquistadors." *The New World* (spring 1990). This article is also available online at http://muweb.millersville.edu/~columbus/data/art/ADORNO01.ART (accessed on November 5, 2004).

Web Sites

Guaman Poma de Ayala, Felipe. *The First New Chronicle and Good Government.* Translated and edited by David Frye, 1999. http://www-personal.umich.edu/~dfrye/guaman.htm (accessed on November 5, 2004). Offers a short excerpt from Poma's chronicle.

The Mayas and
Their Ancestors

Of the great ancient civilizations of the Americas, the Mayas were the first to develop a writing system that could completely reproduce their spoken language, and they were the only group of Americans who accomplished this during pre-Columbian times (the period before Spanish explorer Christopher Columbus arrived in the Americas in 1492). From the Classic Maya era (250–900 C.E.) on, the Maya people were using an effective numbering system (which included a zero symbol), sophisticated and accurate calendars, and a system of recording their history and stories. The Mayas were by no means the originators of these systems. Writing, numbers, calendars, and many other features of Maya civilization existed in earlier Mesoamerican civilizations, particularly among the Olmecs and the Zapotecs. The Mayas simply adopted concepts that were already being used in Mesoamerica and then developed them with great skill.

During the Classic Maya era, powerful kings ruled the great cities of Tikal, Copán, and Palenque. They commissioned artists and architects to erect great monuments and stelae, stone pillars carved with images or writing. Some of

73

Quick Facts about the Mayas and Their Ancestors

- The Mayas were one of several ancient civilizations that arose in Mesoamerica, an area that included parts of present-day Mexico (mainly its southern and central regions), Guatemala, Honduras, El Salvador, and Belize. Some experts report that about thirty civilizations rose and fell in Mesoamerica during prehistoric times (the period before the existence of written records). Each one had its own distinct culture—arts, language, beliefs, customs, and institutions, but they shared many key cultural elements, such as primary gods, mythology, calendar systems, and military traditions.

- Among the early Mesoamerican civilizations that came before the Mayas were the Olmecs and the Zapotecs. The Olmecs thrived from about 1200 to 400 B.C.E. along the southern gulf coast of present-day Mexico. The Zapotecs were a predominant force in the Oaxaca Valley from about 500 B.C.E. to 700 C.E.

- The Mayas lived in city-states (independent, self-governing communities consisting of a single city and the surrounding area) and towns in a vast area of about 200,000 square miles (518,000 square kilometers). This region included the present-day southeastern Mexican states of Campeche, Quintana Roo, Yucatán, Chiapas, and Tabasco; the nation of Belize; the northern part of Guatemala (Petén); and the western portions of Honduras and El Salvador.

- The Mayas never lived as a unified people. Experts believe that thousands of years ago there was a single Mayan language, but over the years the Maya people separated into groups with distinct cultures and new Mayan languages developed among the groups. There are thirty-one distinct Mayan languages. They are so different from each other that people speaking in different Mayan languages cannot understand each other.

- Maya history is often divided into three eras: the pre-Classic era: c. 2000 B.C.E.–250 C.E.; the Classic era: c. 250–900 C.E.; and the post-Classic era: c. 900–1521 C.E. In the Classic era the predominant Maya cities were Tikal, Copán, and Palenque; in the post-Classic era the dominant cities were Chichén Itzá; and Mayapán in the Mexican state of Yucatán.

the first glyph-writing (carving or drawing figures to represent words, ideas, or sounds) in Mesoamerica was used to record the names of enemies who had been killed in wars. The later glyph texts carved upon stelae and monuments were created to glorify the Maya kings and to carefully record the history of their succession, or passing power from one ruler to the next.

Around 900 C.E. the cities of the Classic Maya era collapsed after a series of disasters. At that point, many Maya groups moved north into the area that is now the Mexican state of Yucatán. Other Maya groups, such as the Quiché, remained in various locations in the highlands of present-day Guatemala. In the post-Classic era (900–1521), the Mayas no longer created stelae for their writing. Instead, they wrote their glyphs in illustrated books called codices (singular: codex) recording their knowledge of astronomy (study of the stars and the planets), calendar systems, history, and religion. Scholars believe that these codices contained vast amounts of Maya learning and culture.

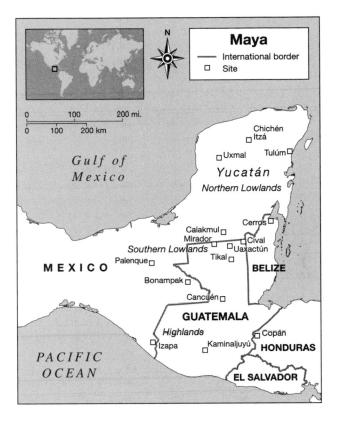

Map showing the major sites of Maya civilization in Mesoamerica. *Map by XNR Productions. The Gale Group.*

The Spanish conquistadores (Spanish word for "conquerors") first arrived in the Maya world around 1517, beginning many years of violent conflict. By 1546, the Spanish conquistadores occupied most of the Yucatán peninsula. After a fierce defense of their lands, the Mayas were forced to live under Spanish rule. Spanish missionaries, people who worked to spread their religious beliefs, quickly set to work converting the Mayas to Christianity. In 1549 a missionary named Diego de Landa (1524–1579) arrived in the Yucatán. Like many other missionaries, Landa believed it was necessary to completely eliminate the Maya heritage and culture in order to convert the people to Christian beliefs. He was ruthless in his pursuit of this goal. First he ordered the destruction of hundreds of sacred Maya shrines. Then he ordered that all the Maya codices be collected and burned. Landa believed that the codices were particularly evil. Thousands were destroyed by his order; in fact, only three Maya codices are known to have survived to modern times.

The traditional Maya culture was severely disrupted under the Spanish; some of the Maya ways of preserving their traditions could not be carried out under the harsh eye of the new government. The scribes and priests who knew how to read and write glyphs eventually died. Finally there was no one left who could read the glyphs that the earlier Mayas had left behind. The histories that Maya kings, priests, and scribes carefully recorded in their codices and on stelae, doorways, and monuments would not be read again for centuries.

The seven entries in this chapter follow the chronological progression of glyph-writing among the Mayas and their ancestors. The first entry features a simple glyph carving in a ceramic artifact found in 2002 at an Olmec site. This **Olmec Stone Roller Stamp** is the earliest known writing of the Americas. The next three entries of this chapter present samples of the **Bar and Dot Number System**, the **Sacred Calendar**, and the **Long Count** system of measuring time, including a diagram of a stela with a full date written in Maya format and glyphs. These entries provide an introduction to the workings of the sophisticated three-calendar system of the Mayas. The fifth entry in this chapter features photos and illustrations of **Copán stelae and monuments** commissioned by the powerful Copán king named 18 Rabbit (ruled 695–738). The illustrations show an intricate sculpture portrait of the king and columns of glyph text carved on the back of the monument. Also featured in this entry is a photograph and discussion of the Hieroglyphic Stairway in Copán, Honduras, the longest inscription of the Classic Maya era. Following this entry is a biography of the great king of Palenque, **Pacal**, whose famous Temple of Inscriptions contains exquisite artwork and a detailed history of the king. Finally, the chapter ends with an excerpt from the ***Popol Vuh,*** a copy of the sacred book that the Quiché Mayas created after the Spanish conquest, probably copying an older codex of unknown origin. This text represents the Mayas' desperate attempt to preserve the traditions, religion, and history of their people. It is considered one of the greatest works of literature coming from the culture of pre-Columbian America, and it is powerful proof of the great loss that occurred with the destruction of the Maya codices.

Timeline: The Mayas and Their Ancestors

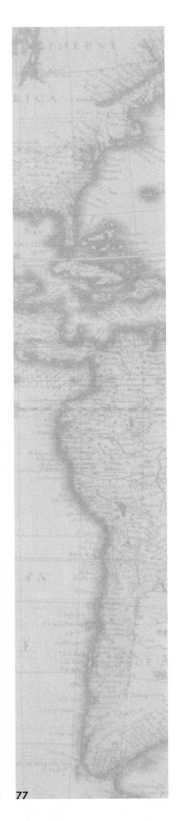

1500–1200 B.C.E. The earliest distinct Olmec culture emerges in San Lorenzo, along the Gulf of Mexico, south of Veracruz.

650 B.C.E. The first known example of writing from the Americas is carved by an Olmec artist onto a **stone roller stamp**.

600 B.C.E. Another early example of a glyph representing a **sacred calendar** date found at a Zapotec site dates back to this time.

500 B.C.E. Building begins on the Zapotec city Monte Albán in the Oaxaca Valley.

c. 2680–2526 B.C.E.
Building of the Great
Pyramids near Giza, Egypt

776 B.C.E.
Greece's first recorded
Olympic games are held
at Olympia

3000 B.C.E.   **800** B.C.E.

400 B.C.E. The numerical concept of zero emerges in Mesoamerica. The **bar and dot number system** has been in place for centuries.

c. 400 B.C.E. The Olmec city La Venta experiences upheaval and never recovers. The Olmec civilization rapidly declines.

36 B.C.E. An Olmec **Long Count** inscribed with this date was found in the Mexican state of Chiapas.

250–900 C.E The classic Maya era takes place, in which the cities of Tikal, Palenque, and Copán flourish in the southern highlands of the Maya world.

615 Maya king **Pacal** begins his rule of Palenque, in present-day Chiapas, Mexico; the city builds its greatest architecture during his long reign.

695 18 Rabbit begins his rule of Copán, bringing about a new age of art and writing, particularly on the **stelae and monuments** of the city.

c. 900 The classic Maya era ends when the dominant cities of the southern highlands, including Tikal, Palenque, and Copán, are abandoned. The Mayas of the south scatter and Chichén Itzá in the present-day Mexican state Yucatán becomes the most powerful city in the Maya world.

1000 A profound Toltec influence takes over Chichén Itzá.

c. 1200 The city of Mayapán in the present-day Mexican state of Yucatán replaces Chichén Itzá as the Maya capital. After this time, Mayas are less centered in cities and Maya groups become scattered.

1517 Mayas successfully fight off the forces of Spanish explorer Francisco Fernández de Córdoba. Soon epidemics of small pox and the measles break out among

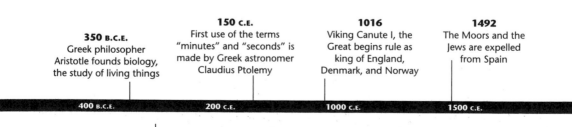

350 B.C.E.
Greek philosopher Aristotle founds biology, the study of living things

150 C.E.
First use of the terms "minutes" and "seconds" is made by Greek astronomer Claudius Ptolemy

1016
Viking Canute I, the Great begins rule as king of England, Denmark, and Norway

1492
The Moors and the Jews are expelled from Spain

400 B.C.E.   200 C.E.   1000 C.E.   1500 C.E.

the Mayas, eventually killing as many as 90 percent of the people.

1526 Another large Spanish attack on the Mayas is repelled and the Spanish flee.

1531 The Spanish take the Maya city of Chichén Itzá, but the Mayas rise against them and force them to flee.

1532 The Spanish missionaries establish missions in the Maya world and begin strenuous efforts to convert the Mayas to Christianity.

c. 1550s The members of three noble Quiché Maya families set to work writing down the story of their creation and history as it had been written earlier in a sacred codex (painted book). The book they produce is called the *Popol Vuh.*

1562 Spanish missionary Diego de Landa begins a book-burning campaign, destroying thousands of Maya codices in his efforts to eliminate the Maya religion. Only three known Maya codices survive.

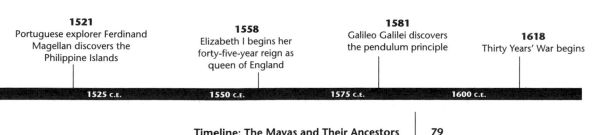

1521
Portuguese explorer Ferdinand Magellan discovers the Philippine Islands

1558
Elizabeth I begins her forty-five-year reign as queen of England

1581
Galileo Galilei discovers the pendulum principle

1618
Thirty Years' War begins

1525 C.E.   1550 C.E.   1575 C.E.   1600 C.E.

Olmec Stone Roller Stamp

Photograph of an Olmec stone roller stamp and a drawing of its rolled-out seal

Artifact date c. 650 B.C.E.; found at San Andres, Tabasco, Mexico

In 2002 anthropologist Mary Pohl (1942–) and a group of fellow archaeologists (scientists who dig up and examine artifacts, remains, and monuments of past human life) were working in San Andres, a site near the ancient Olmec city of La Venta in the western part of the Mexican state of Tabasco. They found a ceramic cylinder (tube-shaped object) with raised, carved symbols on it. Nearby they found small fragments of flattened jade inscribed with similar symbols. The ceramic cylinder is believed to have been a roller stamp or seal. When it was rolled in ink or dyes, it could be used to print the symbols from its raised carvings onto cloth, or even human skin as a kind of body decoration. Scientific testing indicated that the cylinder and other artifacts found nearby dated back to 650 B.C.E.

What made this find so remarkable was that the archaeologists recognized the symbols on the cylinder as glyphs (figures used as symbols to represent words, ideas, or sounds). Prior to the roller stamp cylinder, the earliest known example of writing had been found in Zapotec sites a few hundred miles away. A Zapotec carved stone slab with a glyph on it was at least fifty years more recent than the roller stamp. Pohl, who

Some experts believe the 2002 discovery of the roller stamp proves the Olmecs were the originators of glyph-writing in Mesoamerica.

has studied the Olmec cylinder extensively, believes it represents the earliest known example of writing in the Americas.

The Olmecs were a Mesoamerican civilization that thrived between about 1200 and 400 B.C.E. in swampy jungle river basins in the tropical coastal plains of the modern-day states of Veracruz and Tabasco in Mexico. Olmec artifacts discovered in the twentieth century have provided evidence that the Olmecs had developed many early skills and were the actual originators of many of the Mesoamerican institutions. For example, the Olmecs seem to have been the first Mesoamericans to build ceremonial centers, citylike centers usually run by priests and rulers, in which people from surrounding areas gathered to practice the ceremonies of their religion, often at large temples and plazas built specifically for this purpose. The Olmecs are believed to have been the first to form a political state with a formal government and elite rulers (people in a socially superior position who have more power and privileges than others). From recent evidence, it seems possible that Mesoamerican ball games, calendars, and number systems all originated within the Olmec society. Some experts believe the 2002 discovery of the roller stamp also proves the Olmecs were the originators of glyph-writing (recreating some parts of the spoken language by creating carved or drawn figures to represent words, ideas, or sounds) in Mesoamerica.

Things to remember while examining the photograph of an Olmec stone roller stamp and a drawing of its rolled-out seal:

- Note that when rolled in ink or dye, the ceramic cylinder prints out a picture of a bird with lines streaming from its beak. The lines connect the bird's beak to two symbols that appear to be the bird's dialogue. This concept is called a speech scroll. Speech scrolls resemble dialogue balloons used in present-day comic books and cartoons. Dialogue balloons represent the idea of speech or sound emerging from the mouths of humans or animals. Speech scrolls were widely used in later Mesoamerican writing to depict dialogue.

- Mary Pohl and her team of archaeologists believe the symbols in the Olmec speech scroll on the roller

Photograph of the Olmec stone roller stamp from a site in San Andres, Tabasco, Mexico. *Photograph by Richard Brunck. Courtesy of Dr. Mary Pohl, FSU.*

stamp are glyphs representing words. They found a strong resemblance between these symbols and the later Maya glyphs. Archaeologists were able to use Maya glyphs to aid in translating the Olmec roller stamp symbols.

• The sideways U shape at the end of the top speech scroll resembles the Maya glyph for the word "king."

Drawing of the rolled-out seal from the Olmec stone roller stamp, showing what the stamp would look like rolled out. *Drawing by Ayax Moreno. Courtesy of Dr. Mary Pohl, FSU.*

- The three dots under the sideways U shape represent the number three in the Mesoamerican bar and dot number system. In this system, a bar represents the value of five and a dot represents the value of one. One bar with three dots would signify the number eight. (See **Bar and Dot Number System** entry.)

- Pohl believes the symbol below the three dots is a glyph representing the day name "Ajaw" from the sacred 260-day calendar used by the Olmec. Every Mesoamerican society from the Olmecs forward used a calendar system that combined two calendars: the sacred 260-day calendar and the practical 365-day solar calendar. The 260-day calendar was composed of twenty consecutive day names combined with the numerals one to thirteen. For example, a given day such as "3 Jaguar" was formed of two parts: the numeral three with the day name Jaguar. The written form of a day name consisted of a glyph and a bar and dot numeral (see **Sacred Calendar** entry). "3 Ajaw" is probably a reference to a particular day. Many Mesoamerican groups named their children after the day name of their birth date—a child born on 6 Monkey, for example, would bear that name. Thus, "King 3 Ajaw" is likely the name of an Olmec king.

- In Mesoamerican symbolism, birds often represented royal figures and gods. Pohl believes the stamp is a royal seal, probably used by the people of San Andres to show their loyalty to the king of nearby La Venta.

What happened next ...

Chronologically, the next known example of glyph-writing in Mesoamerica was an artifact found in the Zapotec site of San José Mogote in the northern arm of the Oaxaca (pronounced wah-HAH-kah) Valley. Dating back to about 600 B.C.E., only fifty years after the Olmec cylinder, the artifact consists of a carved stone slab set on the floor of a public walkway. The carving is of a victim of human sacrifice. The man's eyes are closed and his mouth is open in a distorted manner portraying either horror or pain. Blood flows from the hole in his chest where his heart has been removed. At his feet there is a glyph, which experts have translated as the day name "1 Earthquake." Experts believe the glyph represents the victim's name and that he was probably a chief of a community the Zapotecs defeated in combat. The Zapotecs set the carved slab on the floor to be walked upon by everyone who passed, showing their complete victory over their enemy and their glory as conquerors. Scholars believe Zapotec writing originated as an attempt to record their victories in battle.

Did you know ...

- Many Mesoamerican scholars agree with Mary Pohl that the Olmec roller stamp may represent the first writing in the Americas. Other experts are not convinced. Mesoamerican epigrapher (a person who deciphers ancient forms of writing) Stephen Houston argues there is no proof the symbols on the roller represent true written language; instead, they may just be an example of a sophisticated form of iconography. Iconography is a system of expression in which easily recognized images are associated with ideas that are central to a culture. An example of iconography is the use of a halo adorning an angel in a painting. A viewer familiar with Christian symbols will immediately know what the halo means. Houston argues that the images on the roller might be recognized symbols rather than proof of an early language.

- In "Olmec Origins of Mesoamerican Writing," a paper written by Pohl and fellow Mesoamerican scholars Kevin O. Pope and Christopher von Nagy, Pohl asserts that the Olmec glyphs do indeed represent spoken language. "The speech scrolls on the San Andres seal represent speech pictographically [through pictures] and clearly signify that the signs they encompass represent words to be spoken as opposed to iconography."

Consider the following ...

- Make a list of the forms of communication other than writing or speaking that we use in modern times. Include some examples, such as traffic signs and warning sirens, for each form of communication on your list. How do we know what these things mean?

- If you were named using the Olmec system, your birthday—October 7, for example—might be your name. Make a glyph-writing representation of your name, using either a numeral or a bar and dot-number and a month glyph you create for yourself.

For More Information

Books

Coe, Michael D. *Mexico: From the Olmecs to the Aztecs.* 4th ed. London and New York: Thames and Hudson, 1994.

Fagan, Brian M. *Kingdoms of Gold, Kingdoms of Jade: The Americas before Columbus.* London and New York: Thames and Hudson, 1991.

Sabloff, Jeremy A. *The Cities of Ancient Mexico: Reconstructing a Lost World.* Rev. ed. New York: Thames and Hudson, 1997.

Periodicals

Popson, Colleen P. "Earliest Mesoamerican Writing?" *Archaeology* (March/April 2003). This article is also available online at http://www.archaeology.org/0303/newsbriefs/olmec.html (accessed on November 3, 2004).

Web Sites

Pohl, Mary E., Kevin O. Pope, and Christopher von Nagy. "Olmec Origins of Mesoamerican Writing." http://www.anthro.fsu.edu/research/meso/Pohltext.doc (accessed on November 3, 2004).

Bar and Dot Number System

Illustrations showing how the Mayas used the Mesoamerican bar and dot number system for mathematics

Date of origination: 1200–400 B.C.E.

The bar and dot system of writing numbers was in use in Mesoamerica as far back as the Olmec civilization (1200–400 B.C.E.) and prevailed in a wide variety of regions. The bar and dot number system was devised in conjunction with the Mesoamerican calendar systems (see **Sacred Calendar** and **Long Count** entries). Perhaps one of the most notable features of the Mesoamerican number system and mathematics is the value of zero, which developed around 400 B.C.E. Mesoamericans were among the earliest civilizations to use the concept of zero. The Olmec, Zapotec, and Maya number systems were all basically the same. There were minor variations in the way numbers were laid out, the way zeroes were represented, and the ornamentation around the numbers, but many of these were individual or regional preferences.

Perhaps one of the most notable features of the Mesoamerican number system and mathematics is the value of zero, which developed around 400 B.C.E.

Things to remember while examining the illustrations showing how the Mayas used the Mesoamerican bar and dot number system for mathematics:

- The bar and dot number system shown in the drawing labeled "Drawing A: Maya digits with Yucatec Maya names" is one version of the system used by the Mayas and other Mesoamericans. The names of the numbers are in the Yucatec Mayan language, the most commonly used of the thirty-one Mayan languages.

- In the bar and dot system, the Mayas expressed all numbers using only three figures—the bar, the dot, and a symbol for zero (often a shell). The bar represents the value of five, while the dot represents the value of one. The Mayas often filled in the spaces between the dots with various shapes, like the crescents shown in Drawing A. These crescents and other fillers have no value and are merely decorative.

- Reading the bar and dot figures between zero and nineteen is easy. The number twelve, as shown in Drawing A, is written using two bars and two dots placed side by side. Each bar has a value of five, so together they have a value of ten. Each of the two dots beside them has a value of one, so the bars and dots add up to twelve. The crescent between the two dots simply fills in the blank space.

- The bars and dots in the numbers pictured in Drawing A are placed side by side, but in "Drawing B: Maya mathematics" they run from bottom to top, with the bars on the bottom and the dots placed over them. In many Maya texts, the scribes (people who did the writing) wrote their bar and dot numbers in both bottom-to-top and side-to-side formats within the same passage.

- The Maya numbering system was vigesimal, or base-twenty. Our numbering system is decimal, or base-ten. Like our numbers today, the Maya number system used a place value system. With a place value system, the numeral 4 can be used to mean 4, 40, 400, or 4,000, depending on its position in a number. In the decimal system, to write the number 1,234, a 1 is placed in the 1000s column, a 2 in the 100s column, a 3 in the 10s column,

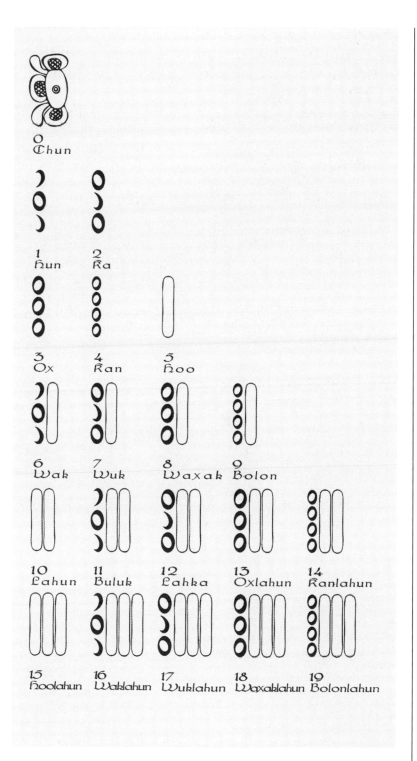

Drawing A: Maya digits with Yucatec Maya names.
Calendario Maya
(www.calendariomaya.com).

Drawing B: Maya mathematics. *The Gale Group.*

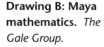

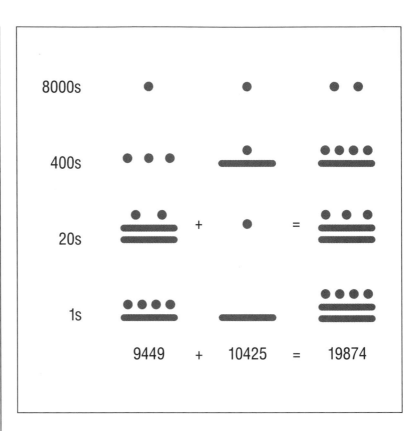

and a 4 in the 1s column. Those are each numeral's place value. In Maya mathematics, numbers were written in powers of 20. The column values are 1s, 20s (20 x 20), 400s (20 x 200), 8,000s (20 x 400), 160,000s (20 x 8,000), and so on.

- Drawing B shows how the numbers beyond 20 are formed. In the first column, 9,449 is expressed with a 1 in the 8000s column (1 x 8,000 = 8,000); a 3 in the 400s column (3 x 400 = 1,200); a 12 in the 20s column (12 x 20 = 240), and a 9 in the 1s column (1 x 9 = 9). Thus, 8,000 + 1,200 + 240 + 9 = 9,449.

- Addition in the Maya bar and dot system is simple. The numbers are set side by side and then combined by columns. In Drawing B, 9,449 is added to 10,425 by simply adding the dots and bars in each column. Subtraction is a process of eliminating, rather than combining, the dots and bars. The Maya did not use fractions.

- The zero figure allowed the expression of a number such as 400, which would be written with one dot in the 400s column and shells or other symbols recognized as zero in the 20s and 1s columns below it.

What happened next ...

At some point in their history, Maya priests modified the vigesimal system so it would work with their calendar system. All the place values remained the same except 20 x 20, or 400, which became 20 x 18, or 360, to approximate the solar year (see Sacred Calendar and Long Count entries).

The Mayas expressed numbers using the bar and dot system, but they also used glyphs (figures used as symbols to represent words, ideas, or sounds) or pictures of gods associated with particular numbers. Sometimes the Mayas used both the bar and dot numbers and glyphs in the same number. This caused more confusion for archaeologists trying to decipher their writing.

While the Mesoamericans were using the bar and dot number system, the Europeans were still using the Roman numeral system. The Roman numeral system did not have a zero and did not have place values like the bar and dot system and the Arabic numeral systems. It was not until around 1200 that Europe switched to the Arabic numeral system used today.

Did you know ...

- People often count using their fingers. Scholars believe the Mesoamericans used the number value of one for the dot, indicating one finger, and five for the bar because it is the number of fingers on a human hand. They believe the vigesimal system was used because human beings have twenty digits—fingers and toes—on which to count. In the Yucatec Mayan language, the word for the number twenty (*Winik*) is the same as the word for "human being." This probably means the number twenty encompasses all the fingers and toes of a human being.

Consider the following ...

- If a shell stands for the value zero, how would you write the number twenty in the bar and dot system?

- Try your skills at working in the Maya's vigesimal bar and dot number system. Creating a chart like the one in Drawing B, do the following addition problem: 5,421 + 11,157. For help getting started with this problem, read on. To write the first number in the problem—5,421—in the bar and dot system, find the highest possible place value for the number in the left-hand column of the chart. Since the number is not divisible by 8,000, you will start with the 400s column. Divide 5,421 by 400 to find the highest whole number by which it is divisible. The number is 13 (13 x 400 = 5,200), so you will put two bars and three dots, or 13, in the 400s column. You have 221 left, so you can put two bars and a dot (11) in the 20s column (11 x 20 = 220). Then put one dot in the 1s column to complete the number. Can you finish the problem?

For More Information

Books

Coe, Michael D., and Mark Van Stone. *Reading the Maya Glyphs*. London and New York: Thames and Hudson, 2001.

Galvin, Irene Flum. *The Ancient Maya*. New York: Benchmark Books, 1997.

Web Sites

Fought, Steven. "Maya Arithmetic." *The Math Forum*. http://mathforum.org/k12/mayan.math/ (accessed on November 3, 2004).

"Maya Mathematics." *Maya Astronomy Page*. http://www.michielb.nl/maya/math.html (accessed on November 3, 2004).

"The Maya Number System." *Oracle Think Quest Education Foundation*. http://library.thinkquest.org/J0112511/mayan_number.htm (accessed on November 3, 2004).

Sacred Calendar

Illustration of the Maya tzolkin, *or sacred calendar*
Date of origination: prior to 500 B.C.E.

No one knows for certain where the first Mesoamerican calendar systems arose, but two very likely places are the Olmec homeland, along the southern gulf coast of Mexico, and the Zapotec city of Monte Albán in Mexico's Oaxaca (pronounced wah-HAH-kah) Valley. Virtually every Mesoamerican civilization from the Olmecs forward used a calendar system that combined two calendars: the sacred 260-day calendar now known as the *tzolkin* and the practical 365-day solar calendar called the *haab.*

The Maya used three calendars in combination: the *tzolkin,* the *haab,* and the **Long Count** (see entry), a way of counting the days from the beginning of time. While the Maya did not invent these calendars, they were responsible for making them work nearly perfectly and for adding many features. In the Maya world, specially trained priests were responsible for keeping track of the days in the combined three-calendar systems and for determining what days were best for certain ceremonies or major events, like marriages or battles. Combining the three calendars and many other variables, the priests put together a system in which numerous

Because the Maya priests were very good at their work, the Maya calendars were actually slightly more accurate than modern calendars are. The Maya calendars were also much more complicated—definitely not designed for use by ordinary, untrained people.

cycles of time meshed like the cogs (series of teeth that fit between the teeth on another wheel so that one wheel can move the other) of a modern machine. Because the priests were very good at their work, the Maya calendars were actually slightly more accurate than modern calendars are. The Maya calendars were also much more complicated—definitely not designed for use by ordinary, untrained people.

The earliest and most basic part of the system was the 260-day-year *tzolkin,* the Maya's sacred calendar. The *tzolkin* is known to have existed in Mesoamerica as early as 500 B.C.E. Scholars believe it was the first Mesoamerican calendar, preceding the solar calendar and the Long Count. No one knows why the Mesoamericans chose a 260-day year for their sacred calendar; however, experts are certain that this calendar played a vital role in Maya cultural life. The *tzolkin* is the only Maya calendar that has remained in use into present times, even after the Gregorian calendar (the one used internationally in modern times) had become the primary calendar in Central America. The Maya priests used the *tzolkin* for the purpose of divination—the study of signs to determine whether a particular day was appropriate for an important event or ceremony and to attempt to foretell the future. In that sense the calendar had a function similar to that of astrology, a popular pseudoscience based on the zodiac (a pseudoscience is a set of theories and methods that cannot be scientifically tested or proved; astrologers study the positions of the stars and the planets to determine their influence on human affairs).

Most modern people believe that time progresses in a forward direction—from earlier to later. The Maya, however, believed that they lived in cycles of time, with no one point in time being unique. For example, one of the units of time that they measured was a four-hundred-year period called a *baktun.* They believed that after four hundred years had passed, the events of that period would happen again—occurring in the same order and on the same particular days in the next four-hundred-year period. There were numerous cycles besides the *baktun,* all going on at the same time and each one influencing the others; therefore, only the most scholarly priests devoted fully to analyzing the Maya calendars could make any sense of the complicated cycles and the events associated with them. The Maya firmly believed that if they could understand what happened in the past, they might be able to interpret the present and predict future events.

Things to remember while examining the illustration of the Maya *tzolkin*, or sacred calendar:

- There are 260 days on the *tzolkin*. The names of every one of the 260 days in the cycle can be determined using the interlocking wheel diagram of the sacred calendar.

- To begin, look at the large outer wheel, and note that there are twenty glyphs (figures used as a symbol to represent words, ideas, or sounds) on it. Below each glyph is a day name.

- On the inner wheel, thirteen day numbers are represented with Arabic numerals (modern numbers) and with the Maya's **Bar and Dot Number System** (see entry). As an alternative to the bar and dot system, the Maya sometimes used special number glyphs that represented the heads of Maya gods. It is likely that the day numbers were associated with specific deities, as were the day names.

- Imagine the inner wheel turning, making its round on the outer wheel. Each bump on the inner wheel will roll into an indentation below one of the day names. The position that is shown in the picture—1 Imix—represents the first day of the sacred calendar. The second day is 2 Ik', the third day is 3 Ak'bal, and so on.

- When the thirteenth bump (or cog) on the inner wheel rolls into place, it will be at the day name Ben on the outer wheel; thus the thirteenth day is called 13 Ben. The number wheel then begins its rotation again, though the day-name wheel does not. The fourteenth day is 1 Ix, the fifteenth day is 2 Men, and so on. When the wheel arrives back where it started on the outer circle, the number 8 will be lined up with Imix; this position—8 Imix—represents the twenty-first day of the cycle.

- If the small inner wheel continued to rotate within the larger wheel, the result would be 260 (13 x 20) different

The Maya *tzolkin,* or sacred calendar. *Calendario Maya (www.calendariomaya.com).*

combinations of numbers and day names before any one of them repeated. On day 261, the wheels would align at the original starting position, 1 Imix.

- Every day of the *tzolkin* calendar was associated with a deity and other factors that were thought to determine the day's events. When planning for war, marriages, or large ceremonies, Maya priests studied the calendar intensely, trying to foresee the best days for these events to take place.

- Mayas were sometimes named after their day of birth; for example, a person might be called 7 Ahaw.

What happened next ...

Though the *tzolkin* was the first calendar to arise in Mesoamerica, the solar calendar was not far behind. The solar calendar, also known as the *haab* or the vague calendar, measured a 365-day year. The *haab* had eighteen twenty-day months. At the end of the eighteenth month came a five-day period called *Uayeb* (also spelled *Wayeb*) to finish out the year. This short period was considered a very unlucky time.

The eighteen *haab* month names were Pop; Uo; Zip; Zotz; Tzec; Xul; Yaxk 'in; Mol; Ch 'en; Yax; Sek; Ceh; Mac; K' ank' in; Muan; Pax; Kayab; and Cumhu. The *haab* days were numbered from zero to nineteen and combined with the month name. The first day of the year, therefore, was 0 Pop; then came 1 Pop, 2 Pop, and so on through 19 Pop. Then the second month began: 0 Uo, 1 Uo, and so on.

After the *tzolkin* and *haab* calendars had been around for some time, the Maya priests combined them in their Calendar Round. To understand this round, imagine that it functioned like the inner and outer wheels of the sacred calendar. The 365-day *haab* was longer, so it served as the outer wheel, and the 260-day *tzolkin,* a circle made up of all the combined day names and numbers, was the inner wheel. In this combined calendar system every day had two names—its name on the *tzolkin* and its name on the *haab*—for example, 9 Imix 5 Zotz. Under this two-calendar, two-name system, it would be fifty-two years before 9 Imix 5 Zotz, or any other date, would recur.

Did you know ...

• There are about forty calendar systems in use in the twenty-first century. The five most-used calendars are the Gregorian, Hebrew, Islamic, Indian, and Chinese calendars. For international agreement of dates, however, the Gregorian calendar is dominant worldwide.

• The Gregorian calendar is based on a calendar system initiated by Roman statesman Julius Caesar (100 B.C.E.–44 B.C.E.). The Romans had been using an ancient Greek method of measuring time, but it had fallen out of sync with the seasons—a month that had once signaled spring, for example, was falling in the middle of summer. In 45 B.C.E. Caesar added ninety days to the calendar, much to the confusion of the Roman people. Then he introduced a calendar (called the Julian calendar) with twelve months and a leap day (an extra day added at the end of February) every fourth year. The Romans originally counted their years back to the date of the founding of Rome, about 753 B.C.E. In 315 C.E. Rome adopted Christianity under the Roman emperor Constantine I (c. 280–337). At that time the Romans began to count the years back to the birth of Christ rather than the founding of Rome.

- The Julian calendar accounted for a year with 365.25 days, but the solar year is actually 365.242199 days. Over the centuries the difference caused the calendar to become out of sync with the seasons again. In 1582 Pope Gregory XIII (1502–1585) reformed the Julian calendar. By his decree, the day after October 4, 1582, was October 15, taking ten days out of the calendar year. He also changed the leap year system so that leap years would only occur in years that were divisible by four; years divisible by one hundred were only leap years if they were divisible by four hundred.

Consider the following ...

- Try to imagine a world without a calendar system. Make a list of ordinary activities that would be impossible for people to carry out if society did not have ways of measuring time. How important do you think calendars are in a highly populated civilization?

- Create the first thirty days of a Calendar Round. Divide a sheet of paper into two columns. In the first column, write down the names of the first thirty days of the *tzolkin* calendar year. In the second column, write the names from the *haab* or solar calendar year next to the corresponding sacred calendar days. (Hint: The first days in the *tzolkin* column are 1 Imix and 2 Ik'; the first two days in the *haab* column are 0 Pop and 1 Pop.) Combining the two, as in 1 Imix 0 Pop, gives you a Maya date. The Long Count, described in the next entry, will complete the picture.

For More Information

Books
Coe, Michael D., and Mark Van Stone. *Reading the Maya Glyphs.* London and New York: Thames and Hudson, 2001.

Henderson, John S. *The World of the Ancient Maya*. 2nd ed. Ithaca, NY, and London: Cornell University Press, 1977.

Web Sites

"Calendars and the Long Count System." *Tikal Park*. http://www.tikalpark.com/calendar.htm (accessed on November 9, 2004).

"The Maya Calendar." *Maya World Studies Center*. http://www.mayacalendar.com/f-cuenta.html (accessed on November 9, 2004).

Meyer, Peter. "The Maya Calendar." *Hermetic Systems*. http://www.hermetic.ch/cal_stud/maya/chap1.htm#5 (accessed on November 9, 2004).

Long Count

Illustrations showing how the Mayas used the Long Count system to record dates

Date of origination: first century B.C.E.

Virtually all Mesoamerican societies from the Olmecs forward used both the sacred *tzolkin* calendar and a solar calendar, but only a few groups used the Long Count, most notably the Olmecs and the Mayas (pronounced MY-uhs). Many scholars believe the Long Count originated with the Olmecs sometime around the first century B.C.E. Stela C, found at the Olmec site of Tres Zapotes, has long been thought to be one of the oldest dated written documents of the Americas, dating back to 32 B.C.E. An even earlier Olmec Long Count date of 36 B.C.E. was more recently found on an artifact in the present-day Mexican state of Chiapas. In 1986 a huge, four-ton basalt (a fine-grained, dark gray rock) monument was found at La Mojarra, near the Olmec urban center of San Lorenzo. One side of the monument, called La Mojarra stela, features an elaborate carving of an Olmec ruler and twenty-one columns of glyphs, or symbols representing words, ideas, or sounds. The people who carved this monument used the bar and dot number and Long Count systems to record the dates (see **Bar and Dot Number System** entry).

The Long Count was a way to count days from the beginning of time. The Mayas believed that the world had been created and destroyed several times before their era of existence.

The Long Count dates on La Mojarra stela are May 21, 143 C.E., and July 13, 156 C.E.

The Maya's Calendar Round, the combined system of their sacred and solar calendars, worked well for measuring seasons and timing important events (see **Sacred Calendar** entry). Using the Calendar Round, it was possible to distinguish each day from all others for fifty-two years; that is, each day within the fifty-two-year cycle had a different name. The Mayas called these fifty-two-year cycles "bundles." If the Mayas had used only these two calendar systems, they would have been unable to distinguish time frames beyond these fifty-two-year bundles. During a term of two hundred years, for example, the same name might occur two or even three times. To create a larger time frame for their dates, the Mayas used the Long Count.

The Long Count was a way to count days from the beginning of time. The Mayas believed that the world had been created and destroyed several times before their era of existence. For reasons scholars do not yet understand, the Mayas placed the beginning of their era on a date that would be called August 13, 3114 B.C.E. (some sources say August 11, 3114 B.C.E.) on the Gregorian calendar—the calendar that most people use in the twenty-first century.

Long Count dates are expressed in units of time that are modified forms of the vigesimal, or base-twenty, system. The smallest unit of time was 1 day, or 1 kin; the next unit of time, the winal, represented 20 days (20 x 1 day). The tun, originally represented 400 days (20 x 20 days), but it was adjusted from 400 to 360 (18 x 20 days) in order to stay in line with the 365-day solar year. The units of time the Mayas used to measure their history are as follows:

1 kin = 1 day

1 winal = 20 days or 20 kins

1 tun = 360 days (approx. 1 year) or 18 winals

1 katun = 7,200 days (approx. 20 years) or 20 tuns

1 baktun (also spelled bactun) = 144,000 days (approx. 395 years) or 20 katuns

Things to remember while examining illustrations showing how the Mayas used the Long Count system to record dates:

- The Mayas expressed Long Count dates in five numerals, using the bar and dot number system. Modern writers express Long Count dates in five Arabic numerals separated by periods. In both Maya and modern texts, the numerals are arranged from the largest time period (baktun or katun) to the smallest (kin).

- The Mayas marked the beginning of time in their era on a date equivalent to August 13, 3114 B.C.E. In the Long Count system that date is written 0.0.0.0.0.

- The Long Count date shown in the first illustration in the photo section, labeled "Drawing A: Maya Long Count date," is 12.16.3.8.5. It expresses the following time units:

    12 baktuns = 12 x 144,000 days = 1,728,000 days

    16 katuns = 16 x 7,200 days = 115,200 days

    3 tuns = 3 x 360 days = 1,080 days

    8 winals = 8 x 20 days = 160 days

    5 kins = 5 x 1 day = 5 days

    Total days = 1,844,445

- The Long Count date in Drawing A is approximately 1,844,445 days after the beginning of the Maya era (August 13, 3114 B.C.E.).

- To convert Long Count dates to the modern calendar requires some extensive arithmetic; most scholars use a conversion software program.

- Long Count dates written by the Mayas were always accompanied by the dates from the *tzolkin*, or sacred calendar, and the *haab*, or solar calendar.

- The earliest writing in Mesoamerica stemmed from attempts to put a date and name on carvings that illustrated defeated enemies or victorious battles. Soon the Mayas began to chronicle the lives of their kings on stelae, large, stone pillars that they inscribed with images and glyphs and used as monuments. Along with portraits of their kings, the Mayas often carved their birth and death dates, their dates of succession to the throne, and sometimes the dates of important triumphs on the battlefield.

Maya dates were often based on the Long Count system and carved on stone pillars, or stela, such as this one from Tikal, Guatemala. *The Art Archive/Archaeological Museum Tikal Guatemala/Dagli Orti.*

- The second illustration, labeled "Drawing B: Maya Long Count date inscribed on a stela," shows a Maya Long Count date as it would have appeared on a stela. The illustration depicts the Maya date 12.16.3.8.5 9 Chikchan 3 Sek. Like most Maya dates, it is written first in the Long Count, with the *tzolkin* and *haab* dates following.

- Note the large figure at the top of the stela in Drawing B. This is called the Initial Series Introductory Glyph (ISIG). Every Maya date is introduced by this glyph. Its function is to alert the reader that a date is going to follow. The ISIG always looks the same except for a sign in the middle of its upper section; the sign changes each month to show the *haab* month, called the "patron month," in which the date falls. In this stela, the patron month is Sek.

- The stela is read from top to bottom in pairs of glyphs. The pairs are read from left to right. The five figures after the ISIG are the five components of the Long Count date as described above (12 baktuns; 16 katuns; 3 tuns; 8 winals; 5 kins).

- The figure after the Long Count date is the *tzolkin* date 9 Chikchan.

- On the bottom left of the stela in Drawing B, between the position for the *tzolkin* date and the *haab* date, there is a variable element of the date. Scholars place the items that fall in this position of the date stela in a category they call the Supplementary Series. Not all Maya dates have Supplementary Series elements, and even when such elements are found, they cannot always be immediately deciphered—that is, interpreted. In this stela the Supplementary Series element is labeled Lord of the Night G-3. The Lord of the Night G-3 is one of nine G-Glyphs that often appear in this position; each represents one of the

12   Baktuns

16   Katuns

3   Tuns

8   Winals

5   Kins

Drawing B: Maya Long Count date inscribed on a stela. *Calendario Maya (www.calendariomaya.com).*

nine Lords of the Night. Because no one knows the individual names of the Lords of the Night, modern decipherers have labeled them G-1, G-2, and so on. Scholars believe that each of the Lords of the Night had its own special powers, but they are uncertain about the details of these traits. They suggest that the Mayas may have seen the Lords of the Night as protectors: Each Lord appeared once every nine days in the calendar cycle, perhaps to watch over people born on those particular dates. The Lords of the Night are not used in every Maya date, and there are several other types of elements in the Supplementary Series.

- After the Supplementary Series, the *haab* date, 3 Sek, appears in the bottom right corner, completing the Maya three-calendar date.

What happened next …

Dates were a central part of Maya writing and proved to be the key to modern understanding of Maya glyphs. In the 1960s, Maya glyphs still remained a mystery to scholars. Only the easily recognized bar and dot numbers, and subsequently the Maya dates, could be deciphered. At that time, Russian American archaeologist Tatiana Proskouriakoff (1909–1985), was studying a Maya stela in Guatemala and noted patterns of dates that never spanned a period of time longer than a human life. Once she correctly guessed that one glyph, which looked like an upended frog, stood for birth, she was able to identify birth and death glyphs. Working on the same stela, she went on to identify glyphs that revealed the names of Maya rulers, the royal family lineage, details of war and enemy captives, and other historical details. Proskouriakoff provided an essential key to scholars: She discovered that most of the Maya's writing was a record of Maya history and that Maya writing stemmed from recording dates. From this starting point, many more scholars worked together and cracked the Maya code.

In the twenty-first century, scientists use the Julian day number system to measure time. Like the Maya system, the Julian system counts back to a certain date, but in this case the date is January 1, 4713 B.C.E. Many experts believe that the date of the beginning of the Maya era, August 13, 3114 B.C.E., has a day number of 584,285 in the Julian day number system. (Some scholars say 584,283; the exact number remains controversial.) To convert Maya dates to Julian day numbers, 584,285 is added to the number of days totaled in the Long Count. However, to verify the correspondence between Maya Long Count dates and Julian day numbers, historians continue to seek a day in Maya history that has been identified both in the Maya Long Count and in a modern dating system. If the Mayas recorded an astronomical event such as an eclipse, for example, scientists might be able to match that event with modern historical records. (An eclipse is a partial or total blocking of light from one celestial body as it passes behind or through the shadow of another.) If the match was conclusive, scientists could convert Maya dates to the Gregorian calendar.

Did you know ...

- Most of the Long Count dates found on Maya artifacts occurred during the Classic Maya era (c. 250–900 C.E.). They have a baktun count of nine and are dated from 9.0.0.0.0 through 10.0.0.0.0.

- Contemporary Maya people from Guatemala developed the names of the time units, such as baktun, kin, and tun. These terms have gained acceptance from other modern Maya groups.

- The Mayas viewed all time in cycles. Many scholars believe that by Maya calculations 0.0.0.0.0. (or August 13, 3114 B.C.E.) marked the beginning of a great cycle. This great cycle would last for thirteen baktuns (1,872,000 days or about 5,126 solar years). Scholars have determined that the last day of the present age—perhaps the end of the world in Maya beliefs—is coming up in just a few years, on December 22, 2012.

Consider the following ...

- Dates were a vital part of the Maya's sophisticated system of writing. Why do you think the simple recording of dates was so important in the development of writing? What were the Mayas trying to express with their dates?

- What does each of the numbers in the Maya Long Count 9.12.5.8.2 express?

For More Information

Books

Coe, Michael D., and Mark Van Stone. *Reading the Maya Glyphs*. New York and London: Thames and Hudson, 2001.

Henderson, John S. *The World of the Ancient Maya*. 2nd ed. Ithaca, NY, and London: Cornell University Press, 1977.

Web Sites

Calendario Maya. http://www.calendariomaya.com (accessed on December 2, 2004).

Jenkins, Dawn. "The Mayan Calendar." *Maya Astronomy*. http://www.michielb.nl/maya/calendar.html (accessed on November 11, 2004).

"The Mayan Calendar." *Calendars Through the Ages*. http://webexhibits.org/calendars/calendar-mayan.html (accessed on November 11, 2004).

Meyer, Peter. "The Maya Calendar." *Hermetic Systems*. http://www.hermetic.ch/cal_stud/maya/cont.htm (accessed on November 11, 2004).

Copán Stelae and Monuments

Photographs and illustrations of Stela A (front and back views),
featuring Maya king, 18 Rabbit

Artifact date 731 C.E.; located in Copán, Honduras

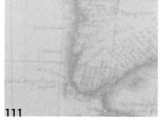

One of the main features of the Classic Maya (pronounced MY-uh) era (c. 250–900 C.E.) was the stela cult—the widespread creation of carved stone monuments known as stelae (plural of stela) that adorned the public areas of the great Maya city-states such as Tikal, Palenque, and Copán. The stelae were huge, inscribed slabs or pillars of stone—the Maya called them "tree-stones." They ranged from 3 to 35 feet (0.9 to 10.7 meters) tall. Much of the Maya glyph-writing (carving or drawing figures to represent words, ideas, or sounds) that survived into present times appears on stelae excavated from Maya sites. Maya text written in glyphs has also been found on other monuments, such as temple doorways and altars—large carved stone blocks that sometimes served as thrones. For more than 150 years Maya scholars studied these artifacts without being able to decipher, or interpret, the glyphs. Now experts are able to read this writing and learn about Maya royal history in the Maya's own words.

A common form of Classic Maya stela featured a carved portrait of a king, the ruler of a city or city-state, dressed in an elaborate headdress and surrounded by symbol-

Copán's artists were masters at creating intricate stone carvings and glyph texts. Because Copán has so many great stone monuments, made with incomparable artistry and inscribed with extensive text, historians call Copán the "Athens of the New World," comparing it to the ancient Greek center of art and astronomy.

ic images. Alongside the images, there was often a passage of glyphs providing the birth, succession, and death dates of the king (see **Long Count** entry for more information on Maya dates), as well as other information, such as the history of a significant event involving the king or some aspect of the city-state's history. Stelae were an important means of communication for Maya rulers, who used them to promote and justify their powerful positions within the city-states.

Though many Classic Maya cities had stelae, the city of Copán is particularly famous for them. Copán is located in northwestern Honduras near the Guatemala border. It was never a big city like Tikal, and its buildings were not as extravagant as those in other cities. But Copán's artists were masters at creating intricate stone carvings and glyph texts. Because Copán has so many great stone monuments, made with incomparable artistry and inscribed with extensive text, modern scholars consider it the literary and artistic center of Maya civilization. Historians call Copán the "Athens of the New World," comparing it to the ancient Greek center of art and astronomy. Drawn by Copán's wealth of intriguing artifacts, archaeologists (scientists who dig up and examine artifacts, remains, and monuments of past human life), epigraphers (people who study and decipher ancient forms of writing), historians, and many other specialists interested in ancient life have spent a great deal of time uncovering and studying the city's past.

The royal history of Copán

Stelae rise up throughout a large area in and around Copán, but they are most numerous and most striking along the walkways of Copán's Great Plaza, a huge, grassy courtyard surrounding a pyramid. Some of the stelae in the plaza are 14 feet (4.3 meters) tall. These remarkable stone artifacts serve as written documents of the city's royal dynasty (a succession of rulers who come from the same family).

Altar Q

One of the most revealing artifacts from Copán is called Altar Q, a large block of carved stone. On each of its four sides the block bears a carving of four men, for a total of sixteen figures. The figures represent the kings who ruled Copán from 426 to about 820 C.E., the era of Copán's highest artistic achievements often called its golden age. The kings are seated around the altar in the order of their reigns. A name glyph is carved below each of the kings. On one side of Altar Q, Copán's founder, K'inich Yax K'uk' Mo', is seen passing the scepter of kingship to Copán's last king, Yax Pac. Set between the founder and Yax Pac is a glyph that represents a Maya date of 6 Kaban 10 Mol, or July 2, 763 C.E., the date of Yax Pac's inauguration as king. Altar Q was probably designed to show Yax Pac's absolute right to rule; the founder of the dynasty hands him his power, proving to the people of Copán that Yax Pac was a legitimate ruler. The other kings, who ruled between Copán's founder and Yax Pac, all appear on Altar Q, but some of their names are still not deciphered.

Altar Q provides a background for K'inich Yax K'uk' Mo' and the founding of the dynasty of Copán kings. K'inich Yax K'uk' Mo' was not originally from the area; he arrived as a powerful foreigner in what was then a small community at Copán. In stela passages he is often referred to as the Lord of the West. In a *Nova* documentary, Maya scholar David Stuart explains what the glyph-writing carved into the top of Altar Q says about the king:

> It begins with a reference to a day in the early 400s, when it says that he took the emblems of office [symbolic objects connected with being a king or other leader] at a place that we think is connected somehow to Teotihuacán or with Central Mexico somewhere. Three days

The Sixteen Kings of the Golden Age of Copán

1. K'inich Yax K'uk' Mo' (Great Sun Green Quetzal Macaw), ruled c. 426–c. 437
2. K'inich Popol Hol, ruled c. 437–455
3. Unknown king, ruled c. 455–465
4. Cu Ix, ruled from c. 465
5. Unknown king, ruled c. 476–485
6. Unknown king, ruled from c. 485
7. Waterlily-Jaguar, ruled c. 504–c. 544
8 and 9. Two unknown kings, ruled c. 544–553
10. Moon Jaguar, ruled 553–578
11. Butz' Chan, ruled 578–628
12. Smoke Imix K'awiil (Smoke Jaguar), ruled 628–695
13. Uaxaclajuun Ub'aah K'awiil (Eighteen Are the Images of the God; generally called 18 Rabbit), ruled 695–738
14. K'ac Joplaj Chan K'awiil (Smoke Monkey), ruled 738–749
15. K'ac Yipyaj Chan K'awiil (Fire Is the Strength of the Sky God K'awiil; generally called Smoke Shell or Smoke Squirrel), ruled 749–763
16. Yax-Pasaj Chan Yoaat (The Sky Is Newly Revealed; also called Yax Pac), ruled 763–c. 820

later, it says, he comes from that place.... A hundred and fifty-three days after he leaves ... he rests his legs. And then it says he is a West Lord, and that's a title that he has throughout the Copán inscriptions throughout history. And then finally, the last two glyphs of the passage read 'Hu'li Uxwitiki,' 'he arrived at Copán.' So there's no question in my mind that K'inich Yax K'uk' Mo' became a king at a very faraway spot in Central Mexico and brought those emblems of office back here to Copán to found the dynasty.

After he arrived at Copán and assumed power there, K'inich Yax K'uk' Mo' began building monuments. It was during his reign that, for the first time in Copán, stelae and monuments were carved with Maya glyphs. But after K'inich Yax K'uk Mo's reign, few if any stelae were built for many generations. Stelae and glyph-writing emerged again with the rule of the tenth king, Moon Jaguar, whose reign began in 553. Moon Jaguar and his successor, Butz' Chan, both built stelae and monuments to create records of their long periods of rule.

In 628 C.E. Copán was ruled by Smoke Imix K'awiil (Smoke Jaguar), a strong ruler who built up the city's economy through trade. During his long and prosperous reign, Copán's artists worked at a steady pace, building huge monuments to glorify the king. Smoke Jaguar wanted to make Copán strong throughout a wide area, so he built monuments on hillsides and mountaintops well outside the city. By the time of his death in 695, Copán ruled over many surrounding communities, apparently including the cities of Quiriguá, Los Higos, and Rio Amarillo. An estimated twenty-seven thousand people lived in the city of Copán and the Copán Valley.

The king of the arts
Smoke Jaguar's son was Uaxaclajuun Ub'aah K'awiil. The name means Eighteen Are the Images of the God, but this king is generally called "18 Rabbit." 18 Rabbit was Copán's thirteenth king and its most famous. He is often called the Maya king of the arts because he focused on promoting arts and literature rather than trade. During his reign, the city's arts underwent a major change in style. In most Maya cities at that time, stela carvings were flat and boxy. The stelae of 18 Rabbit's time and afterward were more rounded, or three-dimensional, like sculptures. The details on them include elaborate dress and ornamentation.

During 18 Rabbit's forty-three-year rule, Copán's Great Plaza became crowded with intricately carved pillars that depicted the king in various costumes and represented him as different gods or ancestors. Most of the stelae were lined up at certain stations within the plaza to commemorate important days in the Maya calendar. The Maya carried out a special ceremony for each new stela, dedicating the monument to the gods. These ceremonies were designed to honor the gods, but they were probably also intended to inspire awe in the people, making it clear to them that their king was a very powerful man.

The glyph passages placed on 18 Rabbit's monuments are generally very brief. In his article "Hieroglyphs and History at Copán," David Stuart (1965–) notes one exceptional glyph passage that 18 Rabbit had inscribed on a step leading into his Temple 22. The passage says "On the day 5 Lamat is the completion of my k'atun [in office]." (Katuns are twenty-year units.) Stuart explains that 18 Rabbit's reference to himself in

Hieroglyphic Stairway at the ruins of the Maya city of Copán, Honduras. © *Craig Lovell/Corbis.*

the expression "my k'atun" is exceptional: "These are the spoken words of Ruler 13 [18 Rabbit] himself, and constitute the only known example of a quotation of an ancient Maya king."

Shortly before his death, 18 Rabbit began a project like no other, the famous Hieroglyphic Stairway. This project was a complete departure from the ornate monuments and terse glyphs that were characteristic of his reign. Many scholars believe that 18 Rabbit wrote the text for the stairway (although some attribute it to Smoke Shell, the fifteenth king). The Hieroglyphic Stairway has been called one of the greatest ancient achievements in the world. With twenty-two hundred glyphs carved into the massive stone blocks of its sixty-three steps, the stairway constitutes the longest known passage of Maya writing. The glyphs describe the royal successions from K'inich Yax K'uk' Mo', the founder of Copán, to Smoke Shell, the fifteenth king of the city. The sixty-first step is dedicated to 18 Rabbit and his rule. Its story, though, is not what 18 Rabbit had planned.

On May 3, 738 C.E., Cauac Sky, the ruler of the small nearby community of Quiriguá, recorded the killing, or "axing," of Ruler 13—18 Rabbit. No one knows exactly what happened, but many historians guess that the powerful king of Copán was captured by the people of Quiriguá and then beheaded in a human sacrifice ceremony (ceremony in which humans are killed as offerings to the gods). The event was not recorded in Copán until the Hieroglyphic Stairway was completed many years later. After 18 Rabbit's death, no one in Copán built any stelae or other monuments for twenty years. The absence of new monuments indicates that the ruling dynasty of Copán probably lost its power temporarily to Quiriguá. The kings at Copán would rise again, but none ever moved 18 Rabbit's stelae from their place of prominence.

Things to remember while examining the photographs and illustrations of Stela A (front and back views), featuring Maya king, 18 Rabbit:

- Stela A is a portrait stela depicting 18 Rabbit. It was dedicated (set apart to be devoted to the gods) in 731 C.E. The front of the stela is the king's portrait; the back is carved with glyphs. The photographs in the gallery section show the actual carved stone stela. The illustrations are drawings of the front and back of the stela, showing the carvings in more detail.

- In modern times most people would say that 18 Rabbit was a bit of an egotist. He set hundreds of artists and other craftspeople and laborers to work creating portrait stelae and then crowded the main plaza of Copán with these images of himself.

- 18 Rabbit is known as the king of the arts. During his reign, artists began to change the style of their stelae. Instead of making flat stone monuments with images scratched into their surface, Copán's artists created intricately carved and sculpted works of art with rounded features, elaborate detail, and deep relief (different levels of surface depth). Note the detail of Stela A and try to imagine what it would be like to carve something that elaborate out of stone.

- In most of his portrait stelae 18 Rabbit appears in ceremonial costumes, sometimes as a god or as one of his royal ancestors. In the front of Stela A, according to Maya scholar Elizabeth Newsome, 18 Rabbit appears as the spirit of his ancestor Butz' Chan, who ruled from 578 to 628.

- Almost every aspect of 18 Rabbit's costume is a symbol. Although modern scholars do not know what all the symbols mean, the people who viewed the stela in the eighth century would have known the meaning of every detail.

- The tall basket-weave crown of 18 Rabbit's giant headdress, shown in the front view, is a Maya symbol of royalty. The faces and bodies that emerge from the headdress probably depict his ancestors. The heads attached to his belt represent either gods or ancestors. The bags hanging from his belt probably held stingray spines, which were used for bloodletting, a process of piercing one's own skin to draw blood in order to offer it to the gods. Mirrors hang from the belt in groups of three, a symbol of the heavens. In front of 18 Rabbit, positioned between his legs, is his serpent bar, which symbolizes the Milky Way.

- At the base of Stela A there is a small chamber where offerings to the gods were placed.

- The back of Stela A is an example of Maya glyph-writing. These glyphs tell the date of the dedication of the stela and provide details of the ceremonies that took place on dedication day. Many stelae were dedicated on calendar dates that were considered significant, such as the end of a katun (twenty-year period) or a baktun (twenty katuns, or approximately four hundred years). These were thought to be times of change and perhaps luck.

- Note that there are two columns of glyphs and that each of the columns features a pair of glyphs side by side. The glyphs are read from top to bottom and left to right.

- Glyphs are generally square figures with rounded corners. Although some glyphs are made up of only one element, or sign, most have several elements. Look at some of the glyphs in the drawing of the back of Stela A. Notice that in each glyph there is usually a large sign that looks like a face or some other design. In some, there are smaller shapes and designs attached to the main element. Together these elements make up one glyph, and the glyph represents a full word or several syllables.

- There are numbers scattered throughout the glyph passage. The numbers are written in the Maya **bar and dot number system** (see entry). Determine how many bar and dot numbers are in the drawing. What numbers are they?

- Continue looking at the drawing of the back of Stela A. In the fourth row up from the bottom of the left-hand column, there is a bar and dot representation of the number eighteen: three horizontal bars (fifteen) with three dots on top of them (three). Underneath the numeral eighteen is a glyph that looks like the profile of an animal face. This is a glyph for the word "Ub'aah." Ub'aah, which often appeared in front of noble or royal names, means "his image." Right next to it within the pairing is the glyph for K'awiil, a snake-footed god who represents the royal dynasty. The name Eighteen Uaxaclajuun Ub'aah K'awiil is thus "Eighteen Are the Images of the God," 18 Rabbit's formal name. While this pair of glyphs expresses the name of 18 Rabbit, another pair directly to the right describes 18 Rabbit. The left-hand glyph represents the concept of "the divine king of Copán," and the

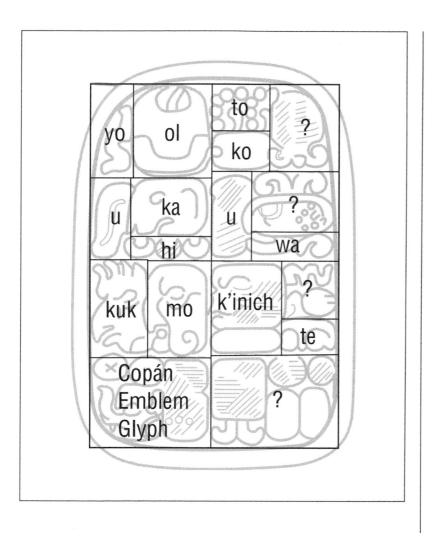

Figure 1: Illustration showing the breakdown of glyph-writing taken from an artifact in Quiriguá, Guatemala. *The Gale Group.*

right-hand glyph represents the word *bacab,* which suggests a high royal ranking.

- Most glyphs are read in parts—the main sign and the attachments; the parts form full words from separate sounds. Figure 1 is a breakdown of glyph-writing taken from an artifact in Quiriguá (pronounced kir-ee-GWAH), Guatemala. In this figure the drawings of the Maya glyphs have been overlaid with the Maya sounds they represent, written in the Roman alphabet that is used in the Americas today. Note the Copán emblem (place name) glyph. The word for Copán is not broken down into syllables; the glyph represents the full concept.

Photograph of the front of Stela A, located in Copán, Honduras.

Early Civilizations in the Americas: Biographies and Primary Sources

Drawing of the front of Stela A.

Photograph of the back of Stela A, located in Copán, Honduras.

Early Civilizations in the Americas: Biographies and Primary Sources

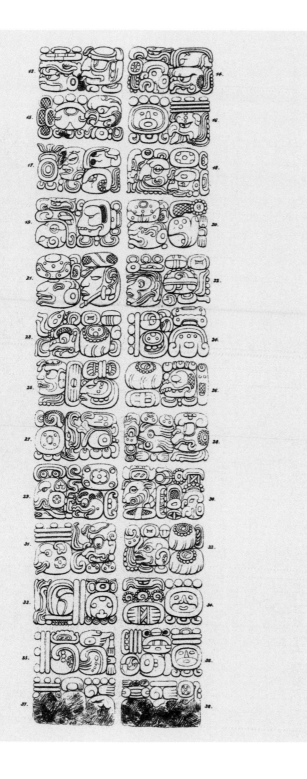

Drawing of the back of Stela A.

What happened next ...

About twenty years after 18 Rabbit's death, the kings of Copán regained control of their city. Under the fifteenth leader, Smoke Shell, who ruled from 749 to 763, 18 Rabbit's Hieroglyphic Stairway was completed. It contains a brief mention of his death, the only known reference to 18 Rabbit's untimely demise known to exist in Copán. The Hieroglyphic Stairway is a magnificent monument to the history of Copán's royalty. Unfortunately, it was built with faulty materials, and it has collapsed repeatedly throughout subsequent history. The stone blocks bearing its glyphs are scattered and broken, and they are now hopelessly out of sequence.

During the rule of Yax Pac, the last king of Copán, turmoil arose in the city. The end of the line for the Copán kings is chronicled in the city's last known royal artifact, dated 822 C.E. Altar L, like Altar Q, depicts the succession of a new king; Yax Pac is shown handing the scepter to the next king, named U Cit Tok'. But history must have intervened. The artist carving Altar L never finished the job, and the new king probably never took office. After 822, no more stelae were built in Copán. Some people continued to live in and around the city, but the great rulers and the golden age of Copán were over.

It is worth noting that the stelae and glyphs of Copán only tell the story of the royalty. There were tens of thousands of commoners living in the Copán Valley surrounding the city. Archaeologists have studied the skeletons of these people and have determined that by the time of Yax Pac's reign, there was widespread hunger and even famine among the farming people of the valley. This probably helped bring about the downfall of the Maya royal government.

Copán was eventually abandoned (some scholars say as late as 1200), and dense tropical forests grew over its monuments. The Spanish conquered much of the Maya territory, but they did not find the abandoned city. In 1839 John Lloyd Stephens (1805–1852), a U.S. travel writer and lawyer with a fascination for ancient sites, and his partner, English architect and artist Frederick Catherwood (1799–1854), traveled to northern Honduras in search of ancient ruins. To their amazement, they stumbled into the ruins of Copán. Since then, four generations of archaeologists have labored to discover the ancient city's history.

Up to the 1970s no one could read the Copán stelae. Only about 10 to 15 percent of the glyphs had been identified. In 2004 scholars can read 80 to 85 percent of Maya glyphs, so the Maya kings at Copán live on, making history with their own words.

Did you know ...

- Maya glyph-writing focused on the royal successions and dates, but it was not limited to these subjects. The glyphs could fully reproduce the Maya spoken language. Archaeologist Ricard Agurcia, quoted in Vincent Murphy's *Mundo Maya* article, "Copán: In the Valley of the Kings," explains: "[The Maya] were fully literate. Had they wanted to write a novel, they could easily have done so with their system of writing."

- One of the leading experts on Maya glyphs is David Stuart. Stuart, the child of Maya scholars, first laid eyes on Maya glyphs in 1969 when he was three years old; he was deciphering Maya glyphs by the age of eight. During high school he made some breakthrough discoveries about the Maya calendar and published important articles about Maya glyphs. At age eighteen he was the youngest winner ever of the MacArthur Fellowship, which is sometimes called the "genius" award, for his work on the Mayas. In 2004 Stuart was working with other experts to try to reconstruct the Hieroglyphic Stairway in Copán and is the Schele Professor of Mesoamerican Art and Writing at the University of Texas at Austin.

Consider the following ...

- The Maya kings at Copán spent a lot of effort creating stelae and monuments. Explain why stelae and glyph-writing may have been so important to them.

- Scholars have discovered the history of the kings at Copán by analyzing artifacts the Mayas left behind. What were some of the important artifacts that told the tale? How did these artifacts reveal the story of the royal dynasty to modern scholars?

- Many people have dedicated their lives to retrieving Copán's story from the city's ruins. Imagine that you are an archaeologist arriving at Copán in 1920, well before the Maya code was cracked. You wish to know who created the stone pillars and what they were trying to say. What steps would you take to learn the history from the shattered ruins? What kind of tools would you need? What would you hope to find?

For More Information

Books

Henderson, John S. *The World of the Ancient Maya.* 2nd ed. Ithaca, NY, and London: Cornell University Press, 1997.

Newsome, Elizabeth A. *Trees of Paradise and Pillars of the World: The Serial Stela Cycle of "18-Rabbit-God K," King of Copan.* Austin: University of Texas Press, 2001.

Periodicals

Stuart, George E. "City of Kings and Commoners: Copán." *National Geographic* (October 1989). This article is also available online at http://muweb.millersville.edu/~columbus/data/art/STU ART01.ART (accessed on November 12, 2004).

Web Sites

"Lost King of the Maya." *Nova Science Programming On Air and Online.* http://www.pbs.org/wgbh/nova/transcripts/2804maya.html (accessed on November 12, 2004).

Murphy, Vincent. "Copán: In the Valley of the Kings." *Mundo Maya.* http://www.mayadiscovery.com/ing/archaeology/default.htm (accessed on November 15, 2004).

Reddick, Greg. "Copán Hieroglyphic Stairway: A New Reading of the Copán Hieroglyphic Stairway with Implications of the Quiriguá Connection to Smoke Imix God K and 18 Rabbit." *Maya Info.* http://www.mayainfo.org/works/copanhs/default.asp (accessed on November 12, 2004).

Stuart, David. "Hieroglyphs and History at Copán." *Altar Q and Copán.* Peabody Museum, Harvard University. http://www.peabody.harvard.edu/Copan/text.html (accessed on November 12, 2004).

"Tour Copán with David Stuart." *Nova Science Programming On Air and Online.* http://www.pbs.org/wgbh/nova/maya/copa_transcript.html (accessed on November 12, 2004).

Pacal

Born March 26, 603 C.E.
Palenque, Mexico
Died August 31, 683 C.E.
Palenque

King of Palenque

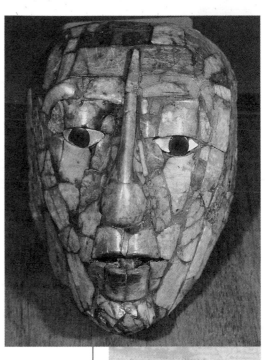

On the Maya Long Count date 9.9.2.4.8 (or July 29, 615 C.E.) in the Maya city of Palenque (pronounced pah-LAIN-kay), K'inich Janahb' Pakal, more commonly referred to as Pacal, ascended to the city's throne. He ruled for sixty-eight years, becoming the most well-known of Palenque's, and perhaps the Maya world's, kings. During his reign and the reign of his oldest son and immediate successor, Chan Bahlum (635–702), the formerly humble town of Palenque became an extraordinarily beautiful Maya ceremonial center (a central place where people from surrounding areas gather to practice their religions, usually at large temples and plazas built for this purpose). Under the direction of these kings, the Mayas in Palenque created some of the finest bas-relief carvings (sculpture in which the background is cut away, creating a slightly raised depiction), sculptures, and architecture in the entire Maya world.

The fact that we now have knowledge about a king who died eight centuries before the Europeans arrived in the Maya world is a testament to the amazing advances made by Maya scholars. In the twenty-first century many Maya schol-

"What is unique about Pakal and [his son and heir] Chan Bahlum is the length of their rule, the coherence of their vision and the permanence of their legacy.… Eighty-six years of ruling consistency and stability created a golden age in Palenque, where history and religion were fused with the architecture."

Shelagh McNally, "City of Kings." Mundo Maya Online.

Mask of Pacal made from jade mosaics. *The Art Archive/Dagli Orti.*

ars are focusing on the glyph-writing that appears on the monuments of Palenque. Glyphs are symbols that represent words, ideas, or sounds, and scholars have learned to decipher these—that is, they have figured out what the symbols mean and can now read the glyph-writing on the ancient monuments. The information they have discovered, combined with revealing artifacts found by archaeologists (scientists who dig up and examine artifacts, remains, and monuments of past human life), helps historians piece together the biographies, or stories, of people from ancient times. The details of Pacal's daily life will probably always remain a mystery, but the story of his kingdom, as recorded by Pacal and his son, can be found among the monuments of Palenque.

Background

Palenque was a medium-sized city built upon a ridge in the foothills in present-day Chiapas, Mexico, overlooking the swampy floodplains of the Usumacinta (pronounced oo-soo-mah-SEEN-tah) River and the tropical plains that extend to the Mexican Gulf Coast. People had lived there since about 100 B.C.E. or earlier. The first known recorded event in the history of Palenque was the rise to the throne of Kuk Bahlum ("Jaguar Quetzal") on March 11, 431 C.E. All Palenque kings that came after Kuk Bahlum claimed descent from him. Palenque did not become a major population center until about 600 C.E. For the next two hundred years the city flourished under very strong leadership and was a dominant force in the Maya world.

Pacal rose to the throne of Palenque by an unusual route. Normally, Maya kingship passed from father to son; women were traditionally excluded from rule. However, in Palenque there were two occasions when women took the throne: Lady Yohl Ik'nal ruled from 583 to 604, and her granddaughter, Lady Sak Kuk, who was Pacal's mother, ruled from 612 to 615. Both women were the legitimate (lawful) daughters of kings, and each assumed full rule as "king" of Palenque. According to most historians, these women must have been very powerful to have held such authority, because women kings were contrary to tradition. Pacal's mother probably felt pressured to give up her seat on the throne to a man. As soon as her son Pacal was twelve years old, Lady Sak Kuk transferred her crown and the kingship of Palenque to him. Pacal's father was not a king, so Pacal's succession to the throne (the conditions under which he became king) would not have been considered legitimate. Therefore, Lady Sak Kuk had to work very hard to make sure the nobility and royal family supported her son's rule. Many historians believe that Lady Sak Kuk continued to rule the city behind the scenes after her son took the throne. She died in 640.

Rebuilding the city and its royal history

In the years after his mother's death, Pacal began to commission (order to be made) the construction of the great monuments for which he is famous. The appearance of the city changed dramatically. Workers built tall, ornate pyramids, a grand palace compound, and striking temples. Along with their visual splendor, many of the buildings featured glyph-writing and images designed to justify Pacal's ascent to the throne. Much of the artwork Pacal commissioned is dedicated to showing that his family descended directly from the gods. Pacal's mother was given the name of a goddess, the First Mother, whom the Mayas believed to be the creator of humanity and divinity; the intention of this renaming was to prove or claim that Pacal's mother was a god in human form. Pacal also claimed that his birth date was the same as that of the First Mother. With these claims Pacal was creating his own myth: if his mother was a goddess and gave birth to him on the date of her own birth, his blood must be semidivine (half human, presumably from his father's side, and half god) and therefore, he reasoned, the gods must have ordained him to rule. In many later works, Pacal is portrayed as a god— sometimes the sun god and other times the maize god.

It was probably not a matter of ego for Pacal to commission a multitude of monuments and artwork focusing solely on himself and his royal descent. He needed to establish that he was a legitimate king, because many times questionable successions to the throne meant years of suffering for a city. Rivals to the throne often instigated revolts, causing widespread bloodshed and disruption of the economy and government. The monuments Pacal asked his workers to build were designed to inspire awe and reverence for the king

Ruins of the Temple of
Inscriptions in Palenque,
Mexico. © *Charles & Josette
Lenars/Corbis.*

among the people of Palenque, so that they would never
question his legitimacy.

The Temple of Inscriptions

By the time Pacal was in his seventies, his city had
grown strong and wealthy. Wars had been fought, and regions
around the city had been conquered. Around 675 Pacal began
to make plans for the building where he would be buried. The
Temple of Inscriptions, as it came to be called, was a temple
set atop a tall pyramid. It took the combined efforts of two
rulers to complete; although Pacal built the pyramid and prepared it for his burial, it was his son, Chan Bahlum, who finished construction of the temple at the top of the pyramid
after Pacal's death. This was the first known instance of a pyramid being used as a burial place in Mesoamerica.

The pyramid on which the Temple of Inscriptions sits
stands about 75 feet (23 meters) tall. It is built in eight "layers,"

The Palenque Kings

Unless otherwise specified, the kings listed below ruled until their deaths.

1. Kuk Bahlum. Born March 31, 397; ruled 431–435.

2. "Casper" (nickname; ancient name not translated), also known as 11 Rabbit. Born August 9, 422; ruled 435–487.

3. Butz'ah Sak Chik. Born November 15, 459; ruled 487–501.

4. Ahkal Mo' Nahb' I. Born July 6, 465; ruled 501–529.

5. K'an Hoy Chitam I. Born May 4, 490; ruled 529–565.

6. Ahkal Mo' Nahb' II. Born September 5, 523; ruled 565–570.

7. Kan Balam I (Chan Bahlum I). Born September 20, 524; ruled 572–583.

8. Lady Yohl Ik'nal. No birth date available; ruled 583–604.

9. Ah Ne Ohl Mat. No birth date available; ruled 605–612.

10. Lady Sak Kuk. No birth date available; ruled 612–615; died 640.

11. K'inich Janahb' Pacal. Born March 26, 603; ruled 615–683.

12. K'inich Kan Balam II (Chan Bahlum II). Born May 23, 635; ruled 684–702.

13. K'inich K'an Hoy Chitam II. Born November 5, 644; ruled 702–711 (captured); died after August 22, 731.

14. K'inich Ahkahl Mo' Nahb' III. Born September 16, 678; ruled 722–731.

one on top of the other getting smaller as they go up. The base of the temple sits on the top layer. A small stairway leads up the face of the pyramid to the temple. On the front of the temple are five large doors or windows. Alternating with these portals are five stucco (plaster) carvings depicting Pacal and some other adults holding a six-year-old child, Chan Bahlum. Chan Bahlum is represented with six fingers on each hand and six toes on each foot, an actual deformity he lived with, showing his human side. But in place of one of his legs is a snakelike creature, a traditional Maya symbol associating Chan Bahlum with the gods. Chan Bahlum probably commissioned these carvings when he was overseeing the completion of the temple; the depictions were meant to fortify his own succession to the throne.

Inside two of the chambers in this temple, archaeologists have found three panels carved with columns of glyphs that provide a detailed history of the Maya people as well as the ruling family of Palenque. The panels are the second longest known inscription (passage of carved writing) of the ancient Mayas (the longest inscription is the Hieroglyphic Stairway at Copán; see **Copán Stelae and Monuments** entry for more information). The reigns of the kings of Palenque from 431 C.E. forward were carefully recorded on the three massive "kings list" panels (see box on page 131) in the Temple of Inscriptions. Archaeologists found these lists in the 1800s, but no one could decipher them for more than a century. In the early twenty-first century, because of the great strides that scholars have made in reading Maya glyphs, the names of the kings are finally known. In fact, as the deciphering continues, the names of the Palenque kings have grown longer and more detailed; different spellings arise regularly.

Pacal's burial chamber

In 1948 a hidden stairway was found inside the Temple of Inscriptions. The stairway leads down into the inside of the pyramid, descending about 80 feet (24 meters) through the pyramid and then below ground to reach Pacal's tomb. In the tomb lies Pacal's huge sarcophagus (a stone coffin). The massive limestone lid covering the sarcophagus is one of the most famous artifacts of the Mayas. The lid itself weighs about 5 tons (4.5 metric tons). It is about 12 feet (4 meters) long, 7 feet (2 meters) wide, and 8 inches (20 centimeters) thick. Carved onto the lid are glyph and pictures, which serve as a record of information that Pacal wanted remembered. At the same time it serves as an outstanding example of Maya art.

The pictorial scene carved into the lid is vivid and highly detailed, depicting Pacal falling from life into death. Below him are the skeletons of two open-mouthed dragons. Their gaping mouths unite to form the door to Xibalbá (the underworld; pronounced shee-bahl-BAH). Inside Xibalbá is the Tree of the World, standing at the center of the universe with its roots in the underworld and its branches rising into the heavens. A celestial bird, the symbol of the heavens, sits on its top branch. Pacal tumbles down into Xibalbá accompa-

The Discovery of Pacal's Tomb

In 1948, archaeologist Alberto Ruz Lhuillier (1906–1979) had been working on the Temple of Inscriptions at Palenque for several years. While working in the temple atop the 75-foot-tall (23-foot-tall) pyramid, he noticed something puzzling: In one of the stone slabs of the temple floor there were four drilled holes filled with stone plugs. Nothing like this existed elsewhere in the temple. Investigating further, Ruz noticed that the temple walls did not stop at the floor, but appeared to continue underneath it. Ruz then guessed that the holes had been drilled there so that the floor could be hoisted up with ropes. He proceeded to pull up the stone floor. Underneath he found a hidden stairway completely filled with rubble (broken up pieces of building material, such as rock, mud, and brick). The rubble had clearly been painstakingly placed there long ago to ensure that no one descended the stairs.

With a team of archaeologists, Ruz spent three years clearing the rubble from the long, steep stairway, which descended 80 feet (24.4 meters) into the pyramid's interior. The job was very dangerous and hot, but it paid off. In 1952 Ruz and his team reached the bottom of the stairway. There they found a large triangular slab door. They drilled a hole through the slab, and Ruz aimed his flashlight through it to look inside.

In "Who Is Buried in Pakal's Tomb?" he describes his first view inside the chamber:

> Out of the dim shadows emerged a vision from a fairy tale, a fantastic, ethereal [lacking in material substance] sight from another world. It seemed a huge magic grotto [cave] carved out of ice, the walls sparkling and glistening like snow crystals. Delicate festoons of stalactites [calcium carbonate deposits hanging down from a cave roof like icicles] hung like the tassels from a curtain, and the stalagmites [calcium carbonate deposits rising up from the cave floor] on the floor looked like the drippings from a great candle. The impression, in fact, was that of an abandoned chapel. Across the walls marched stucco figures in low relief [carved from the wall and therefore somewhat raised from their background]. Then my eyes sought the floor. This was almost entirely filled with a great carved stone in perfect condition.

When the archaeologists made their way through the door, they discovered a stone chamber about 30 feet (9 meters) long and 13 feet (4 meters) wide. The carved stone Ruz had seen through the peephole was an elaborately carved sarcophagus. The team opened the heavy lid with great effort and inside discovered the skeletal remains of a human being. The skull was covered in a mosaic jade mask with shell and obsidian (dark, solid glass formed by cooled lava) eyes. The body was heavily adorned with jade jewelry. The skeleton would later prove to be Pacal's.

nied by a skeleton monster associated with the sun. The idea is that, like the sun disappearing below the horizon at night and rising again at dawn, Pacal will disappear into the underworld (die) and then rise up the Tree of the World (be reborn) at dawn. The Tree of the World gives Pacal access to the heavens, the underworld, and the human world, placing him among the gods.

Around Pacal's sarcophagus, there are portraits of his ancestors. One of the carved scenes is notable. It records the goddess called the First Mother's accession to the throne of Palenque on October 22, 612, and shows young Pacal as the goddess's nine-year-old son. This artistic representation is meant to convey that Pacal had divine ancestry.

Maya experts believe that Pacal had this chamber built with the sarcophagus inside it before he had the pyramid and temple built on top of it. When Pacal died at the age of eighty, his son carried out elaborate burial ceremonies, which included the sacrifice of six young people. Their bodies were placed in a small room in front of the burial chamber. The king was buried wearing an exquisite mosaic jade face mask and was surrounded by a collection of jade burial offerings and other sculptures. An air shaft ran from the burial chamber all the way up to the temple. Experts have several theories about the purpose of this shaft. It may have been created to allow the sun's rays to reach the chamber, so that the space would pass from darkness to light, symbolizing the king's journey into death and his return to life. Other scholars think the shaft may have been intended as a means for the king's spirit to communicate with the world above.

When the archaeological team located Pacal's tomb, Maya experts were not sure whose remains were inside, particularly because the bones appeared to be those of a relatively young man. It was decades later before they could read the glyphs on the sarcophagus. Although there is still some controversy, the glyphs clearly state that the remains inside the sarcophagus are those of Pacal. Pacal's tomb represents the most elaborate Maya burial that has been found yet.

The end of the golden age

In 684 Chan Bahlum began his eighteen-year reign of Palenque. He continued the building his father had begun, and he was responsible for leaving behind many more records and legends of his royal family. Like his father, he covered the walls of his city with tablets inscribed with tales of his descent from the gods. When he died in 702, his younger brother, K'inich K'an Hoy Chitam II (known as Kan Xul) took the throne. Although his reign began well, with more building in the city, the story becomes cloudy after about 711. It is believed that Kan Xul was captured by enemy troops around that time. He was later decapitated. Palenque continued to be a well-populated urban center with new kings on the throne until about 799, but not much building or glyph-writing took place after Kan Xul's reign.

Though the Maya people continued to live throughout the vast Maya world, they abandoned many of their great cities at the turn of the ninth century and Palenque was one of the first to be abandoned. There has been much speculation about the reasons for the cities' demise. Theories for abandoning the cities include famine, natural disasters, uprisings, and invasion. What is known, however, is that the Maya were still present in large numbers when the Spanish arrived in the early sixteenth century. The culture of the Classic Maya era that had thrived in cities such as Palenque, Copán, and Tikal had not survived intact, however. One of the great losses was knowledge of the written language that covered the walls and monuments of these cities. By deciphering what the kings of the ancient Mayas so carefully recorded more than thirteen centuries ago, experts are making connections with the ancient past of the continent one glyph at a time.

For More Information

Books

Fagan, Brian M. *Kingdoms of Gold, Kingdoms of Jade: The Americas before Columbus.* London and New York: Thames and Hudson, 1991.

Henderson, John S. *The World of the Ancient Maya.* 2nd ed. Ithaca, NY, and London: Cornell University Press, 1997.

Web Sites

Cámara Riess, Francisco. "Pacal's Tomb." *Mundo Maya Online.* http://www.mayadiscovery.com/ing/archaeology/default.htm (accessed on November 19, 2004).

Criscenzo, Jeeni. "Temple of Inscriptions." *Jaguar Sun.*

http://www.jaguar-sun.com/temple.html (accessed on November 19, 2004).

McNally, Shelagh. "City of Kings." *Mundo Maya Online.* http://www.mayadiscovery.com/ing/archaeology/default.htm (accessed on November 19, 2004).

"Who Is Buried in Pakal's Tomb?" *Mesoweb.* http://www.mesoweb.com/palenque/features/sarcophagus/pakals_tomb.html (accessed on November 19, 2004).

Popol Vuh

Excerpt from Popol Vuh: The Mayan Book of the Dawn of Life.
Based on the ancient knowledge of the modern Quiché Maya
**Translated and with commentary by Dennis Tedlock, 1985.
Reprinted from** *University of Wisconsin, Eau Claire* **(Web site)**

**Created by the Quiché Maya (date unknown); copied by Francisco
Ximénez c. 1702**

The *Popol Vuh* is the sacred book, or bible, of the Quiché
Maya (pronounced kee-CHAY MY-uh) and is considered
one of the greatest works of literature to have survived from
the pre-Columbian (before the arrival of Spanish explorer
Christopher Columbus in 1492) Americas. The name of the
book, *Popol Vuh* (also spelled *Popul Vuh* or *Popo Vuh*), is usually
translated as "book of council." It is believed that the Quiché
Maya had a copy of the book written in glyphs (figures used as
symbols to represent words, ideas, or sounds) in the years before Europeans arrived in the Americas. It told them of the
creation of the world, of their sacred traditions, and of their
history. When the noblemen of the community of Quiché
sought help in making decisions for their people, a council of
specially trained priests gathered to consult the *Popol Vuh*.

Background

The Quiché Maya were one of many distinct groups
of Mayas. They lived in the western highlands of present-day
Guatemala in the era after the great Maya cities such as Tikal,

"And then the earth
arose because of them, it
was simply their word
that brought it forth. For
the forming of the earth
they said 'Earth.' It arose
suddenly, just like a
cloud, like a mist, now
forming, unfolding."

*Popol Vuh: The Mayan Book of
the Dawn of Life.*

Palenque (pronounced pah-LAIN-kay), and Copán had collapsed and been abandoned, around 900 C.E. The Quiché Maya were of Maya descent, but they had picked up some of the traits of the Toltecs, who had become dominant in many areas throughout the Maya world around 900.

In the post-Classic era (900–1521), the Mayas did not carve any more stone stelae (tall, pillar-shaped stone monuments usually featuring glyph-writing that were used to record the history and deeds of the royalty of classic Maya cities). Nevertheless, the art and glyphs that had once been carved into stone did not disappear. Maya scribes (people hired to write down the language) instead drew their glyphs in books called codices (singular: codex). A codex is a book written and illustrated by hand. The paper for a codex was usually made from the inner bark of fig trees and then treated with a lime coating. A Maya scribe wrote his or her columns of glyphs on a long strip of this paper with a brush dipped in ink. Pictures were also added throughout to illustrate the writing. The paper upon which the glyphs were written was then folded like an accordion to form pages.

In the post-Classic Maya cities, the topics the Mayas wrote about in their glyph-writing changed. The earlier tradition of paying respect to royalty and nobles with art and glyphs disappeared. Instead, priests and scribes recorded the information they needed to conduct Maya rituals (formal acts performed in a ceremony) in accordance with the Maya calendar. The codices recorded farming cycles and the positions of the sun, moon, and planets. Some kept track of solar and lunar eclipses, while others recorded history or foretold the future. (An eclipse is a partial or total blocking of light from one celestial body as it passes behind or through the shadow of another.) No matter what the specifics, absolutely everything about the writing of the codices was spiritual. The people chosen to write them were specially trained priests and scribes who underwent purification rituals before undertaking this sacred work. The Mayas believed the writing itself was done with the aid of the gods; once written, the codices were considered too holy to be placed anywhere but in special rooms in temples. The Maya people did not handle the books; readings from the codices were given by priests at ceremonies and festivals.

The burning of the codices

Spanish conquistadores (Spanish word for "conquerors") under the command of Pedro de Alvarado (c. 1485–1541) arrived in the Guatemala area in the early 1520s and were soon at war with various Maya groups. They attacked the Quiché Maya in 1524. The Quiché Maya mounted a fierce defense, but, because of the superior weapons of the Spanish, they finally had to surrender. The nobles in the city of Utatlán (pronounced oo-that-LAHN) tried to make peace, inviting the Spanish to meet with them to discuss the surrender. But, upon entering the city, the Spanish killed the royal family in front of the people and then burned the city. After this incident, Spanish missionaries—people who work to convert others to their religion—quickly set about converting the Quiché Mayas to Roman Catholicism. In their fervor to stamp out the Maya religion and traditions, the missionaries rounded up all the sacred codices they could find and burned them.

The Spanish missionaries probably did not realize that destroying the books of the Quiché Maya was not simply a matter of burning the paper on which they had been written. The Mayas had kept their stories and traditions alive for many generations through a system of memorization and oral storytelling. In every generation, certain children were selected to be keepers of the traditions; from a young age, they were thoroughly trained to memorize the stories, speeches, and poems of their ancestors. As they grew older, they in turn trained children from succeeding generations, and the literature and history were passed on with remarkable accuracy.

The secret replacement of a sacred work

Along with their efforts to convert the native peoples of the Americas to Christianity, the Spanish missionaries usually taught them to read and write in Spanish. Some of the Spanish priests found a way to write the Mayan languages using their own Latin alphabet (the alphabet that evolved by the Romans and serves for writing most of the languages of western Europe). They taught this writing system to the Mayas so that the Mayas could then read and write Christian prayers in their own language. Sometime around the mid-sixteenth century in the abandoned town of Quiché, the members of three noble Quiché Maya families set to work writing down the story of their creation and history as it had been written earlier in a sacred codex. They wanted to preserve their religion and heritage before it disappeared forever under Spanish rule. Naturally, they hid this writing from Spanish eyes.

Around 1702, a Spanish missionary named Francisco Ximénez (pronounced zee-MAY-nays) lived and worked among the Quiché Maya in their town of Chichicastenango. Ximénez had learned to speak Quiché Maya and was interested in learning about Maya customs. He evidently gained the trust of the Quiché nobles because they allowed him to copy their *Popol Vuh,* which they held to be sacred. No one knows what happened to the Quiché Mayas' copy of the *Popol Vuh* after Ximénez copied it. As far as anyone knows, only the priest's copy, written in Quiché and in Spanish translation, survived to modern times. (There is always the possibility, however, that copies of the *Popol Vuh* and other sacred books remain hidden from the eyes of outsiders to this day.)

Ximénez's copy of the *Popol Vuh* was lost and forgotten for well over a century. In the 1850s it was discovered in a university library in Guatemala City, and subsequently several translations were published in Europe. With the discovery of such an extraordinary piece of literature, the people of Europe and the Americas began to realize the tremendous cultural loss that resulted from European policies during the conquest of the Americas.

The text

Parts of the text of the *Popol Vuh* are difficult to understand for scholars and general readers alike. It is likely that the writers feared to write directly about their traditional beliefs since it could result in punishment and so they wrote in ways that demanded interpretation. The writing is very poetic. Readers can usually visualize the scenes evoked. In reading the *Popol Vuh* there is not necessarily a right or wrong interpretation, but a careful reading yields some fascinating insights.

The following excerpt is the beginning of the book, in which the first attempts by the gods to create the world are described. In the first part of the excerpt the authors reveal a little bit about the circumstances in which they are writing. Then they go on to describe the world before the creation—an empty sky above and quiet oceans below.

Things to remember while reading this excerpt from *Popol Vuh: The Mayan Book of the Dawn of Life:*

- There are two groups of creation gods: those from the ocean and those from the skies. Their names are often invoked in long sequences. The sea gods are named Maker, Modeler, Bearer, Begetter, Heart of the Lake, Heart of the Sea, Sovereign Plumed Serpent (probably a reference to the Maya god known as Kukulcán [pronounced ko-kol-KAN], who was known to the Aztecs as Quetzalcoatl [pronounced kates-ahl-koh-AH-tul], a god associated with the creation of human beings), and others. The sky gods are named Heart of Sky, Heart of Earth, Newborn Thunderbolt, Raw Thunderbolt, and Hurricane. The very earliest gods, called the matchmaker and midwife (one who assists women in childbirth), created these two groups of creation gods.

- As the excerpt begins, notice the way the writers speak of the "Ancient Word," or their old religion. Compare this to the way they speak of Christianity. Remember that at the time they wrote this version of the *Popol Vuh*, the Spanish conquistadores and missionaries did not permit the Quiché Maya to practice their own religion. Yet here they speak of their own gods who "accounted for everything—and did it, too—as enlightened beings, in enlightened words." They state that their reason for writing down the *Popol Vuh* is because the original sacred book is gone: "We shall bring it out because there is no longer a place to see it, a Council Book." Then they speak of writing "amid the preaching of God, in Christendom now." Try to understand their tone or emotions in these words.

- The Quiché Maya nobles who wrote this copy of their sacred book never let anyone know who they were. Note the passage: "There is the original book and ancient writing, but he who reads and ponders it hides his face." This seems to indicate that the original book still existed when they wrote this copy. Yet it might also mean that the book existed only in their memories. The readers and ponderers referred to may be actually this group of writers themselves who "hide their faces" in remaining anonymous.

- The next statement explains the manner in which this version of the *Popol Vuh* was written: "It takes a long performance and account to complete the emergence [coming out] of all the sky-earth." In his commentary on the *Popol Vuh,* translator Dennis Tedlock explains what is meant by this statement. He believes the writers did not copy what the glyphs said directly, because the glyph-writing could only be read by trained priests and would not have made sense to other readers. According to Tedlock these writers were recording what an orator, or a reader of the book, would have been reciting at a "long performance" or a public reading of the book. He observes: "Lest we miss the fact that they are quoting, they periodically insert such phrases as 'This is the account, here it is,' or 'as it is said.'"

- In Maya codices, pictures are used to help express the meaning conveyed by the glyphs. It is likely that in the original glyph version of the *Popol Vuh* there were pictures, but in the surviving copy there are none. While reading this excerpt, note any places in which the writers seem to be referring to a picture.

Excerpt from Popol Vuh: The Mayan Book of the Dawn of Life

PART ONE

*This is the beginning of the ancient word, there in this place called Quiche. Here we shall inscribe, we shall implant the Ancient Word, the potential and source for everything done in the **citadel** of Quiche, in the nation of Quiche people.*

And here we shall take up the demonstration, revelation, and account of how things were put in shadow and brought to light

Citadel: Stronghold; safe place.

by the Maker, Modeler, named Bearer, Begetter,
Hunahpu Possum, Hunahpu Coyote,
Great White **Peccary, Tapir,**
Sovereign Plumed Serpent,
Heart of the Lake, Heart of the Sea,
Maker of the Blue-Green Plate,
Maker of the Blue-Green Bowl

as they are called, also named, also described as

the **midwife,** matchmaker
named Xpiyacoc, Xmucane,
defender, protector,
twice a midwife, twice a matchmaker

as is said in the words of Quiche. They accounted for every-thing—and did it, too—as enlightened beings, in enlightened words.

We shall write about this now amid the preaching of God, in Christendom now. We shall bring it out because there is no longer a place to see it, a Council Book,

a place to see "The Light That Came from
Across the Sea,"
the account of "Our Place in the Shadows,"
a place to see "The Dawn of Life,"

as it is called. There is the original book and ancient writing, but he who reads and ponders it hides his face. It takes a long perfor-mance and account to complete the **emergence** of all the sky-earth:

the **fourfold** siding, fourfold cornering,
measuring, fourfold staking,
halving the cord, stretching the cord
in the sky, on the earth,
the four sides, the four corners,

as it is said,

by the Maker, Modeler,
mother-father of life, of humankind,
giver of breath, giver of heart,
bearer, upbringer in the light that lasts
of those born in the light, **begotten** in the light;
worrier, knower of everything, whatever there is:
sky-earth, lake-sea.

This is the account, here it is:

Peccary: An animal related to the pig family.

Tapir: A hoofed animal with a long snout.

Sovereign Plumed Serpent: A reference to the Maya god known as Kukulcán, who was known to the Aztecs as Quetzalcoatl, a god associated with the creation of human beings having supreme power.

Midwife: One who assists women in childbirth; more generally, one who helps bring forth or produce something.

Emergence: Coming out.

Fourfold: Made up of four parts, or four times.

Begotten: Produced.

Mayas considered the quetzal, a Central American bird admired for its brightly colored feathers, sacred.
© *Michael & Patricia Fogden/Corbis.*

Eloquence: Powerful expression.

Quetzal: A Central American bird with bright green feathers.

Accord: Agreement.

Now it still ripples, now it still murmurs, ripples, it still sighs, still hums, and it is empty under the sky.

Here follows the first words, the first *eloquence:*

There is not yet one person, one animal, bird, fish, crab, tree, rock, hollow, canyon, meadow, forest. Only the sky alone is there; the face of the earth is not clear. Only the sea alone is pooled under all the sky; there is nothing whatever gathered together. It is at rest; not a single thing stirs. It is held back, kept at rest under the sky.

Whatever there is that might be is simply not there: only the pooled water, only the calm sea, only it alone is pooled.

Whatever might be is simply not there: only murmurs, ripples, in the dark, in the night. Only the Maker, Modeler alone, Sovereign Plumed Serpent, the Bearers, Begetters are in the water, a glittering light. They are there, they are enclosed in **quetzal** feathers, in blue-green.

Thus the name, "Plumed Serpent." They are great knowers, great thinkers in their very being.

And of course there is the sky, and there is also the Heart of Sky. This is the name of the god, as it is spoken.

And then came his word, he came here to the Sovereign Plumed Serpent, here in the blackness, in the early dawn. He spoke with the Sovereign Plumed Serpent, and they talked, then they thought, then they worried. They agreed with each other, they joined their words, their thoughts. Then it was clear, then they reached **accord** in the light, and then humanity was clear, when they conceived the growth, the generation of trees, of bushes, and the growth of life, of humankind, in the blackness, in the early dawn, all because of the Heart of Sky named Hurricane. Thunderbolt Hurricane comes first, the second is Newborn Thunderbolt, and the third is Raw Thunderbolt.

So there were three of them, as Heart of Sky, who came to the Sovereign Plumed Serpent, when the dawn of life was conceived:

"How should it be **sown**, how should it dawn? Who is to be the provider, **nurturer**?"

"Let it be this way, think about it: this water should be removed, emptied out for the formation of the earth's own plate and platform, then comes the sowing, the dawning of the sky-earth. But there will be no high days and no bright praise for our work, our design, until the rise of human work, human design," they said.

And then the earth arose because of them, it was simply their word that brought it forth. For the forming of the earth they said "Earth." It arose suddenly, just like a cloud, like a mist, now forming, unfolding. Then the mountains came forth. By their genius alone, by their cutting edge alone they carried out the **conception** of the mountain-plain, whose face grew instant groves of cypress and pine.

And the Plumed Serpent was pleased with this:

"It was good that you came, Heart of Sky, Hurricane, and Newborn Thunderbolt, Raw Thunderbolt. Our work, our design will turn out well," they said.

And the earth was formed first, the mountain-plain. The channels of water were separated; their branches wound their ways among the mountains. The waters were divided when the great mountains appeared.

Such was the formation of the earth when it was brought forth by the Heart of Sky, Heart of Earth, as they are called, since they were the first to think of it. The sky was set apart, and the earth was set apart in the midst of the waters.

Such was their plan when they thought, when they worried about the completion of their work.

Now they planned the animals of the mountains, all the guardians of the forests, creatures of the mountains: the deer, birds, **pumas**, jaguars, serpents, rattlesnakes, yellowbites, guardians of the bushes.

A Bearer, Begetter speaks:

Sculpture of Maya and Aztec god Kukulcán/ Quetzalcoatl depicted as the "plumed serpent." The god was associated with the creation of humanity.
© *Charles & Josette Lenars/Corbis.*

Sown: Scattered, like seeds, on the earth for growth.

Nurturer: Someone who provides care, nourishment, and fostering.

Conception: Creation, or bringing into being.

Pumas: Mountain lions.

A Quiché Maya urn decorated with three quetzal birds. *The Art Archive/Museo del Popol Vuh Guatemala/Dagli Orti.*

"Why this pointless humming? Why should there merely be rustling beneath the trees and bushes?"

"Indeed—they had better have guardians," the others replied. As soon as they thought it and said it, deer and birds came forth.

And then they gave out homes to the deer and birds:

"You, the deer: sleep along the rivers, in the canyons. Be here in the meadows, in the thickets, in the forests, multiply yourselves. You will stand and walk on all fours," they were told.

So then they established the nests of the birds, small and great:

"You, precious birds your nests, your houses are in the trees, in the bushes. Multiply there, scatter there, in the branches of trees, the branches of bushes," the deer and birds were told.

When this deed had been done, all of them had received a place to sleep and a place to stay. So it is that the nests of the animals are on the earth, given by the Bearer, Begetter. Now the arrangement of the deer and birds was complete.

And then the deer and birds were told by the Maker, Modeler, Bearer, Begetter:

"Talk, speak out. Don't moan, don't cry out. Please talk, each to each, within each kind, within each group," they were told—the deer, birds, puma, jaguar, serpent.

"Name now our names, praise us. We are your mother, we are your father. Speak now:

> *'Hurricane,*
> *Newborn Thunderbolt, Raw Thunderbolt,*
> *Heart of Sky, Heart of Earth, Maker, Modeler,*
> *Bearer, Begetter,'*

speak, pray to us, keep our days," they were told. But it didn't turn out that they spoke like people: they just squawked, they just chattered, they just howled. It wasn't apparent what language they spoke; each one gave a different cry. When the Maker, Modeler heard this:

*"It hasn't turned out well, they haven't spoken," they said among themselves. "It hasn't turned out that our names have been named. Since we are their **mason** and sculptor, this will not do," the Bearers and Begetters said among themselves. So they told them:*

*"You will simply have to be **transformed**. Since it hasn't turned out well and you haven't spoken, we have changed our word:*

"What you feed on, what you eat, the places where you sleep, the places where you stay, whatever is yours will remain in the canyons, the forests. Although it turned out that our days were not kept, nor did you pray to us, there may yet be strength in the keeper of days, the giver of praise whom we have yet to make. Just accept your service, just let your flesh be eaten.

"So be it, this must be your service," they were told when they were instructed—the animals, small and great, on the face of the earth.

*And then they wanted to test their timing again, they wanted to experiment again, and they wanted to prepare for the keeping of days again. They had not heard their speech among the animals; it did not come to **fruition** and it was not complete.*

And so their flesh was brought low: they served, they were eaten, they were killed—the animals on the face of the earth.

Mason: Artisan who builds by laying stone or brick.

Transformed: Changed.

Fruition: Completion or full development.

What happened next ...

After the excerpt, the *Popol Vuh* goes on to tell the rest of the story of creation. The creation story, though, is interrupted with the tale of the two ball-playing young men known as the Hero Twins. Their story is one of the foundations of the Maya belief system and is told in other sources, but none with as much detail as in the *Popol Vuh*. In this tale, the Hero Twins are playing ball and they disturb the Lords of Death with their noise. The lords challenge the twins to come to Xibalbá (pronounced shee-bahl-BAH; the underworld) to play a ball game. In Xibalbá the lords put the twins through many tests and ordeals. In some of these tests the twins die, but they always come back to life. Through their quick-thinking, trickery, and courage, the twins outsmart the Lords of Death several times, and finally kill them. Having defeated death, the Hero Twins ascend into the sky from the underworld, becoming the sun and the moon, making the maize (corn) grow, and bringing balance to the world. Their story brings the message that one may defeat death in the afterlife. The Hero Twins' adventures mirror the journey of the sun, which disappears, or dies, every night in the underworld and is resurrected each morning to bring light and life to the Maya people.

After the digression with the tale of the Hero Twins, the creation story in the *Popol Vuh* continues. After the gods create the animals, they attempt to create human beings. First they try to make them from mud and then from wood. Both attempts fail to produce human beings who will honor and pray to the gods, which is what the gods desire. In the third, and successful, attempt, the gods use ground maize as the material to make the first four human beings. These four men are the founders of the Quiché nobility, and, for a time, they are gifted with perfect sight and understanding. Then the gods, fearful of making their creations as capable as themselves, cloud the humans' vision and give them wives. Humankind begins.

The last part of the *Popol Vuh* describes the development of the Quiché people through history. It begins as the first four nobles journey to the city of Tulan Zuyua (which historians believe was Teotihuacán [pronounced tay-uh-tee-wah-KAHN], a sacred city to most Mesoamericans) to find a patron god, or a god who will look after them. There are many other Maya groups there; each group finds its own patron god and, according to the *Popol Vuh,* this is the start of the division of the Mayas into distinct groups with different languages. The Quiché leave the city and migrate for many years, stopping in the western highlands of Guatemala. The latter part of the history details the settlement and the new generations of Quiché gods and nobles. Listed at the end of the book are the noble Quiché families.

Popol Vuh was not the only Maya book to use the Latin alphabet to preserve the religion and traditions written in the Mayan language. The *Chilam Balam* ("Jaguar Priest") was a series of books written in the Yucatán in the century following the Spanish conquest also using the Latin alphabet. The priests of the different Maya communities in the Yucatán each kept their own *Chilam Balam,* recording in it their community's religious traditions and history. Most of the history concerns life under Spanish rule.

Did you know ...

- Of all the Maya codices that existed before the Spanish arrived—and some experts have estimated that there were thousands—very few have survived: the Dresden, the Paris, and the Madrid codices (all named for the cities in which they are now located), and the Grolier, which was found in fragments in Mexico. The origin of the Grolier remains controversial, and the codex may not have been Maya. These codices escaped burning because they were shipped to Europe before the missionaries found them.

- In order to prepare his English translation and commentary of the *Popol Vuh,* Dennis Tedlock traveled to the Quiché Maya country in Guatemala in the late 1970s. Tedlock describes the Quiché Maya as modern people with a variety of interests, though many have remained deeply rooted in their language, customs, and beliefs. Quiché Maya "daykeepers" are people trained to interpret the signs and omens that appear in life and dreams and to help other people to find hidden truths. In a very traditional Quiché town, Tedlock found a daykeeper named Andres Xiloj who was willing to train him as an apprentice (someone who learns a trade or an art by working under the guidance of someone with experience). Tedlock spent four and a half months training as a daykeeper, then asked Xiloj to help him to interpret the *Popol Vuh.* Tedlock's 1985 translation and commentary, the result of years of research, was highly influenced by the time he spent among the Quiché Maya and their daykeeper.

Consider the following ...

- Create a storytelling circle. With your friends or classmates, sit in a circle and present a reading of this excerpt of the *Popol Vuh,* allowing each person to read a short section aloud. Between sections, stop and discuss what you are reading. Describe what the scene might look like and what the gods are trying to do. Ask questions and make comments about the text.

- Try to envision the physical settings described in this excerpt: the beginning scene, in which there is only sky and sea; the creation of the earth; the gods conversing; the creation of the animals; the creations of the homes for the animals; the gods talking to the animals, etc. Make a simple sketch or painting depicting one of these scenes. Write the passage from the text that inspired the picture somewhere within your picture.

- Write a brief summary in your own words explaining the story, or what happens, in this excerpt. Begin with the passage: "There is not yet one person, one animal, bird, fish, crab, tree, rock, hollow, canyon, meadow, forest.... " and continue to the end.

For More Information

Books

Popol Vuh: The Definitive Edition of the Mayan Book of the Dawn of Life and the Glories of Gods and Kings. Rev. ed. Translated by Dennis Tedlock. New York: Touchstone, 1996.

Web Sites

"Background and History of Chichicastenango and the Academia de Arte y Cultura Maya." *Project Guggenheim in Guatemala.* http://www.projectguggenheim.org/pg/Guatemala/History.htm (accessed on November 10, 2004).

Dove, Anna. "Quiche." *E-Museum, Minnesota State University Mankato.* http://www.mnsu.edu/emuseum/cultural/mesoamerica/quiche.html (accessed on November 10, 2004).

"History." *Mundo Maya Online.* http://www.mayadiscovery.com/ing/history/default.htm (accessed on November 12, 2004).

"Popol Vuh: The Mayan Book of the Dawn of Life." Translated and with commentary by Dennis Tedlock, 1985. *University of Wisconsin, Eau Claire.* http://www.uwec.edu/greider/Indigenous/Popol_Vuh/Popol%20Vuh.htm (accessed on November 10, 2004).

The Aztec Empire

The Aztecs migrated into the Valley of Mexico and settled there in 1325. Other groups already living in the valley initially considered the Aztecs crude ruffians with vulgar habits, but the Aztecs quickly disposed of that image by adopting key aspects of the established cultures of the valley—and then taking them a step further in development. The Aztecs wanted more than acceptance in their new home. They were warriors at heart, and their main goal was to rule.

In their travels through the Valley of Mexico, the Aztecs had learned about the Toltec empire, which thrived in the region from about 900 to 1200 C.E. (An empire is a vast, complex political unit extending across political boundaries and dominated by one central power, which generally takes control of the economy, government, and culture in communities throughout its territory.) Most of the Mesoamericans they met believed that the Toltec emperor Topiltzin-Quetzalcoatl (lived in the mid- to late-900s) had descended from the gods; therefore, they considered his descendants the only true rulers of the valley. The Aztecs even-

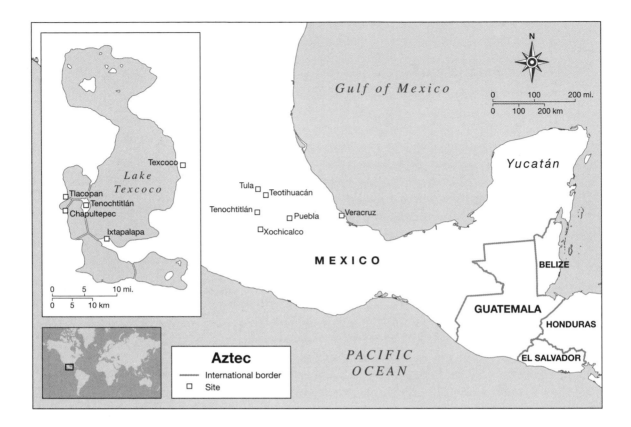

Gulf of Mexico

Yucatán

Lake
Texcoco

Texcoco

Tlacopan
Tenochtitlán
Chapultepec

Ixtapalapa

Tula
Teotihuacán

Tenochtitlán

Puebla

Veracruz

Xochicalco

MEXICO

BELIZE

GUATEMALA

HONDURAS

PACIFIC
OCEAN

EL SALVADOR

0   5   10 mi.
0   5   10 km

0   100   200 mi.
0   100   200 km

N

Aztec
------- International border
☐   Site

Map showing the sites of the ancient Aztec civilization in Mesoamerica. *Map by XNR Productions. The Gale Group.*

tually rewrote their history to prove that they were descendants of the Toltecs. Toltec history, as interpreted by the Aztecs, became central to the Aztecs' own history. Thus, this chapter on the Aztecs begins with the story of the Toltec ruler **Topiltzin-Quetzalcoatl.**

The line of Aztec kings was established in 1376, but for more than fifty years after that, a powerful group known as the Tepanecs dominated the Aztecs and most of the other peoples around Lake Texcoco. The Aztecs were not able to start empire-building until 1428, when they formed the Triple Alliance, joining forces with the nearby cities of Texcoco and Tlacopán. The Triple Alliance destroyed the Tepanecs, and the Aztecs soon became the most powerful group in the Valley of Mexico. In 1440 the emperor **Montezuma I** (c. 1397–1469) took the throne. During his long reign, the Aztec civilization reached its peak of development. It was prosperous and highly advanced in arts and sciences. The Aztec culture was based on war, however. The Aztec

Quick Facts about the Aztecs

- The Aztecs are more properly called the *Mexicas* or the *Culua-Mexica*. They are called Aztecs in this volume for the sake of recognition.

- The Aztecs established the city of Tenochtitlán in 1325. About one hundred years later they began to build their empire, and they remained the dominant force in the Valley of Mexico until the Spanish conquest of 1521.

- Tenochtitlán, the Aztec capital, was located on an island in Lake Texcoco in the Valley of Mexico. When the Spanish conquistadores first arrived there in 1519, about two hundred thousand people were living in the city. After destroying Tenochtitlán and conquering the Aztec people, the Spanish built their own capital on the same spot and called it Mexico City.

- The Valley of Mexico is a huge oval basin set between mountains in the Sierra Mountain ranges in central Mexico. The area contains some of Mexico's most fertile land. In the sixteenth century a large portion of the Mesoamerican population lived in the valley. It was the most densely populated region of Mexico, with groups of many different backgrounds residing there.

- At its peak, the Aztec empire included most of central Mexico, including large portions of the present-day Mexican states of Oaxaca, Morelos, Veracruz, and Puebla and parts of Guatemala in the south. It stretched east to west from the Gulf of Mexico to the Pacific coast. The empire included about five hundred cities, some very large. The largest city was Tenochtitlán.

armies conquered cities throughout a vast area and demanded that the defeated communities send them payments of goods on an annual basis, providing wealth for the capital city of Tenochtitlán. For the Aztecs, war had another purpose as well—to provide victims to offer their gods. During Montezuma's reign, the Aztecs killed prisoners of war in great numbers in human sacrifice ceremonies.

At the center of the Aztec culture was their calendar system. One of the most famous artifacts of Tenochtitlán is the giant **Aztec Sun Stone** (often called the Calendar Stone), which was found buried under Mexico City in the eighteenth century. The elaborately sculpted stone is covered with images from the calendar that reflect the Aztec concept of cycles of time. Though scholars of the Aztecs do not know how the Sun Stone was used, they have been able to interpret many of the sequences of symbols, pictures, and glyphs (symbols that represent words). Reading the pictures on this stone is an excellent introduction to reading other Aztec writings.

The Aztecs created codices (singular: codex), painted books in which they recorded their history, calendar system, and religious observations. Though their writing system was highly complex, the Aztecs could not completely reproduce their spoken language on the page. Aztec writers relied heavily on pictorial representations of words and concepts; they used glyphs for the names of places and people and for dates. Skilled readers presented the Aztec codices to audiences after memorizing the content; they used the pictures and symbols in the books to help them along with their oration (readings aloud). Unfortunately, the Spanish destroyed all but about fifteen Mesoamerican codices. The *Codex Borgia* was spared and is considered one of the finest examples of a pre-Hispanic (before the Spanish conquest) codex. However, scholars have not been able to discover the meaning behind its portraits of gods, rituals, and calendar symbols. The *Codex Mendoza,* created after the Spanish conquest under the supervision of Spanish missionaries (people who try to convert others, usually in a foreign land, to their religion), is much easier to understand. It presents a detailed look at the history, economy, and daily life of the Aztecs. The entries on the *Codex Borgia* and the *Codex Mendoza* present illustrations from these codices.

Some Aztec codices were meant to be "sung," or chanted. During the later years of the empire, a group of young men developed a tradition of song-like poetry to express their philosophical ponderings about the gods and the meaning of life. By far the best known of the Aztec poets was **Nezahualcoyotl** (meaning "Hungry Coyote"; 1402–1473), the poet king of Texcoco.

The Aztec empire lasted less than one hundred years. The last four entries of this chapter focus on the Spanish conquest of Tenochtitlán. A biographical sketch of **Montezuma II** (1466–1520) describes the emperor who had the misfortune to be on the throne when the Spanish conquistadores arrived in 1519. While the Spanish conquest was Montezuma's undoing, it brought a young Amerindian woman into the spotlight. **Malinche,** or Doña Marina (c. 1501–c. 1550), who had been living as a slave with the Mayas, became the interpreter for the Spanish expedition under the command of Hernán Cortés (1485–1547); she eventually became Cortés's mistress. Malinche was in the middle of some dramatic and important historical moments, often assisting with negotiations between Spanish and Aztec leaders. Yet she would have been forgotten had it not been for the efforts of **Bernal Díaz** (1492–c. 1581), a Spanish eyewitness who carefully wrote down the events that occurred during the conquest. Presented in this chapter is Díaz's description of the historic first meeting between the Cortés expedition and the Aztecs at Tenochtitlán. The final entry features **Aztec poetry**—three mournful poems by Aztec poets writing soon after the conquest. Most histories of the conquest have been presented from the conquerors' point of view. The sorrow expressed in these poems is a reminder of the terrible consequences that resulted from the destruction of the Aztec civilization.

Timeline: The Aztec Empire

400–700 The city of Teotihuacán in the Valley of Mexico rules over a vast economic empire that includes much of the southern two-thirds of Mexico, most of Guatemala and Belize, and some parts of Honduras and El Salvador.

c. 750 The powerful city of Teotihuacán in the Valley of Mexico is destroyed and abandoned.

c. 968 Toltec ruler **Topiltzin-Quetzalcoatl** establishes the Toltec capital at Tula in the Valley of Mexico.

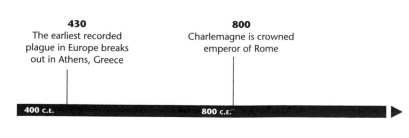

430
The earliest recorded plague in Europe breaks out in Athens, Greece

800
Charlemagne is crowned emperor of Rome

400 C.E.   800 C.E.

1064	After upheaval in the Toltec capital of Tula, most Toltecs abandon their city.
1325	The Aztecs establish their city of Tenochtitlán on an island in Lake Texcoco in the Valley of Mexico.
1376	The Aztecs place Acamapichtli, their first *huey tlatoani* (ruler) on the throne.
1428	The Aztecs become the most powerful group in Mesoamerica. They form the Triple Alliance with Texcoco and Tlacopán and rapidly build a vast empire of an estimated fifteen million people.
1433	King **Nezahualcoyotl** takes the throne in Texcoco in the Valley of Mexico, beginning an era of artistic, educational, and cultural development in that city.
1440	**Montezuma I** becomes the ruler of the Aztecs; during his reign the empire expands and Tenochtitlán grows more prosperous.
1479	Aztec emperor Axayácatl commissions the **Sun Stone**, a massive stone sculpture depicting the cycles of the Aztec universe.
1502	**Montezuma II** takes the throne of the Aztec empire.
1510s	The Mixtec codex, or painted book, later called the ***Codex Borgia*** is created by unknown priests/artists from southern or central Puebla or northern Oaxaca. The Mixtec-Aztec book is an almanac of religious and calendar knowledge.
March 1519	Spanish conquistador Hernán Cortés, while traveling in the Gulf of Mexico on his way to Tenochtitlán, receives a "gift" from the Mayas of a young woman called **Malinche**. She assists him as his

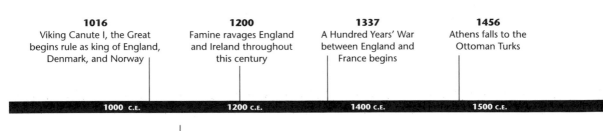

1016	**1200**	**1337**	**1456**
Viking Canute I, the Great begins rule as king of England, Denmark, and Norway	Famine ravages England and Ireland throughout this century	A Hundred Years' War between England and France begins	Athens falls to the Ottoman Turks

1000 C.E.   1200 C.E.   1400 C.E.   1500 C.E.

interpreter and becomes his mistress during the Spanish conquest of Tenochtitlán.

September 1519 Cortés enlists the help of the Tlaxcalans, enemies of the Aztecs who will be his allies during the conquest.

November 1519 Cortés's expedition arrives at Tenochtitlán. Within a few weeks the Spaniards imprison Aztec ruler Montezuma II.

June 1520 Montezuma II is killed during an uprising against the Spaniards. The Spaniards flee from Tenochtitlán.

July 1520 Epidemics of smallpox and measles strike the Aztecs. In the twenty years that follow, the Aztec population is reduced to one-half its former size.

May 1521 Cortés's forces attack Tenochtitlán.

August 1521 The Aztecs surrender to the Spanish. The conquistadores finish destroying the city of Tenochtitlán and begin building their own capital city, Mexico City, on top of the ruins.

1522 Spanish missionaries begin their efforts to convert the native people of Mesoamerica to Christianity. They destroy thousands of Aztec codices, or painted books, and prohibit all religious practice, hoping to break all connections to non-Christian religion. Hundreds of thousands of Mesoamericans convert to Catholicism.

1541 Viceroy (regional governor who represents the king of the ruling country) Antonio de Mendoza of Mexico City commissions a history of the indigenous (native) people in his region. *Codex Mendoza,* a book painted and written by native Mesoamericans under the supervision of a Spanish missionary is the result, cover-

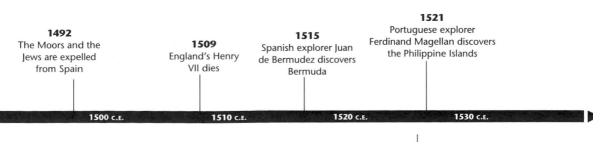

1492
The Moors and the Jews are expelled from Spain

1509
England's Henry VII dies

1515
Spanish explorer Juan de Bermudez discovers Bermuda

1521
Portuguese explorer Ferdinand Magellan discovers the Philippine Islands

1500 C.E.   1510 C.E.   1520 C.E.   1530 C.E.

ing the history, economy, and daily life of the people of the Aztec empire.

1560–1580 Over twenty years, a group of native Mesoamericans collect traditional Aztec songs and record them in *Cantares mexicanos*. Some of these are the **"Elegies on the Fall of the City,"** probably written shortly after the Spanish conquest of Tenochtitlán in 1521 to mourn the destruction of the city.

1568 **Bernal Díaz,** one of the conquistadores that defeated the Aztecs at Tenochtitlán, completes his famous history, *Historia verdadera de la conquista de Nueva España* (*The True History of the Conquest of New Spain*).

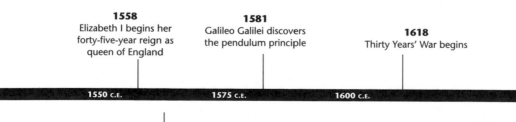

1558
Elizabeth I begins her forty-five-year reign as queen of England

1581
Galileo Galilei discovers the pendulum principle

1618
Thirty Years' War begins

1550 C.E.   1575 C.E.   1600 C.E.

Topiltzin-Quetzalcoatl

Born c. 947 C.E.
Valley of Mexico
Death date unknown

Legendary ruler of the Toltecs

S ometime in the early 900s, a group of warriors from the northern regions of Mexico arrived in the Valley of Mexico. One of their first acts was to invade and destroy the abandoned ruins of Teotihuacán (pronounced tay-uh-tee-wah-KAHN), which was considered the holiest of cities by most Mesoamericans. In time these invaders, who would come to be known as the Toltecs (pronounced TOHL-tecks) established their own cities of Culhuacán (pronounced cool-whah-CAHN) and Tula. Until about 1200 they were the dominant rulers of the Valley of Mexico. The Toltecs were the last group to rule over an extended area of the valley before the Aztecs came to power there around 1325.

Historians and archaeologists (scientists who dig up and examine artifacts, remains, and monuments of past human life) have not managed to find much physical evidence to help them formulate the story behind the Toltecs. The Toltecs had no known writing system, and most of their artifacts (items that they made, such as tools, weapons, or monuments) were taken by the Aztecs and used to build the Aztec

"In Tollan, in myth, and perhaps in life, Quetzalcoatl stood for learning, culture and, in particular, opposition to human sacrifice."

Hugh Thomas, Conquest: Montezuma, Cortés, and the Fall of Old Mexico.

Aztec image of Quetzalcoatl. © *Corbis.*

????

capital, Tenochtitlán (pronounced tay-notch-teet-LAHN). The Toltec empire had dissolved and its people had scattered centuries before the Spanish arrived in Mesoamerica in the early 1500s and began trying to record the American past.

Much of what is known of the Toltecs comes from the oral traditions (history and stories passed by spoken word from generation to generation) of the Aztecs, who revered the Toltecs as their ancestors. The Aztec tales, which were passed along verbally through several centuries before being recorded, seem to freely blend history with mythology (traditional, often imaginary stories dealing with ancestors, heroes, or supernatural beings). Some scholars of ancient civilizations believe that the Aztec traditions about the Toltecs contain a certain amount of factual truth; others are not so sure.

The legendary life of Topiltzin-Quetzalcoatl (pronounced toe-PEEL-tzin kates-ahl-koh-AH-tul) is both troublesome and fascinating in the way it mixes mythology and history. (A legend is a story commonly believed to be true but may have become part fable or myth as it has been passed down the generations.) Topiltzin-Quetzalcoatl, if the man actually existed, was the ruler of the Toltecs in the tenth century. Quetzalcoatl is one of the major gods of Mesoamerica. The Aztec stories about Topiltzin the man and Quetzalcoatl the god are so entwined that it is impossible to separate them. There are many variations of these tales. Some portray Topiltzin-Quetzalcoatl as a god in human form; others describe him as a mortal man. All versions describe the Toltec ruler's acts in a legendary way; in essence, Topiltzin-Quetzalcoatl served as a superhero in Aztec stories and traditions.

Many versions of the life of Topiltzin-Quetzalcoatl begin with his father, Mixcoatl (pronounced meesh-COE-ah-tul; meaning "Cloud Serpent"), the leader of a group of warriors from the north who led the invasion of Teotihuacán. Mixcoatl established a new city in the Valley of Mexico around 930; the city was called Culhuacán. Mixcoatl was murdered by his brother, who then took over the rule of the city. Mixcoatl's wife, Chimalma, who was pregnant at the time, fled from Culhuacán only to die in childbirth. Her child, Ce Acatl (pronounced say ah-CAH-tul; the given name of Topiltzin-Quetzalcoatl; the name translates as the calendar date "1 Reed" in Nahuatl, the Aztec language), was raised by his grandparents.

As a young man Ce Acatl studied in the city of Xochi-calco (pronounced zoe-chee-CAHL-coe), where he became a high priest of the cult of the god Quetzalcoatl. (A cult is a group that follows new religious doctrines and practices, often to the extreme.) It was then that he adopted the god's name. Returning to Culhuacán as Topiltzin-Quetzalcoatl, he killed his uncle and took back the throne as the legitimate Toltec king. Around 968 Topiltzin-Quetzalcoatl founded the capital city of Tula in the far north of the Valley of Mexico (in the present-day Mexican state of Hidalgo). From Tula, Topiltzin-Quetzalcoatl established control over a number of communities of various ethnic origins who lived in the areas surrounding the city. He slowly turned these conquests into the Toltec empire.

The religious reformer

After taking the throne, Topiltzin-Quetzalcoatl remained a dedicated priest of the cult of Quetzalcoatl. The cult is thought to have emerged during the "dark ages" in the Valley of Mexico, the period after about 700, when the great city of Teotihuacán collapsed, leaving the valley in turmoil. Quetzalcoatl was the god associated with human life, rebirth after death, the arts, and peaceful existence; placing their faith in this god may have brought hope to the people living in the valley. As both king of the city and priest of the cult, Topiltzin-Quetzalcoatl brought religious reform to the people of Tula, refocusing Toltec religion to include holiness and morality—in other words, goodness. One of his reforms was to outlaw human sacrifice. He asserted that no humans needed to suffer to satisfy Quetzalcoatl; he assured the people that the god wanted nothing more than butterflies or snakes as offerings.

Many citizens of Tula embraced Topiltzin-Quetzalcoatl's reforms, but for others in the city, the king's decree on human sacrifice became a source of conflict. A large group of Tula residents worshiped the god Tezcatlipoca (pronounced tez-caht-lee-POE-cah; meaning "Smoking Mirror" or "Smoked Mirror"). Tezcatlipoca represented night, death, sorcery (magical powers gained with the help of evil spirits), and war; his followers believed strongly in the practice of human sacrifice.

The flight from Tula

According to some Aztec accounts, those in Tula who worshiped Tezcatlipoca planned an uprising against Topiltzin-Quetzalcoatl. Because the king was beloved by many, the rebels used trickery to try to remove him from the throne. They succeeded: Topiltzin-Quetzalcoatl is said to have fled into exile in the year 987. There are many versions of the tale of his flight. A few examples follow, illustrating the various views of Topiltzin-Quetzalcoatl as a human, a superhero, and a god.

In one version of the tale, the rebels tried to trick the honorable and pure king into committing shameful acts that would discredit him in front of his people. As a priest in the cult of Quetzalcoatl, Topiltzin-Quetzalcoatl had sworn to remain celibate (refrain from sexual relations). Knowing this, his enemies tricked him into drinking *pulque* (pronounced PUHL-kay), an alcoholic beverage made from cactus juice. Topiltzin-Quetzalcoatl had never had alcoholic beverages before, and he became very drunk and unaware of his actions. When he awoke the next morning, however, it was clear to him that he had broken his vow of celibacy. Ashamed, he decided he was no longer fit to rule his empire, and he sailed east into exile from his land. This is the human Topiltzin-Quetzalcoatl.

In another version of the tale, the god Tezcatlipoca takes on a human form to oppose the heroic Topiltzin-Quetzalcoatl. After a struggle between them, Topiltzin-Quetzalcoatl kills Tezcatlipoca, but the god of sorcery casts a spell on his own body before he dies, making it impossible for the people of Tula to remove the rotting corpse (dead body) from their city.

This Toltec carving depicts Topiltzin-Quetzalcoatl in godlike form. *The Art Archive/National Anthropological Museum Mexico/Dagli Orti.*

Quetzalcoatl, the God

Quetzalcoatl was a god worshiped by every group of Mesoamericans. He is particularly associated with Teotihuacán, the Toltecs, and the Aztecs, as well as the Mayas in Chichén Itzá. Translated literally, his name means "quetzal bird-snake." Mesoamericans considered the quetzal, a Central American bird known for its bright green feathers, sacred so the name probably means "divine serpent"; however, Quetzalcoatl's worshipers usually referred to the god as the "feathered serpent." To the Toltecs, Quetzalcoatl was the creator god. In one legend, Quetzalcoatl travels to the underworld to collect the bones of dead human beings. The god drips his own blood onto the bones and restores them to human life, becoming the father of humanity in a new world. Quetzalcoatl was also the god of civilization, holiness, and peace. In Toltec and Aztec mythology Quetzalcoatl was strongly associated with the wind and sometimes takes the form of the wind god, Ehecatl (pronounced eh-weh-KAH-tul).

The body begins to smell very bad, and people who go near it die, but no amount of effort can move it. Topiltzin-Quetzalcoatl decides to leave the city to save it from Tezcatlipoca's sorcery. He sails off to exile in the east on a raft made of serpents. In this version, Topiltzin-Quetzalcoatl shows superhuman capabilities.

In another version of the story, Topiltzin-Quetzalcoatl is driven from Tula by the god Tezcatlipoca and his human followers. He goes into exile in a land on the east coast of Mexico. Then, promising to return, he sets himself on fire, and his heart rises as Venus, the morning star. This shows Topiltzin-Quetzalcoatl as god.

The Toltecs after Topiltzin-Quetzalcoatl

After Topiltzin-Quetzalcoatl left the Toltec capital to live in exile, the fierce, warlike groups of Tula took control of the empire. War became a regular part of life for all the people of Mesoamerica, and the battles became increasingly vicious and bloody. At this time, too, the Toltec priests began to demand more and more human sacrifices. The empire continued to expand through conquests, but the people under Toltec rule were not unified by culture or mutual goals.

Tezcatlipoca: Quetzalcoatl's Rival

The Toltecs worshiped many gods, but the two gods who reigned supreme during the peak years of the empire were Quetzalcoatl and Tezcatlipoca. Tezcatlipoca was the Toltec god who opposed and rivaled Quetzalcoatl. The two gods ruled over human beings with about equal powers. The shield Tezcatlipoca carried was a dark mirror, which he used to view or reflect human activities. He may have functioned as a judge, handing out his own brand of justice to people. Tezcatlipoca was also the god of night and sorcery, and he was known for his warlike nature. He was said to have the power to destroy the world, and it was considered very dangerous not to worship him. The followers of Tezcatlipoca introduced mass human sacrifices to please the god.

Many scholars believe that the accounts of the struggle between the gods Quetzalcoatl and Tezcatlipoca and the eventual banishment of Quetzalcoatl from the Toltec world are more or less based on the historical facts of the Toltec empire. In their view, the original group of northern people who arrived in the Valley of Mexico was probably led by Topiltzin-Quetzalcoatl's father, Mixcoatl. These newcomers adopted the more peaceful ways of the Valley of Mexico after settling there. Their rulers were priests, and Quetzalcoatl, the peaceful god, was their representative. However, as new ethnic groups from the north migrated into the Valley of Mexico and settled in the city of Tula, a more warlike culture arose. These groups were probably responsible for banishing the priest-rulers of the early Toltec period, such as the legendary Topiltzin-Quetzalcoatl, and replacing them with a ruling class of warriors. Tezcatlipoca was the chief god of their new, warlike state. Accounts of the exile of Quetzalcoatl, god and ruler, relate the beginning of a new, more violent era in the Valley of Mexico.

Sometime in the 1100s the Toltec empire collapsed. According to the Aztec legends, only a few noble Toltec families remained in the Valley of Mexico after the fall. Most Mesoamerican rulers after the fall of the Toltec empire claimed descent from the Toltec kings, regardless of their actual background. The Toltec claim to descent from Quetzalcoatl was believed to give them a divine authorization to rule.

Early Civilizations in the Americas: Biographies and Primary Sources

The legend continues

Topiltzin-Quetzalcoatl continued to be a presence in Mesoamerica long after his exile from Tula. According to legends, the king left Tula and went into exile somewhere in the west. His promise to return was part of Maya and Aztec tradition and both civilizations were influenced by this expectation.

The Maya conqueror/god Kukulcán

Around 900, the great Maya cities in Guatemala and Honduras collapsed, and the new center of the Maya world became the area that is now the Mexican state of Yucatán. Sometime late in the 900s, a conqueror called Kukulcán (pronounced koo-kool-CAHN; the Mayan translation of the name Quetzalcoatl) invaded the Yucatán area. He made the city of Chichén Itzá (pronounced chee-CHEN eet-SAH) his capital. According to some accounts, the Maya people had been awaiting the return of their god Kukulcán, and so they did not give resistance to this conqueror when he entered their city. Under Kukulcán's rule the city prospered and underwent a thorough rebuilding. Around that time the art and culture of Chichén Itzá became distinctly Toltec in style. Most historians believe that the change was due to an increase in trade and other relations between the Toltecs and the Mayas. However, some scholars believe that it might have been caused by a historical event: the arrival of the former Toltec ruler, Topiltzin-Quetzalcoatl, who was welcomed by the Mayas as a returning god.

The Aztec legend

According to the Aztec legends, when Topiltzin-Quetzalcoatl fled from Tula, he promised to return to his people in the year 1 Reed, the Mesoamerican date for which he was named. Images of the god Quetzalcoatl vary: Many depict him as a feathered serpent, but on occasion he was also represented as a fair-skinned human man with a beard (most natives of the Americas did not have facial hair, so this was a rarity). More than five centuries after Topiltzin-Quetzalcoatl fled in 987, the Aztec date 1 Reed arose in the year 1519 (Aztec dates recur every fifty-two years; see **Aztec Sun Stone** entry). That was the year that Spanish conqueror Hernán Cortés (1485–1547), a man with fair skin and a beard, arrived

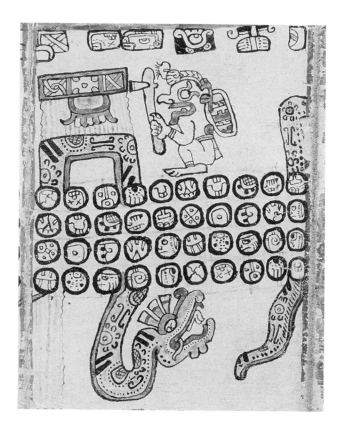

Maya codex depicting the god Quetzalcoatl (known to the Mayas as Kukulcán) as a feathered serpent. *The Art Archive/Museo de America Madrid/Dagli Orti.*

in Mexico seeking gold and power. Many historians have reported that Aztec leader Montezuma II (1466–1520; pronounced mohk-the-ZOO-mah) believed Cortés might be the powerful and revered god Quetzalcoatl making his promised return. The king therefore welcomed Cortés, and the lack of Aztec resistance against the Spanish led to the end of the Aztec civilization. The tale of Montezuma's mistake, though well-known, is by no means accepted by all historians.

What to believe?

Historians and many other experts have studied the legends of Quetzalcoatl in great depth, examining the sixteenth-century sources written by Spanish missionaries (people from Spain who tried to convert the American natives to Christianity) who interviewed Aztec survivors of the conquest or by Aztecs who learned to write in Spanish after the conquest. There are many reasons not to believe these stories represent historical events. For example, scholars have found that in the fifteenth century, an Aztec emperor created a new history for the Aztecs to promote his political ends and demanded that all storytellers memorize his version of history. He wished to promote his divine authority to rule as a descendant of the Toltecs and probably shaped the story in his own interest. A century later, when the Spanish tried to preserve Aztec histories by writing them down, they may well have inserted some of their Christian sense of what was good and evil into the tales, and therefore changed them greatly.

On the other hand, some historians believe that the tales of Topiltzin-Quetzalcoatl should be taken seriously as oral history, because details in each legend agree just enough with the known physical facts of Toltec history. While few scholars read the legends looking for literal truths, many study them for the insight they provide into Aztec—and perhaps Toltec—culture. Others may look upon these stories as art—compelling oral literature that has been passed down through the ages. Still others believe that the Toltec leader Topiltzin-Quetzalcoatl was a real man who made such a tremendous impression on the people and history of Mesoamerica that his name lives on in the region more than a thousand years after his exile.

For More Information

Books

Coe, Michael C. *Mexico: From the Olmecs to the Aztecs.* 4th ed. London and New York: Thames and Hudson, 1994.

Fagan, Brian M. *Kingdoms of Gold, Kingdoms of Jade: The Americas before Columbus.* London and New York: Thames and Hudson, 1991.

Meyer, Michael C., and William L. Sherman. *The Course of Mexican History.* 5th ed. New York and Oxford: Oxford University Press, 1995.

Nicholson, H. B. *Topiltzin Quetzalcoatl: The Once and Future Lord of the Toltecs.* Boulder: University of Colorado Press, 1999.

Thomas, Hugh. *Conquest: Montezuma, Cortés, and the Fall of Old Mexico.* New York: Simon and Schuster, 1993.

Periodicals

Smith, Michael E. "Comments on the Historicity of Topiltzin Quetzalcoatl, Tollan, and the Toltecs." *The Nahua Newsletter* (November 2003). This article is also available online at http://www.albany.edu/~mesmith/1-Re-NahNewsToltec.pdf (accessed on November 5, 2004).

Web Sites

Gardner, Brant. "Quetzalcoatl's Fathers: A Critical Examination of Source Materials." *Atzlan E-Journal.* http://www.cc.ukans.edu/~hoopes/aztlan/tripart.htm (accessed on November 17, 2004).

Quetzalcoatl: The Man, the Myth, and the Legend. http://weber.ucsd.edu/~anthclub/quetzalcoatl/quetzal.htm (accessed on November 17, 2004).

"Topiltzin Ce Acatl Quetzalcoatl." *Wikiverse: A World of Knowledge.* http://topiltzin-ce-acatl-quetzalcoatl.wikiverse.org/ (accessed on November 17, 2004).

Tuck, Jim. "The Quetzalcoatl 'Trinity.'" *Mexico Connect.* http://www.mexconnect.com/mex_/history/jtuck/jtquetzalcoatl.html (accessed on November 17, 2004).

Montezuma I

Born c. 1397 (some sources say 1390)
Tenochtitlán, Valley of Mexico
Died 1469
Tenochtitlán

Aztec head of state

Montezuma I. *Getty Images.*

Montezuma I, or Montezuma Ilhuicamina (also spelled Moctezuma or Motecuhzoma; pronounced mohk-the-ZOO-mah ill-whee-cah-MEE-nah), ruled the Aztecs from 1440 to 1469. His full name means "angry archer who shoots an arrow in the sky." Montezuma lived and ruled in the large and heavily populated Aztec capital, Tenochtitlán (pronounced tay-notch-teet-LAHN), which was located on an island in Lake Texcoco in the Valley of Mexico. In the decades before he took over as the Aztec ruler, the Aztecs had become very powerful in the region and had begun building an empire, a network of the cities and communities throughout the valley they had conquered. The conquered cities were forced to pay them regular payments of goods, bringing great wealth to Tenochtitlán. During his reign, Montezuma expanded the empire well beyond the Valley of Mexico. His rule led to even greater prosperity in Tenochtitlán and to cultural advancement for the people of the empire.

"Montezuma conferred with Nezahualcoyotl [Montezuma's cousin, the king of Texcoco] as to the best means of preventing the return of such a calamity, and they agreed to build immense dams ... the remains of which ... are still a wonder to engineers."

Stanley L. Klos, editor,
Appleton's Cyclopedla of American Biography.

The emperor's royal background

In 1397, the approximate year of Montezuma's birth, the Aztecs were living under the rule of a powerful group called the Tepanecs. The leader of the Tepanecs, Tezozomoc (pronunciation tez-oh-ZOE-mok), had allowed the Aztecs to establish their own monarchy in 1376, though they were to remain under his rule. The Aztecs elected Acamapichtli (pronounced ah-cahm-ah-PEECH-tlee; ruled c. 1376–1391) as their new leader. One of Acamapichtli's sons was Montezuma's father, Huitzilihuitl (pronounced hwheets-eel-ee-WHEE-tul), who ruled from 1395 to 1417. Montezuma's mother was a princess named Miahuaxihuitl (pronounced mee-ah-whash-ee-WHEE-tul). When Huitzilihuitl died, Montezuma's brother Chimalpopoca (pronounced chee-mahl-poe-POE-cah; ruled c. 1417–1423) took the throne as king of the Aztecs. During his reign, Chimalpopoca became involved in a plot to overthrow the ruling Tepanecs. When they discovered his intentions, they assassinated him.

During Chimalpopoca's reign, Montezuma and one of his half brothers, Tlacaelel (1397–1487; pronounced tlah-cai-EL-el) had worked together to gain the support of a group of young, militant nobles. This group chose Montezuma's uncle Itzcoatl (pronounced eetz-coe-WHAH-tul) as the next leader of the Aztecs. Itzcoatl, whose name means "obsidian serpent" (obsidian is a dark natural glass formed from cooled lava), was the illegitimate son of Acamapichtli, but this fact did not diminish his power. With the backing of the militant young nobles, he took aggressive action on behalf of the Aztecs. In Itzcoatl's second year as king, the Aztecs overthrew the Tepanecs, formed the Triple Alliance with the cities of Texcoco and Tlacopán, and founded the Aztec empire, with Itzcoatl serving as the first of its emperors.

Just under the emperor was a position called the *cihuacoatl* (pronounced see-whah-koe-AH-tul). Although this word means "snake woman," the position was always filled by a man. The *cihuacoatl* was a powerful adviser who ruled over the military and domestic affairs of the empire, acting as a kind of deputy to the emperor. Montezuma's half brother Tlacaelel served in this role under Itzcoatl. Montezuma served as Itzcoatl's top general, leading the Aztec army. These three great commanders—Itzcoatl, Tlacaelel, and Montezuma I—

built the Aztec empire into a vast and powerful civilization over a period of about forty years.

Taking command of the empire

When Itzcoatl died in 1440, the Aztec nobles chose Montezuma to be the *huey tlatoani,* or "Great Speaker." This was the name they used for their emperor, because the emperor spoke for the Aztecs and for all the people living in the empire. After he was chosen, but before he was officially crowned, Montezuma took charge. His first act as leader of the Aztecs was to lead his armies in a war against the city of Chalco. Although Montezuma had already proved himself an excellent military commander, Tlacaelel advised him to begin his rule by personally leading a campaign and bringing home prisoners who could be sacrificed to the gods during the corona-tion (crowning) ceremony. Montezuma was successful in his campaign, and his unlucky prisoners became part of the bloody royal ceremony.

Succession of Aztec Kings

When an Aztec king died, the throne did not automatically pass to his oldest son. In fact, being born into Aztec royalty did not ensure any special privilege. The royal family was huge. Emperors frequently had hundreds of wives, and some were said to have thousands of children. To be considered for a top government office, the emperor's heir would have to have been a top performer in combat or experienced in managing government affairs. A council of about thirty nobles chose the new emperor from among four nobles who had held the top positions under the deceased former emperor. These candidates were usually the sons, nephews, or brothers of the deceased emperor.

Montezuma was considered a wise ruler and a modest man. He lived in a simple, clean palace and had only a few wives. Montezuma's reign was strongly influenced by two advisers. One was his cousin **Nezahualcoyotl** (pronounced neh-zah-hwahl-coy-OH-tul; 1403–1473; see entry), the ruler of the allied city of Texcoco. The other was his half brother Tlacaelel, his *cihuacoatl,* or chief military and political adviser. Both men were brilliant, but their ideas of ruling were very different.

As emperor, Montezuma put the Triple Alliance between Tenochtitlán, Texcoco, and Tlacopán into action. The alliance controlled an ever-expanding area of central Mexico, and it imposed obligations on each new city it conquered. When the allied forces defeated a community, they demand-

Tlacaelel: The Snake Woman

Many scholars believe that Montezuma's half brother Tlacaelel was the mastermind of the Aztec empire, responsible for raising Aztec society from a small warrior band to a huge, warlike state capable of overpowering almost all other Mesoamerican cities. Legend has it that Tlacaelel was offered the kingship at several times during his life, but that he refused, preferring to work behind the scenes, directing the Aztec kings Itzcoatl, Montezuma I, and their two successors. Despite his reluctance to take the lead position, everyone around him knew his power and did as he said.

It was Tlacaelel's idea to revise Aztec history. He set out to eliminate all traditions that referred back to the Aztecs as a group of ruffians who came from an unknown region in the north. It was a traditional Mesoamerican belief that the Toltecs, a group of Mesoamericans who had ruled over the Valley of Mexico from about 900 to 1200, had been appointed by the gods to rule the valley. Most Mesoamerican kings claimed to descend from the Toltecs. Therefore, Tlacaelel created a new history about the Aztecs' origins, claiming that the Aztecs had arisen from Toltec ancestry and were ordained to rule a large empire. To make sure that this revision would take hold, he called in every storyteller in the empire and dictated the new, official Aztec "history" to them and prohibited them from telling the old history. Then he made certain that the royal Aztec family married into the families of the few remaining Toltec nobles in the region. Thus he transformed the leaders of the Aztec warrior band into powerful, semidivine royalty.

Most historians note a dark side to Tlacaelel's genius. They believe he was responsible for promoting the cult of the god Huitzilopochtli (pronounced weets-ee-loh-PAWCH-tlee). Worship of this god required human sacrifice—killing people and offering their bodies as a gift to Huitzilopochtli. Acting under Tlacaelel's influence, the Aztecs sacrificed human beings on a larger scale than had ever been done before—killing possibly tens of thousands of people each year. Tlacaelel also seems to have come up with the concept of "flower wars," prearranged battles between friendly cities that were waged solely to provide sacrifice victims for both sides. As the Aztecs grew to be the most powerful force in Mesoamerica, the philosophy of Tlacaelel dominated daily life. Sons were raised to be warriors; their highest goal was to capture prisoners in battle so that Aztec officials could sacrifice these victims to Huitzilopochtli.

ed that the people who lived there pay tribute. Paying tribute meant providing goods or labor to support the empire. This obligation was often ongoing, with "payments" due on a regular basis, like a tax. Under their alliance agreement,

Tenochtitlán and Texcoco each received two-fifths of the tribute, while Tlacopán received one-fifth. The cities of the alliance became rich under this arrangement.

Providing for the people

The Valley of Mexico had a population of about one million people during Montezuma's reign. The area controlled by Montezuma contained about ten urban centers, including Tenochtitlán, and many smaller communities as well. According to Brian M. Fagan in *The Aztecs* (1984), it was "the largest and densest population concentration in the entire history of pre-Hispanic [before the Spanish conquest] America." The large population in a relatively small area posed a great challenge for Montezuma: He had to figure out how to produce enough food for everyone, from only a small amount of land. Fagan presents Montezuma's solution: "The only way to feed everyone was by efficient, government-controlled agriculture." Montezuma was a capable administrator, managing the day-to-day operations of the empire's resources. He employed inspectors throughout the empire to make sure that every bit of land was planted and that extra food was sent to the capital, where it was stored until needed. He imported new cuttings of plants from faraway places—exotic flowers, cacao trees (evergreen trees that grow beans from which cocoa, chocolate, and cocoa butter are made), and even fruit trees so that the Aztecs could establish orchards with a variety of fruits.

An era of disasters

In 1446 Lake Texcoco flooded the city of Tenochtitlán. Rain and hail ruined the harvests, and famine struck the Valley of Mexico. Montezuma asked his cousin Nezahualcoyotl for help. Nezahualcoyotl directed the construction of a 9-mile-long (14.5-kilometer-long) dike (wall or embankment built to prevent flooding) that was designed to control the water level and to lessen the saltiness of the water so it could be used for farming. The eastern sections of Lake Texcoco lay in the bottom of the valley, where salt accumulated. The new dike shut out the salt floods and created a freshwater lake. The dike included gates for protection during rainy seasons. The immense project took almost ten years and tens of thousands of workers to complete.

After the dike was finished, Montezuma continued to work with Nezahualcoyotl on the construction of a 3-mile-long (4.8-kilometer-long) pipeline to bring more freshwater into the city, so the people would have an adequate supply of drinking water. Together Montezuma and Nezahualcoyotl accomplished one of the greatest feats of engineering in the pre-Hispanic Americas. Thanks to their planning and management skills, large populations were able to thrive in the valley and in Tenochtitlán.

While the dike and pipeline projects were still going on, the Aztecs had to deal with a series of natural disasters. Grasshoppers and frost destroyed two harvests. Snow and rain caused terrible flooding one year; and for the next two years the Aztecs faced an extended drought (long period of little or no rainfall). For three years the crops in the Valley of Mexico failed. People had no food, and some even sold their children to distant tribes for corn. Many people died. In desperation, the Aztec nobles and priests kept increasing their human sacrifice ceremonies, hoping to persuade the gods to call a halt to the disasters. By the third year of the famine, the Aztecs were practicing mass sacrifices on a frequent basis, sometimes with hundreds of victims in one ceremony. When the famine ended and healthy crops appeared in the valley, the Aztec priests and rulers believed the sacrifices had been responsible for bringing prosperity back to the valley. From then on, the Aztec practice of human sacrifice took on large-scale proportions. (The exact number of victims per year is still a matter of debate, but many estimates run in the thousands and even tens of thousands.)

Feeding the sun god

Soon after the disasters ceased, Montezuma began reconstruction and enlargement of the temple dedicated to the Aztecs' principal god, Huitzilopochtli. According to Aztec lore, Huitzilopochtli led the wandering Aztecs to their home at Tenochtitlán. He was not originally the chief Aztec god, but under the direction of Tlacaelel, he was given top status, and the Aztec people were taught to worship him as the powerful sun god and the god of battle. Worship of Huitzilopochtli became the hallmark of Aztec spirituality; conquered cities and states were forced to worship him.

The temple Montezuma renovated was called the Templo Mayor, or the great temple. It had originally been built in 1325 when the city was first founded. The initial structure had been small and plain, but it grew with every king's reign. No other Aztec emperor, however, accomplished as spectacular a renovation as Montezuma I's in 1454.

Templo Mayor sat atop a huge pyramid made up of more than one hundred steps. It was a double pyramid with two temples at its top shaped as mountains. One was dedicated to Tlaloc (pronounced TLAH-lock), the rain god, and the other to Huitzilopochtli. Montezuma needed a great number of workers to carry out the reconstruction of the great temple, so he ordered all communities and cities under the control of the Aztec empire to provide workers and material for the building of the new temple. Over a period of years, it would have taken thousands of workers to reconstruct this building.

In the end, the Templo Mayor was huge and commanding, inspiring awe in everyone who saw it.

According to Aztec traditions, the steps leading up to the temple were continually stained red with the blood of the victims who were sacrificed there. When Huitzilopochtli became the primary Aztec god, there was a tremendous increase in the number of human sacrifices in the Aztec empire. As the sun god, Huitzilopochtli was believed to be reborn every morning to make his trip across the heavens. At night, he was the warrior god, descending into the underworld to do battle with death and darkness so that he might rise again the next morning. His daily effort was believed to require vast amounts of fuel, or food. The Aztecs believed that the only food that could maintain Huitzilopochtli was the beating hearts of sacrificed warriors.

The human sacrifice ceremony required four priests to hold the victim and one skilled priest to make the sacrifice. The skilled priest plunged an obsidian knife into the victim's chest and then reached under the ribs to pull out the still-beating heart. The priest held the heart up, sprinkling the blood in the direction of the sun, and then placed it in the mouth of the statue of Huitzilopochtli or smeared it on a figurine of the god.

Conquests

Worried about future famines, Montezuma decided to ensure a reliable food supply by conquest and the collection of tribute. In 1458 he and his army attacked and conquered the province of Panuco, thus extending the Aztec empire to the sea. In 1461 the army conquered the lands of the Totonacs to the south, along with the people of Coatzacoalcos, and four years later Montezuma defeated the Chalca. In 1466, Montezuma fought his last war, defeating the Tepeaca.

Montezuma's laws of conduct

Over the years the Aztecs in Tenochtitlán had developed strict standards about living orderly, disciplined lives. Their oral literature—the stories they passed down by spoken word from generation to generation—is full of rules and guidelines about proper behavior. Streets were to be kept clean, children were to be well-behaved, daily baths were the norm, and drunkenness and adultery were forbidden. People were expected to follow the rules, and the punishments were severe if they failed to do so. While Montezuma was in power, he made certain that the Aztec sense of order and morality was made into law so that it could be preserved.

Montezuma's laws of conduct also drew lines between various levels of Aztec society. Under these laws, people of high birth were easily distinguished by their dress. Ornate clothing was reserved for the noble classes. (Montezuma himself wore the finest jewels, finely woven cotton clothing, and a headdress with bright feathers.) Commoners were prohibited from wearing cotton cloth, sandals, or clothes that extended below the knee. Only noblemen could reside in homes of more than one story or use fine glazed ceramic vessels for their food.

Death

Montezuma I died in 1469 and was succeeded by his nineteen-year-old grandson Axayácatl (pronounced ash-eye-AH-ca-tul), whose rule of the empire from 1469 to 1481 would also be highly influenced by the powerful adviser Tlacaelel. Axayácatl was the father of **Montezuma II** (1466–1520; see entry), the ruler of the Aztecs at the time of the Spanish invasion and conquest. In Aztec history, Montezuma I is sometimes overshadowed by his namesake, who is remembered because his reign took place at the end of the empire. However, Montezuma I can be credited with many more accomplishments than his great grandson.

During Montezuma's reign he expanded the Aztec empire, instituted laws, and changed Aztec religion. He gave Tenochtitlán a dike and a water pipeline that allowed the city to grow and prosper. He also made arrangements for a backup food supply to protect citizens from famine in the event of a crop failure. Montezuma is still remembered for his impressive building projects, especially the temple to the god Huitzilopochtli. However, he also played a large part in some of the less appealing aspects of the Aztec empire. He promoted the idea that war and the taking of prisoners was the main task of the Aztecs in order to ensure a constant supply of sacrificial victims for Huitzilopochtli. This remained the overriding purpose of the Aztecs until the Spanish conquered the empire in 1521.

For More Information

Fagan, Brian M. *The Aztecs*. New York: W. H. Freeman, 1984.

Kandell, Jonathan. *La Capital: The Biography of Mexico City*. New York: Random House, 1988.

Meyer, Michael C., and William L. Sherman. *The Course of Mexican History*. 5th ed. New York and Oxford: Oxford University Press, 1995.

Thomas, Hugh. *Conquest: Montezuma, Cortés, and the Fall of Old Mexico*. New York: Simon and Schuster, 1993.

Townsend, Richard F. *The Aztecs*. London and New York: Thames and Hudson, 2000.

Web Sites

"Tenochtitlan: Templo Mayor." *Metropolitan Museum of Art Online*. http://www.metmuseum.org/toah/hd/teno_2/hd_teno_2.htm (accessed on November 17, 2004).

Aztec Sun Stone

Photograph and illustrations of the Aztec Sun Stone, commonly known as the Calendar Stone
Artifact date c. 1479; located in Mexico City, Mexico

The Aztec Sun Stone, commonly known as the Calendar Stone, is one of the most famous artifacts of the ancient Aztec empire. The huge stone—carved from a fine-grained, dark gray rock called basalt—weighs 24 tons (21.8 metric tons) and measures about 13 feet (4 meters) in diameter. Although it is often called the Calendar Stone, the Sun Stone probably did not function as a calendar. It was an artistic representation of an Aztec idea of the universe measured in cycles from the beginning of time. To the Aztecs, time was much more than a way to count the days, years, and seasons. Every day, month, and epoch was associated with a god. In the Aztec view, an event did not occur only once. When something happened, the Aztecs believed it was simply a variation of an event that had happened before, over and over again on a cyclical basis. To the Aztecs, history was not a recording of events like it is in modern times. The Aztecs viewed history as the placement of events within the context of their cycle. Knowing these cycles was key to understanding the present and the future. Working with the Aztec calendar was therefore considered a sacred task and was carried out by priests.

The Sun Stone has become a national symbol of pride in Mexico, representing the great civilization of the Aztec people.

The Aztec calendar system

The Aztecs used a two-calendar system. One of the Aztec calendars was the 260-day sacred round called the *tonalpohualli* (pronounced toe-nah-poe-WHAHL-lee). Like the **Sacred Calendar** (see entry), the *tonalpohualli* used combinations of twenty day names and the numbers one to thirteen to name each day. There were 260 combinations (20 x 13) before the cycle began again. Each day of the year was associated with a god and with various traits. If a child was born on a day considered unlucky, for example, it was assumed his or her life would be unlucky. The sacred calendar was used by the Aztec priests for seeing into the future and choosing lucky days for weddings, wars, and other important events.

A second Aztec calendar, the *xihuitl* (pronounced shee-WHEE-tul) or solar calendar, was used to measure the agricultural seasons and to time ceremonies and festivals. It had a 360-day year composed of eighteen twenty-day months. At the end of the year there were five extra days, called *nemontemi*. This five-day period, designed to finish off the 365-day solar year, was thought to be a very unlucky time. During this time, the Aztecs did not work or plan important events.

The ends of cycles

The basic Aztec system of measuring time combined both the sacred and solar calendars. Every fifty-two years all possible combinations of both sacred and solar day names and numbers had been used, and the cycles of the dual calendar system would start over. Each period of fifty-two years was called a "bundle of years." At the end of each bundle, there was a twelve-day period before the next calendar cycle started, a time not recorded on any calendars. The Aztecs believed that in these twelve-day periods the world would be destroyed unless they performed specific sacrifices and rituals. A ritual is a ceremonial act, such as burning incense as an offering to the gods.

As the end of a bundle approached, the Aztecs were filled with dread, fearing the sun might fail to rise after the last night of the bundle. On this last night they followed a long ritual called the New Fire Ceremony. As evening approached, the people in every Aztec home broke all their dishes. Every fire in every house, workshop, and temple was put out. On a mountaintop in the Valley of Mexico the priests began an all-night prayer for the sun to rise. In their homes throughout the valley, the Aztec people sat awake and prayed. Even children were not allowed to sleep through this night, unless evil spirits might invade their bodies. All anxiously watched to see if the sun would rise. When it arose, cries of joy and thankfulness filled the valley. On the mountaintop, a human being was sacrificed (killed) to show gratitude to the gods. A fire was lit, and torches taken from this new fire were used to light all other fires. For the Aztecs, the New Fire Ceremony marked the beginning of a new cycle and gave them hope of survival for another fifty-two-year bundle. The last New Fire Ceremony before the Spanish conquest was in 1507.

The five suns

The Aztecs believed there had been four worlds and four suns before the present one, and each world and its sun had been destroyed. The world of the first sun was called the epoch of the ocelot, or jaguar. It ended when the wild animals went on a rampage and devoured all human beings. The god associated with the world of the first sun is Tezcatlipoca (pronounced tez-caht-lee-POE-cah), meaning the "smoking mirror" or "smoked mirror." The world of the second sun was the epoch of wind and was destroyed by terrible hurricanes. It was associated with the wind god Ehecatonatiuh (pronounced eh-weh-KAH-tone-ah-tee-wah) and with Quetzalcoatl (pronounced kates-ahl-koh-AH-tul), the "feathered serpent." The world of the third sun was the epoch of the rains of fire, associated with the god of rain, Tlaloc (pronounced TLAH-lock). Volcanoes poured lava onto the human dwellings and destroyed the world of the third sun. Finally, the world of the fourth sun was the epoch of water, and its god was Atonatiuh (pronounced ah-toe-nah-TEE-wah). Torrential rains caused terrible flooding, thus destroying the world of the fourth sun.

In the days after the destruction of the world of the fourth sun the gods met to make their plans for a fifth. They chose two gods—one rich and the other poor and sickly—to sacrifice themselves so the world would be renewed. When it came time for the rich god to sacrifice himself, he could not bring himself to jump into the sacrificial fire. However, the poor sickly god jumped straight into the fire. The gods waited to see if the sacrifice caused the renewal of the world, but nothing happened. Realizing his sacrifice was demanded, the rich god finally jumped into the fire. Again, the rest of the gods waited to see if the sun would rise and the world would be renewed, but nothing happened. At last, all the gods, one by one, threw themselves into the fire. After these sacrifices, the poor, sickly god who had first jumped into the fire arose out of the ashes in great splendor as Tonatiuh (pronounced toe-nah-TEE-wah), the new sun, bringing light and life to the world. The world of the fifth sun had begun.

The Sun Stone

The Aztecs called their great stone carving *Cuauhxicalli* (pronounced cwah-uh-shee-CAHL-lee), which means "eagle bowl." The Aztec emperor Axayácatl (pronounced ash-eye-AH-ca-tul; ruled c. 1469–1481) commissioned the sculpting of the stone, and it was completed in Tenochtitlán (pronounced tay-notch-teet-LAHN) around 1479. No one knows how or where the Aztecs displayed the stone, but many believe it was placed upon the Templo Mayor, the huge and elaborate temple devoted to the sun and war god, Huitzilopochtli (pronounced hweets-ee-loh-PAWCH-tlee). It was hung in a vertical position facing south and painted in bright reds, blues, and yellows.

When the Spanish defeated the Aztecs in 1521, they began to build their capital, Mexico City, on the site of Tenochtitlán, the former Aztec capital. The Spanish leaders demanded that the Sun Stone be buried—thinking the presence of what appeared to be a religious artifact might make their efforts to convert the Aztec people to Christianity more difficult. They also believed the stone disc might have been used in human sacrifice ceremonies. The Sun Stone remained buried under the growing metropolis of Mexico City for 250 years. By the time it was discovered, many of the meanings of its symbols and designs had been forgotten and were difficult to interpret. Though many scholars believe they understand the meaning of the Sun Stone, many aspects are still disputed.

Things to remember while examining the photograph and illustrations of the Aztec Sun Stone:

- The Aztec Sun Stone is a representation of the Aztec universe in the form of the Sun. Its round shape is representative of the cycles it depicts. Look at both the photograph of the stone and its artistic reconstruction. Note that the images radiate out from the center in rings. The rings are pointed out by the sunrays, the V-shaped pointers.

- The figure at the center of the Sun Stone is generally interpreted to be Tonatiuh, the god of the fifth sun. Tonatiuh is the center of the stone because, like the sun, the god is the center of the world around which all life revolves. Notice how Tonatiuh's tongue sticks out. Its shape is formed like an obsidian blade. Obsidian blades, made from dark, solid glass formed by volcanoes, were often used in Aztec human sacrifice ceremonies. The blade symbolizes Tonatiuh's constant demand for human blood. (See the illustration labeled "Tonatiuh's Face" for a closer view.)

- Looking at the illustration showing a reconstruction of the Sun Stone, note the four rectangular shapes surrounding the image of Tonatiuh. These are called the *Nahui-Ollin,* or Four Movements, and represent the four epochs, or suns, that preceded the present world of the fifth sun. The *Nahui-Ollin* are as follows (in counterclockwise order): the ocelot, or jaguar, in the rectangle on the upper right of Tonatiuh represents the world of the first sun; the god of wind in the upper left rectangle represents the world of the second sun (see the illustration labeled "First Ring" for a closer view of the wind god, Ehecatonatiuh); the god of fire in the lower left rectangle represents the world of the third sun; and finally, the god of water in the lower right rectangle represents the world of the fourth sun.

- On each side of Tonatiuh's face is an image within a circle. Each image depicts one of Tonatiuh's claws (he was considered the "eagle who soars"). The claws are clutching a human heart, which is probably a reference to human sacrifice.

- Note the large upside-down V-shaped pointer over To-natiuh's head. It points to the second ring from the center. The second ring is composed of twenty squares, each containing an image representing one of the twenty day names that make up each of the eighteen months in a solar year. (See the illustration labeled "Second Ring" for a closer view of the day name, Tochtli, or "rabbit.") In clockwise order starting from the top just to the right of the pointer, these names are:

> *Xochitl: flower*
> *Quiahuitl: rain*
> *Tecpatl: flint*
> *Ollin: movement*
> *Cozcacuauhtli: vulture*
> *Cuauhtle: eagle*
> *Ocelotl: jaguar*
> *Acatl: cane/reed*
> *Malinalli: herb/grass*
> *Ozomatli: monkey*
> *Itzquintli: hairless dog*
> *Atl: water*
> *Tochtli: rabbit*
> *Mazatl: deer*
> *Miquiztli: death*
> *Coatl: snake*
> *Cuetzpallin: lizard*
> *Calli: house*
> *Ehecatl: wind*
> *Cipactli: crocodile*

- Going outward from the center, surrounding the day-name glyphs, is a ring with forty squares. Each of the squares contains five dots. There are many explanations for these—one explanation is that they represent forty-five-day weeks. Note the four large pointers that lie between this ring and the outer ring. These represent the four directions: north, south, east, and west.

- The third ring is broad with a light background and contains three types of elements. The eight large, solid V-shaped objects pointing to the outer ring represent sunrays. Between the rays are eight rectangular-shaped objects. Each has a base, topped by three squares with

Tonatiuh's Face

a white ball on top of the squares. These are *chalchihuites* (pronounced chahl-chee-WHEE-tays, meaning "precious ornaments") made of jade plates. The holes visible in them were used for leather straps that attached them to the stone. The *chalchihuites* represented beauty and light. On the sides of the ornaments are smaller upside-down V shapes representing splashed blood, probably associated with human sacrifice. The splashed blood symbols appear to be feeding the symbols of fire above them in the ring. (See the illustration labeled "Third Ring" for a closer view of the splashed blood symbols.)

• The square object at the very top of the outer ring is a dedication plate with the date 13 Acatl (13 Cane or Reed; notice the thirteen dots representing the number), which would be 1479 C.E. on modern calendars. Experts believe this was the year the Sun Stone was completed and dedicated to the gods. (See the illustration labeled

"Outer Ring" for a closer view of the dedication plate.) On each side of the dedication plate are images depicting bundles of herbs with flower buds. Slightly farther away from the dedication plate on each side are two large white bands that represent scrolls or bound strips of natural paper.

• The outer border of the Sun Stone is made up of two fire serpents, or *xiucoatl* (pronounced shee-oo-COE-ah-tul). Their tails meet at the top of the stone and their heads meet at the bottom. The bodies surround the stone. Each serpent is made up of ten segments, and in each of these segments there is a *tlachinolli,* or a flaming sign. At the bottom of the stone the serpents' heads meet. The image of a god comes out of each head. These gods are face to face as if in combat. They are believed to be two aspects of the sun god, Tonatiuh. One is Tonatiuh, the "eagle who ascends" each morning, and the other is Tonatiuh, the "eagle who falls" in the evening.

Illustration showing a reconstruction of the Aztec Sun Stone. *The Art Archive/National Anthropological Museum Mexico/Dagli Orti.*

- The Sun Stone was displayed hanging upon a wall. There are eight holes at the edge of the calendar in which the Aztecs placed sticks that stood straight out from the stone. Light from the sun falling on these sticks casts shadows across the stone, causing it to function like a sundial (an instrument using the shadows cast upon it to tell the time of day).

What happened next ...

After the Spanish conquest of Tenochtitlán in 1521, the Spanish soldiers, led by Hernán Cortés (1485–1547), destroyed the Aztec buildings. They built their own capital, Mexico City, right on top of Tenochtitlán. Cortés is said to have built his home on top of emperor Montezuma II's (pronounced mohk-the-ZOO-mah; c. 1466–1520) palace, and the Spanish cathedral was built on top of the ruins of Templo Mayor. For 250 years, most of the city of Tenochtitlán re-

The First Ring: showing Ehecatonatiuh. The Second Ring: showing Tochtli, or rabbit, one of the twenty day names of the Aztec Sun Stone. *The Gale Group.*

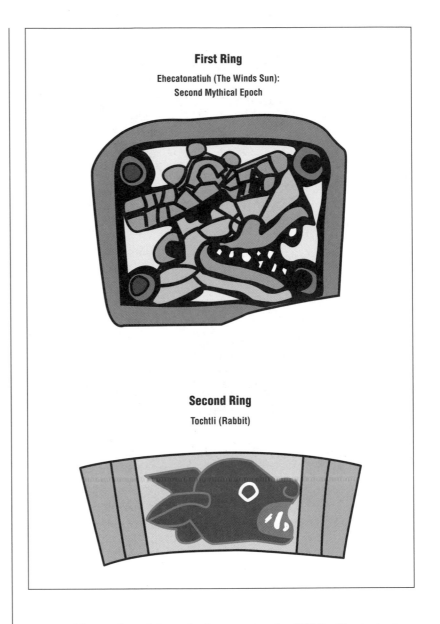

First Ring

Ehecatonatiuh (The Winds Sun):
Second Mythical Epoch

Second Ring

Tochtli (Rabbit)

mained buried and largely forgotten. In 1790 efforts to improve drainage in Mexico City's central plaza (called the Zócalo) resulted in the discovery of two Aztec sculptures buried beneath the plaza. One of the sculptures was the Sun Stone. For about a century, the Sun Stone remained in Mexico City's Zócalo, displayed on the wall of the Metropolitan Cathedral.

In 1949 the Sun Stone was placed in Mexico City's National Museum of Anthropology, where it remains in the

Third Ring

Splashed Blood Symbols

Outer Ring

Dedication Plate

twenty-first century. The Sun Stone has become a national symbol of pride in Mexico, representing the great civilization of the Aztec people. The stone is a magnificent work of art and demonstrates the profound knowledge of astronomy (study of the stars and the planets) and mathematics of its makers. It is an enduring monument to the great achievements of the Aztec empire.

Did you know ...

- The Spanish wanted to bury the Sun Stone because they thought it was a sacrificial altar upon which people had been killed in grisly ceremonies by Aztec priests. They were wrong.

- Tenochtitlán's enormous Templo Mayor lay buried under the central plaza of Mexico City even longer than the Sun Stone. It was not until February 21, 1978, that electrical workers digging under the plaza came upon a large stone carving that had once stood at the bottom of the stairway leading up the pyramid to the base of the temple. The city's authorities permitted archaeologists to excavate the temple in the busy center of Mexico City. After lying underground for more than 450 years, Templo Mayor eventually became a favorite tourist site. Further excavations may continue to reveal precious pieces of Aztec history.

Consider the following ...

- Make your own calendar stone. You will need a large piece of paper, scissors, a pencil and eraser, and colored pencils or crayons. Cut out a large circle of paper (the larger the better), and lay it out on a flat surface where you can work. Create another circle in the center and two or three more rings moving outward toward the rim. Place a sun or moon in the center circle with rays radiating outwards. Decorate the outer rings with pictures of things related to time (clocks, suns, moons, flowers, colorful leaves, snowflakes, pumpkins, birthday candles).

- The Sun Stone is an artifact—something left behind by earlier people that tells people today something about its creators. What does the Sun Stone tell us about the Aztec people?

For More Information

Web Sites

"Aztec Calendar." *Artcamp.* http://www.artcamp.com.mx/AZ/4.html (accessed on November 22, 2004).

Johnson, Charles William. "The Legend of the Four Suns: Math, Geometry, and Design." *Earth / Matrix: Science in Artwork.* http://www.earthmatrix.com/foursuns/xtract24.htm (accessed on November 22, 2004).

Rojas, Sal. "The Great Aztec Sun Stone." *BrownPride.com.* http://www.brownpride.com/history/history.asp?a=aztecs/sunstonehistory (accessed on November 22, 2004).

Senior, Meghan. *Time and the Aztec Mind: The Aztec Calendar Sun Stone in Context.* http://rubens.anu.edu.au/student.projects97/aztec/ACalStone.html/ACAL.html (accessed on November 22, 2004).

"Technology: Calendars." *Oracle Think Quest.* http://library.thinkquest.org/27981/calendar.html (accessed on November 22, 2004).

Codex Borgia

**Illustration of days and gods in the Aztec calendar, from the
Codex Borgia
Created c. 1510**

Codices (singular: codex) are ancient books that relate information about the religion, rituals, history, astronomy, and calendar systems of vanished peoples. Codices from Mesoamerica, such as the *Codex Borgia,* are a leading source of information about the cultures that existed there prior to the arrival of the Spanish in the sixteenth century. Before the Spanish conquest most Mesoamerican codices were painted on paper made from the bark of fig trees or from animal skins. For a deerskin book, for example, strips of deerskin were attached end to end to make one long strip. The strip was then treated with white lime-plaster and folded like an accordion. Priests or scribes made the codices, using natural pigments from vegetables and minerals to color their paints. Their paintbrushes came in a variety of sizes; the bristles were often made of rabbit fur. Many codices had covers made from wood or animal skin.

Common people never handled codices; the books were often considered sacred. In most cases, priests created the codices and kept them safely stored. Priests also trained scribes to read, write, and paint these books. In Aztec society,

"The *Codex Borgia* has long been recognized as one of the most elegant and beautiful of the few surviving pre-Columbian painted manuscripts. Its special significance has been seen in its detailed depiction of highland Mesoamerican gods and the ritual and divination associated with them."

*Bruce E. Byland. "Introduction
and Commentary."* The *Codex
Borgia:* A Full-Color
Restoration of the Ancient
Mexican Manuscript, *by
Gisele Díaz and Alan Rodgers.*

scribes called *tlacuilos* were usually assigned to particular temples or government offices, where they would paint codices detailing anything from religious customs to lists of stored goods. The scribes were well trained and highly honored. The codices they made were kept in special places, probably in the temples or in homes of the head priests, for the use of priests.

Destruction of the codices

After the Spanish conquistadores defeated the Aztecs, the Mayas, and many other Mesoamerican groups in the early sixteenth century, one of their missions was to convert the Mesoamericans to Christianity. Spanish soldiers and missionaries soon began to destroy the sacred objects of the traditional Mesoamerican religions. Most Spaniards viewed the Mesoamerican gods as devils. They were horrified by the practice of human sacrifice, appalled by the sacrifice ceremonies they witnessed during which victims' hearts were cut from their chests while they were still alive (the hearts were then offered as a gift to the gods). The Spanish missionaries were particularly intent upon destroying the codices, which they feared would serve as constant reminders of the traditional beliefs and practices of the Mesoamericans. Thus, Mesoamerican codices were burned by the thousands, and the Americas lost a priceless connection to the past.

Very few codices survived the Spanish conquest. Only about fifteen codices created before the conquest were saved. Even these were not spared on purpose; Spanish soldiers sent them back to Europe as souvenirs of conquest before the book burnings began. After the conquest, a few Spanish missionaries joined forces with the Mesoamericans to create pictorial records of Mesoamerican history and traditions. Many codices were produced from these efforts in the decades after the conquest; more than four hundred post-conquest, or colonial, codices are still in existence. (See **Codex Mendoza** entry for more information on colonial codices.)

The surviving pre-Hispanic codices

Experts have divided the surviving pre-Hispanic codices (those created before the Spanish conquest) into three categories: Maya religious codices, Mixtec historical codices, and the Borgia Group. The Mayas wrote thousands of codices through the centuries of their civilization, but only three (or possibly four) survived: the Dresden, Paris, and Madrid codices (and perhaps the Grolier, although its Maya origins are in question). The Maya codices are religious documents in which the priests or scribes set out and analyzed their calendar systems, often associating gods and other supernatural forces with calendar days in order to understand the present and predict the future.

In their codices the Mayas used an advanced glyph-writing system. Glyphs are figures that function as symbols, representing either full words or the syllables or sounds of a word. By combining the sound glyphs, the Mayas could fully reproduce their spoken language in writing without the use of pictures. The Mayas were the only Mesoamericans to achieve this.

The second group of surviving codices is the work of the Mixtecs. The Mixtec civilization originated sometime around the ninth century and was still in existence when the Spanish arrived in Mesoamerica in the sixteenth century. The Mixtecs lived in southern Mexico in the present-day Mexican states of Oaxaca, Puebla, and Guerrero. They did not have one central government; their civilization was made up of many territories, and each territory had its own royal family to rule over the local people. The seven or eight historical Mixtec codices that survive in the twenty-first century were painted in the territory of Mixteca Alta (Upper Mixteca). They are records of the local history and the ancestry of the royal families. Their writing system is considered by many scholars to be a source of Aztec writing, or at least to be very closely associated with it.

The writing system of the Mixtecs, like the Aztecs, was by no means easy to interpret. Within a single page of a Mixtec codex there were often hundreds of small and large images. Each one of these images had a meaning. They were understood by the reader to represent gods, calendars dates, places, ceremonies, and historical people and events. Thus, though the books could not be read in sentences, a lot of information could be found upon the page. The Mixtecs used a combination of pictographic and ideographic writing systems. In pictographic writing, a small picture visually represents a word. A simple image of a flame, for example, represents the word "fire"; a square topped by a triangle might serve as the sign for "house." In ideographic writing systems, images or symbols stand for objects or ideas rather than specific words; the reader must have prior knowledge of what the symbol means in order to read it. For example, a V shape might represent fire. The Mixtecs, like the Aztecs, also used glyphs in their codices. The glyphs often represented the names of people and places or dates.

Although the Mixtec writing system was complex, it did not fully represent the spoken language of the Mixtec people. Therefore, the writer could not paint, or write out, the whole story. Instead, reading the codices involved intensive memorization. Highly trained priests or storytellers memorized the traditions contained in the books. Then, when they narrated a text to the public, they used the codex as a tool to remind them of the details of the narration.

The Borgia Group: religious codices

The third group of preconquest codices is the Borgia Group, a collection of five codices. The writing style used in these texts is similar but not identical to the style of the Mixtec history codices; the content is religious rather than historical. These codices were created between 1200 and 1500 in the area of the present-day states of Puebla and Oaxaca (pronounced wah-HAH-kah) in the Mexican highlands.

Priests used the Borgia Group codices to help keep track of the complex system of gods and ceremonies for which they were responsible. There were hundreds of gods in the religions of Mesoamerica. Some were universal—every Mesoamerican group worshiped them—while others were local. Each god was associated with various traits, activities, and natural phenomena. For example, one god might be the god of sleep, the god of war, and the god of rain. The gods were portrayed differently by Mesoamerican artists depending on what aspect of themselves they were representing. A god might appear in bird form, for example, as the god of night, and in human form as the flower god.

There were hundreds of ways to worship each god, and it was important to worship in precisely the right way. Mesoamericans considered the natural disasters that threatened their existence—flooding, droughts (long periods of little or no rainfall), volcanic eruptions, earthquakes, and frosts—to be the acts of the gods. In their belief system, people could control nature only by making the gods happy, and the only way to accomplish that was by performing the correct rituals. A ritual is a ceremonial act, such as burning incense as an offering to the gods. Some rituals were simple offerings to the gods performed by families in their homes, but many rituals were part of an elaborate ceremony, with each part carefully performed in a certain order and in a particular way.

Knowing the correct rituals to perform in every circumstance was extremely difficult. Consequently, the priests were highly educated in various aspects of the supernatural forces and devoted their lives to the study of religious rituals. Over the years, some priests became experts in particular areas of worship. Priests who had specialties pooled their learning, and older, more experienced priests trained the new priests. The Mesoamerican religious system became more and more detailed and complex, and the codices reflected this fact. Only those highly skilled through years of training could read and interpret them.

The mysteries of the *Codex Borgia*

The Borgia Group is named after the most elaborate codex of the group, the seventy-six-page *Codex Borgia*. The *Codex Borgia* has been studied intensively by Mesoamerican scholars, but much of it remains a mystery. Scholars are uncertain about where the book originated. No one has been able to pinpoint an exact location, but most experts believe the book comes from southern or central Puebla or northern Oaxaca. Many languages were spoken in that general area, and no one has identified what language was spoken by the book's creators. Though many people think the *Codex Borgia* is a Mixtec creation, others see an Aztec influence, and many scholars identify the work as Mixtec-Aztec. Scholars are not even certain when it was created. Because it has no sign of Spanish influence, they place it sometime before 1520. Most believe the book was made in the decades just before the Spanish conquest.

The *Codex Borgia* was intended as a guidebook for priests, laying out the various religious rituals in association with the periods of time measured by the sacred 260-day calendar. In his introduction to *The* Codex Borgia: *A Full-Color Restoration of the Ancient Mexican Manuscript* (1993), Bruce E. Byland calls the ancient document a "reference book" of rituals. The codex was also used as a tool for divination—the practice of interpreting signs and omens to predict the future. The book evidently aided in the divination process by presenting the calendar cycles in various combinations with the associated gods and other supernatural influences. No one understands how this actually worked.

Some scholars believe the *Codex Borgia* presents detailed astronomical observations (information on stars and planets and their positions) in connection with the calendar system. Several experts have developed complicated theories about the meanings attached to some of the pages of the codex, but few of these theories have found widespread acceptance among scholars.

The content of the book

The *Codex Borgia* is based on a 260-day sacred calendar, which the Aztecs called the *tonalpohualli* (pronounced toe-nah-poe-WHAHL-lee), or the "book of days." Twenty day names combined with the numerals one through thirteen make up the days of the year on the *tonalpohualli*. Using every combination of the thirteen numbers with the twenty day names in a specific sequence created the 260 days of the year. Each day of the year was associated with a god and with various traits. If a child was born on a day considered to be unlucky, for example, it was assumed that the child would have an unlucky life. Mixtec and Aztec priests used the sacred calendar to look into the future and choose lucky days for weddings, wars, and other important events. Everything presented in the *Codex Borgia* is associated with the *tonalpohualli;* the gods and rituals are all presented in association with the calendar periods.

The *Codex Borgia* also contains a great deal of information about the characteristics of the gods. Hundreds of Mesoamerican deities appear in the book, including Xochipilli / Tonacatechutli (pronounced show-chee-PILL-ee / toe-nah-cah-

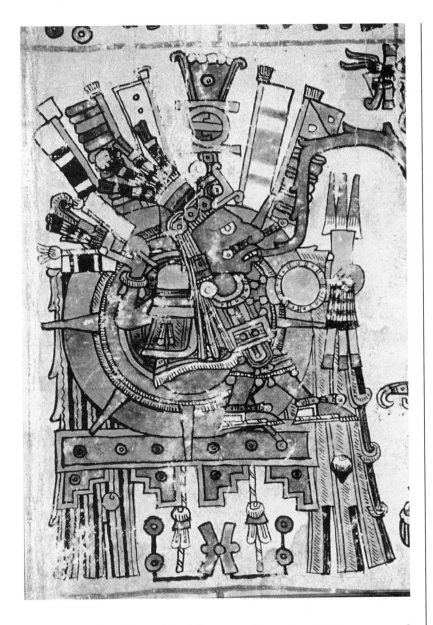

tay-CHOO-tli), the god of flowers; Quetzalcoatl (pronounced kates-ahl-koh-AH-tul), the feathered serpent; Tlaloc (pronounced TLAH-lock), the rain god; Tezcatlipoca (pronounced tez-caht-lee-POE-cah), the "smoking mirror"; and Tonatiuh (pronounced toe-nah-TEE-wah), the sun god or the god of the fifth sun.

The pictures of the *Codex Borgia* represent some of the most remarkable artwork of the era. They frequently focus upon sacrifice or bloodletting (piercing the skin to draw blood as an offering to the gods), and many portray shocking, frightening, or violent scenes. They are dramatic and expressive, conveying their messages through elaborate images. Experts agree that the *Codex Borgia* is the work of a great Mesoamerican artist.

It is important to remember while looking at the pictures that even scholars who specialize in studying the *Codex Borgia* do not understand how it was used.

Things to remember while examining the illustration of days and gods in the Aztec calendar, from the *Codex Borgia:*

- At the top of the picture, in boxes, are the twenty day-name signs used in the *tonalpohualli*. If you read them from the bottom right to left and repeat that sequence up the page, they are in the order in which they fall on the calendar. The day names are as follows: (bottom row, right to left) Alligator, Wind, House, Lizard, Serpent; (one row up from bottom, right to left) Death, Deer, Rabbit, Water, Dog; (second row from top, right to left) Monkey, Grass, Reed, Jaguar, Eagle, Vulture; (top row, right to left) Movement, Flint, Rain, Flower.

- The picture is the first page of a ten-page calendar. Remember that codices were created on a single long strip of paper that was folded like an accordion. If the other nine pages of this calendar were unfolded, the calendar could be read as one long document. The calendar was read from right to left.

- Each of the ten pages, like the one in this picture, contains twenty-six day-name signs, shown in two groups of squares containing the signs for thirteen days. The thirteen-day periods are called *trecenas*.

- The first *trecena* (thirteen squares) is the strip of squares that runs across the bottom of the picture and up the left side. The second *trecena* begins at the left side, just above the end of the first *trecena*, and runs to the right and up the opposite side.

- The creator of this calendar did not put the day numbers into the squares, but the numbers can be determined. Since there are thirteen day numbers, the reader of the

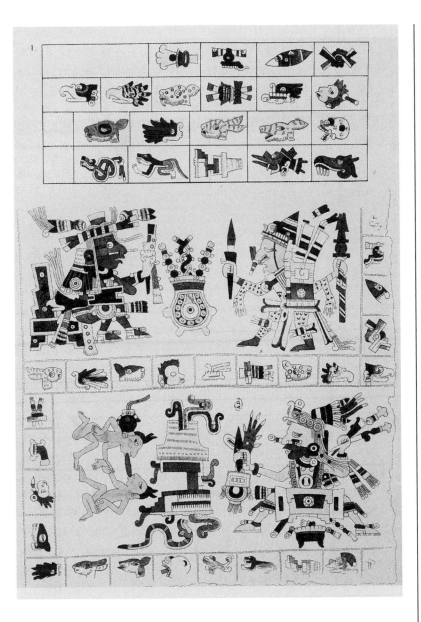

A page from the *Codex Borgia*, with pictographs representing days and gods from the Aztec *tonalpohualli*, or 260-day sacred calendar. *The Art Archive/Bibliotheque des Arts Decoratifs Paris/Dagli Orti.*

calendar would know that a new number cycle would begin every thirteen squares.

- Beginning at the right-hand side of the bottom strip, the first day name is Alligator. With its assumed number, the day is 1 Alligator. Continuing across the bottom strip, the days are 2 Wind, 3 House, 4 Lizard, 5 Serpent, 6 Death, 7 Deer, 8 Rabbit, 9 Water. Going up the left-hand strip, the four squares are 10 Dog, 11 Monkey, 12 Grass, and 13 Reed, completing the first *trecena*.

- If you were looking at the full calendar, the next sequence of thirteen days would begin at the bottom right of the next page (not shown here) on 14 Jaguar. The sequences of *trecenas* running across the bottom and up the left-hand side would continue through all ten pages of the calendar. Then, starting at page ten, they would run across the middle strip and up the right-hand side, returning to the page shown here.

- The second *trecena,* running from left to right across the page, begins with 1 Rabbit. Continuing across, the days are 2 Water, 3 Dog, 4 Monkey, 5 Grass, 6 Reed, 7 Jaguar, 8 Eagle, and 9 Vulture. Going up the right-hand side of the page are 10 Movement, 11 Flint, 12 Rain, and finally 13 Flower, the last day of the 260-day year.

- Each *trecena* serves as a border for an image. The upper *trecena* frames two deities in elaborate costume with a large symbol between them. The lower *trecena* wraps around an elaborately dressed god who is facing a symbol and two small human figures. The large figures are the gods that influence the *trecena*. Experts believe that all the symbols and images surrounding them may have been used in foretelling future events.

- Some of the images surrounding the gods come from the day-name signs. In the lower *trecena,* notice the large symbol separating the god from the two smaller figures on the left. It is very similar to the day-name sign for House.

What happened next ...

After the Spanish conquest, an unknown person sent the *Codex Borgia* to Europe. It was lost for nearly three centuries. In 1805 it was found in the estate of the recently deceased Italian cardinal and historian Stefano Borgia (1731–1804). Evidently Borgia had gotten the codex from an Italian family. Not realizing the value of the book, the family had given it to their servants, who in turn gave it to their children as a plaything. As a result the *Codex Borgia* was severely damaged, and three pages of it were burned. In his will, Cardinal Borgia left the codex to the Vatican (the government of the independent papal state where the Roman Catholic pope resides). The *Codex Borgia,* named after the cardinal, remains at the Vatican, in the Apostolic Library.

The *Codex Borgia* is now five centuries old. During its three hundred years as a lost document in Italy, it was tattered, folded, torn, and burned by people who did not know that it was a priceless document of Mesoamerican history. Many of the images on the original document have rubbed off or been otherwise damaged. In photographed reproductions of the original it is difficult to discern the faint or blurred images. Therefore, most of the pictures from the *Codex Borgia* that are available to the public are actually photographs of hand-painted copies of the original. The artists who copy the pages of the original codex are scholars with considerable knowledge about Mesoamerican codices. Where the images on the original have been rubbed out or folded, the artists have to make educated guesses to fill in some of the blanks. The artists use the same colors that were used in the original codex. Although the restorations (copies) are not exactly like the original, they have at least one advantage: The copies present a better idea of what the codex looked like in pre-Hispanic times, before it was damaged.

Did you know ...

- On Mixtec and Aztec calendars, sacred and solar day names and numbers were paired in every possible combination to yield a fifty-two-year cycle; that is, every fifty-two years, the name-number pairs would repeat. With this system, dates extending more than fifty-two years into the past or future could not be distinguished from dates in the current cycle. Mixtec and Aztec calendars did not have a **Long Count** (see entry) counterpart like the Maya calendars. The Maya Long Count counted back to a zero date, which would be August 13, 3114 B.C.E. on a modern calendar. Using the Long Count, the Mayas were able to place their sacred and solar dates in the context of a large time frame.

- During the Spanish conquest of Mesoamerica, many Mesoamerican priests were killed or badly abused because some of the Spanish soldiers believed the native priests were ministers of the devil because they worshiped gods that were not acceptable to the Christian religion.

Consider the following …

- Form a group with some of your classmates and focus on the details of the picture from the codex. What parts of this page look like they might be part of a picture-writing system? Are there any objects in the picture that you recognize? What kinds of personalities do you think these gods have? What seems odd to you about the picture? Let each member of the group ask one question about a particular image within the picture, and then let everyone discuss the question.

- Make your own codex. You will need four sheets of paper, staples or glue, a ruler, a pencil, and a set of colored pencils or crayons (or paints and a paintbrush). Begin by stapling or gluing the sheets of paper end to end to make them into one long strip. Then measure 6-inch (15-centimeter) segments with your ruler and mark them off with your pencil. Starting at the right, fold the strip of paper accordion-style along the markings until the whole strip is folded. Now spread out the sheet on a large working surface and get ready to write and draw or paint your codex. Choose a theme—motorcycles, fish, baseball, foods, holidays, or whatever you like. Imagine that you are going to give your codex to someone who does not know anything about the theme you chose. On each page of your codex draw pictures to explain and demonstrate your theme. Label your pictures with captions or descriptive phrases.

For More Information

Books

Díaz, Gisele, and Alan Rodgers, eds. "Introduction and Commentary." In *The* Codex Borgia: *A Full-Color Restoration of the Ancient Mexican Manuscript.* With introduction and commentary by Bruce E. Byland. New York: Dover Publications, 1993.

Duran, Diego. *Book of the Gods and Rites and the Ancient Calendar.* Norman: University of Oklahoma Press, 1971.

Periodicals

Aveni, Anthony F. "Other Stars Than Ours." *Natural History* (April 2001). This article is also available online at http://www.findarticles. com/p/articles/mi_m1134/is_3_110/ai_73064227 (accessed on November 22, 2004).

Galarza, Joaquin. "Colour-Coded Languages: Pre-Columbian Writing Systems." *UNESCO Courier* (April 1995). This article is also available online at http://www.findarticles.com/p/articles/mi_m1310/is_ 1995_April/ai_16920763 (accessed on November 22, 2004).

Web Sites

"Ancient Mesoamerican Writing: Borgia." *GBOnline.* http://pages.prodigy. net/gbonline/ancwrite.html (accessed on November 22, 2004).

Bauman, Paul Gerald. "Archives: The Last Bastion of Memory." *Historia Online.* http://www.eiu.edu/~historia/2004/memory.pdf (accessed on November 22, 2004).

"John Pohl's Mesoamerica: Ancient Books: Highlands México Codices." *FAMSI: Foundation for the Advancement of Mesoamerican Studies.* http://www.famsi.org/research/pohl/jpcodices/index.html (accessed on November 22, 2004).

"Realms of the Sacred in Daily Life: Early Written Records of Mesoamerica." *University of California, Irvine.* http://www.lib.uci.edu/libraries/ exhibits/meso/sacred.html (accessed on November 22, 2004).

Codex Mendoza

*Illustration of the founding of Tenochtitlán,
from the* Codex Mendoza
Manuscript compiled c. 1541

When the Aztecs arrived in the Valley of Mexico around 1325, they adopted the writing systems of the people already living there. Like their neighbors, the Aztecs created large folding books called codices (singular: codex) and painted their text on long pages made from bark leaf paper or deerskin. Their system of writing relied heavily on the use of pictures to convey meaning and it included some glyphs (symbolic figures) as well. The Aztecs glyphs represented words, but they were usually used only for people or place names or calendar dates. Unlike Maya glyph-writing, the Aztec system did not include glyphs for individual syllables or the separate sounds that make up words. Therefore it could not fully reproduce the spoken language of the Aztecs.

Using images that could be interpreted by the reader and glyphs to stand for specific people, places, and dates, the Aztecs could put a lot of information on a codex page, but it took a trained reader who had memorized the contents of the codex to make sense of it. In her book *Aztec World* (1994), Elizabeth Hill Boone describes how the codices were used:

"The hand of a single master painter is apparent throughout; his assistants prepared the pigments and applied color in flat washes. Informants who had lived most of their lives under Aztec rule interpreted the pictures in Nahuatl, and a Spanish priest then translated the text into Spanish."

"Realms of the Sacred in Daily Life: Early Written Records of Mesoamerica," University of California, Irvine *(Web site).*

Picture from an Aztec codex showing the Aztec migration to the Valley of Mexico. *© Gianni Dagli Orti/Corbis.*

[When] the Aztec pictorial histories were read aloud to an audience, they were interpreted, and their images were expanded and embellished in the oration of the full story. The pictorial histories were painted specifically to be the rough text of a performance.... Those who read the manuscripts had already memorized the histories, the stories, painted therein, and they knew the discourses as familiar roads.

Colonial codices

The Spanish conquest of Mesoamerica began with the defeat of the Aztecs in 1521. Following the conquest, the Spanish king sent teams of missionaries to the Americas to convert the native people to Christianity. When Spanish soldiers and missionaries witnessed Mesoamerican storytellers reading from codices, they feared that the painted books would keep old traditions alive and obstruct their efforts to convert the Mesoamericans to Christianity. Therefore, in the decades after the conquest, the Spanish destroyed almost all the codices in Mesoamerica. Codices made before the Spanish conquest are very rare: Only about fifteen are known to have survived, and none of those were made by the Aztecs.

Ironically, after most of the codices were burned, some Spanish missionaries and nobles began to take an interest in the culture and history of the people they had conquered. While many Spanish chroniclers (people who record historic events in writing) simply wrote their own books based on their observations of the Mesoamericans, others enlisted native artists to create traditional pictorial books. Spanish missionaries usually supervised these projects. The native artists created the pictures and explained their meaning, and the missionaries wrote down the explanations in Spanish, directly on the pictures and in separate commentaries. The missionaries eventually figured out how to write Nahuatl (pronounced NAH-wah-tul; the language of the Aztecs and many other groups in the empire) using their own Latin alphabet to spell out the sounds of the Nahuatl words. After that, the text in some codices was written in Nahuatl. Sometimes the text was written in both Nahuatl and Spanish.

Of all the codices jointly produced by Spanish missionaries and native artists, about 420 have survived to the present. These books are called "colonial" codices because Mesoamerica had become a colony of Spain. (A colony is a territory ruled by a foreign power.) The colonial codices are an interesting blend of Spanish and Mesoamerican traditions. The Spanish introduced European paper, so the codices have pages like a modern book instead of long, accordion-like folds. The Spanish missionaries usually wrote separate commentary in their own language, interpreting Mesoamerican history for Spanish readers. The Aztec artist-scribes, called *tlacuilos,* painted the books in traditional Mesoamerican style, using dyes made from the pigments of vegetables and minerals.

The first colonial codices were the work of native artists and informants (people who informed Spanish missionaries and other writers about their history and traditions) who had experienced life in the Aztec empire before the conquest. However, as the years passed, these people began to die off, and the next generation of native artists who worked on the books did not have firsthand knowledge of the old traditions. As a result, the pictures and stories in the colonial codices gradually showed more and more European influence.

The Viceroy Mendoza

In the 1530s the Spanish settled in the heart of the former Aztec empire. They named this colony New Spain. From there they ruled over an ever-expanding territory in Mesoamerica. The Spanish built Mexico City, the capital of New Spain, right on top of the old Aztec capital, Tenochtitlán (pronounced tay-notch-teet-LAHN). New Spain's first viceroy (governor, or representative of the Spanish king's rule), Antonio de Mendoza (c. 1490–1552), took office in 1535. He was a strong and competent ruler who was interested in ruling the native people wisely (though he supported many of the Spanish practices that exploited Mesoamerican labor and diminished their civil rights).

In 1541 Mendoza decided to commission (assign as a job) a book devoted to the history, economy, daily life, and culture of the Aztec people. Twenty years had passed since the Spanish defeated the Aztecs at Tenochtitlán, and Mendoza knew the project had to be undertaken soon, while preconquest Aztecs were still alive. Mendoza planned to present this work as a gift to the Spanish king, Charles V (1500–1558), so that the king could gain a better understanding of the people who had come under his rule in New Spain.

The book that Mendoza commissioned is now known as the *Codex Mendoza*. Most experts believe it took a team of skilled artists to create the book. A description of the likely team appears on a University of California, Irvine, Web site called "Realms of the Sacred in Daily Life: Early Written Records of Mesoamerica": "The hand of a single master painter is apparent throughout; his assistants prepared the pigments and applied color in flat washes. Informants who had lived most of their lives under Aztec rule interpreted the pictures in Nahuatl, and a Spanish priest then translated the text into Spanish." The team worked on the codex in Mexico City. The document they produced consisted of seventy-two pages of pictures and sixty-two pages of Spanish commentary.

The contents of the codex

The *Codex Mendoza* is organized into three parts, all covering the times before the Spanish conquest. The first part is a history of the Aztecs, including the foundation of their capital city of Tenochtitlán. The second part provides accounts of the tribute (obligatory payments of goods or labor) paid to the Aztec empire by all its conquered territories; it includes a chronicle of the conquests the Aztecs made and lists the ruling years of all the Aztec kings. The third part of the codex is unique among the colonial codices. It presents an in-depth report of what daily life was like in and around Tenochtitlán. This section includes pictures and explanatory text on many different topics, including child rearing, law and order, farming, weaving, clothes, music, and food.

One of the only topics the *Codex Mendoza* does not cover is the Aztec religion. Religion was a major part of daily life in the Aztec culture, so the omission is strange. Many other codices cover the Aztec religion and its practices. However, the Spanish had burned most of the preconquest codices in Mesoamerica precisely because the books contained information about traditional Mesoamerican religions. After that, the native people were not allowed to practice these religions. As the viceroy of New Spain, Mendoza had a duty to enforce this prohibition, so it is likely that he preferred to avoid the subject of religion in the codex. The scribes were probably instructed not to write on the topic. Despite this large omission, the *Codex Mendoza* is one of the most informative colonial codices. It contains the most illustrations, and no other source provides so many details about the daily life of the Aztec people.

The founding of Tenochtitlán

The *Codex Mendoza* begins with the story of the founding of Tenochtitlán. The Aztecs arrived there in 1325 after years of roaming. According to their own accounts, the Aztecs had resided on the lake island of Aztlán (meaning "the place of the white herons," or "the place of whiteness") before traveling to the Valley of Mexico. In Aztlán they lived under the watchful eye of their supreme god, Huitzilopochtli (pronounced hweets-ee-loh-PAWCH-tlee; the name means "Hummingbird of the South"), who was the god of war and the sun god. Sometime in the early twelfth century Huitzilopochtli directed the people to leave Aztlán to go off in search of a new home. The god instructed them to continue their search until they found an eagle perched on a cactus that bore a large red fruit. So the Aztec people started their long journey. Four priests carried Huitzilopochtli, in hummingbird form, and as they walked, the god occasionally gave them directions. Before long, they had wandered into the Valley of Mexico.

The Aztecs made temporary homes in several areas of the Valley of Mexico. Over the years they gained a reputation as skilled warriors. They aspired to rule the entire valley, but other residents of the valley considered the Aztecs to be vulgar wanderers. They found many of the Aztecs' practices revolting, particularly their methods of performing human sacrifices (killing humans as offerings to the gods). Sometimes the Aztecs offended the local residents so much that violence erupted. By the beginning of the fourteenth century, the Aztecs had been chased out of most of the settled areas in the valley.

With nowhere else to go, the Aztecs camped out on the marshy shores of Lake Texcoco, a muddy place where no one else wanted to live. It was there, according to their legends (stories handed down from earlier times) that they received Huitzilopochtli's sign—on a small island on the lake, they saw an eagle perched on a cactus that bore a large red fruit. In the year 1325, after more than two hundred years of searching, the Aztecs settled on the lake island, calling it Tenochtitlán, which means "among the stone cactus fruit."

Things to remember while examining the illustration of the founding of Tenochtitlán, from the *Codex Mendoza:*

- The Aztec artist(s) who painted the *Codex Mendoza* worked in a pictorial script, using pictures to tell a story and glyphs to add to the story or identify people, places, and dates.

- The artistic style of the codex is easily identified as Aztec. The images contained within a picture are placed on a flat, empty background—there is no attempt to create perspective or dimension. The artists drew the outlines of their pictures first and then filled them in with colors. Human beings are depicted in profile (shown from the side rather than the front). Human heads are usually large—not in lifelike proportion to their bodies.

- In the illustration, the eagle in the center sits on a cactus with a red fruit, representing the sign that the god Huitzilopochtli told the Aztecs to seek in their search for a home. The eagle sign has become one of the most famous images of Aztec history. It now appears in the middle of the Mexican flag and serves as Mexico's coat of arms (emblem on a shield that serves as the sign of a nation). The scribes who compiled the *Codex Mendoza* did not depict the eagle eating a snake, as it is depicted on the Mexican flag. Some experts believe the snake was added to the legend long after the Spanish conquest.

- The eagle and cactus emblem is located at the center of a large X that extends across the illustration. The diagonal lines of the X represent the canals that separated Tenochtitlán into four major districts.

- Just below the eagle and cactus is the image of a shield with arrows behind it. Underneath the image, the word "tenochtitlan" is written in the Latin alphabet. The shield denotes the power of the Aztecs to defend their city.

- The lords of Tenochtitlán are seated in the four sections created by the X. Their names are written down the front of their tunics. An Aztec name glyph appears just behind the head of each lord.

- To the left of the cactus sits the first ruler of Tenochtitlán, whose name was Tenochtli (meaning "cactus fruit"). His mat is different from the mats of the other nobles, probably signifying that his was a woven palm leaf mat, a type of mat used by royalty in many Mesoamerican cultures.

- To the right of the eagle is a rack bearing a human skull. The Aztecs placed the decapitated heads of many of their sacrifice victims on racks called *tzompantli* (pronounced zahm-PAHN-tli). The image is meant to show the Aztecs' strength in having many sacrifice victims to offer the gods.

- Underneath the main picture is a depiction of the Aztecs conquering the towns of Culhuacán (pronounced cool-whah-CAHN) and Tenayuca in the Valley of Mexico. The Aztec warriors are the larger figures

holding swordlike weapons. The smaller figures are their captives. Behind the human figures are two glyphs formed from images of pyramids with their temples in flames and falling over. These glyphs stand for the word "conquered." Above one of the burning temples is the name "colhuacan pueblo," and over the other is the name "tenayuca pueblo." (Pueblo is the Spanish word for town or village.)

- Like most Mesoamerican documents, this illustration of the founding of Tenochtitlán is placed within the context of a calendar. Note the border squares that go around the whole picture. Within each square is a date, with a day-name glyph and a number made from dots. There are fifty-two date squares surrounding the picture, each representing one of the fifty-two years from 1325 to 1377. These are approximately the years of the reign of Tenochtli, the first leader of the Aztecs in Tenochtitlán, who died in 1375.

What happened next ...

After the *Codex Mendoza* was completed, Mendoza sent it off in a ship to Spain. However, it never reached its destination. French pirates attacked the ship and stole its cargo, including the codex. Eventually, the codex fell into the hands of André Thevet (1502–1590), the geographer to the king of France. Thevet signed and dated the codex in the year 1553, and his name appears on the document, at its upper left side. Thevet later gave the *Codex Mendoza* to English geographer Richard Hakluyt (c. 1552–1616), who was living in Paris at the time. It passed through more hands before it arrived at the Bodleian Library at Oxford University in England, in 1659. The manuscript remains there in the twenty-first century.

On November 2, 1821, after winning its independence from Spain, the nation of Mexico adopted as its official coat of arms the image of an eagle atop a cactus plant, eating a snake. There have been a few changes in its design, but it remains largely the same, a reminder of Mexico's great Aztec civilization.

Did you know ...

- The border around the founding of Tenochtitlán illustration demonstrates the Aztec belief that history occurs in cycles. The border is made up of fifty-two squares, each representing one year in the fifty-two-year cycle. The Aztecs used their two calendars—the sacred (260-day year) and solar (365-day year) calendars—in combination, pairing sacred and solar day names and numbers to identify each unique day in the cycle. Every fifty-two years, after every possible combination of names and numbers had been used, the cycle would start over. Each period of fifty-two years was called a "bundle of years." At the end of each fifty-two-year period, there was a twelve-day period before the next bundle would begin. During these days at the end of a cycle, the Aztecs believed the sun might die and the world might be destroyed unless the right sacrifices and other rituals were performed. On the last night of the bundle, the Aztecs carried out the New Fire Ceremony. As evening approached, every fire in every house, workshop, and temple was put out. On a mountaintop in the Valley of Mexico the priests began an all-night prayer for the sun to rise. Everyone waited to see if the sun would appear. When the sun rose the next day, a human being was sacrificed to show gratitude to the gods. A fire was lit, and torches taken from this new fire were used to light all other fires. For the Aztecs, it was the beginning of a new era, a moment that gave them hope of survival for another fifty-two-year bundle.

Consider the following ...

- Using a modern writing system, you can express anything you wish, but people often choose to use pictures and other methods of communication not related to language. For example, in airports, the simple figures of a woman and a man tell you where the restrooms are and which one you should use. Traffic signs and signals sometimes use symbols instead of language. Think of other ways that pictures, colors, or sounds communicate specific meanings without the help of writing.

- Prepare for an Aztec-style performance reading. Draw a series of very simple pictures that depict some of the events in the story about the founding of Tenochtitlán. Then tell the story to a group of your friends or classmates. Do not read the story; tell it from your memory, using the pictures you have drawn to help you remember all the details.

For More Information

Books
Berdan, Frances, and Patricia Rieff Anawalt. *The Essential Codex Mendoza.* Berkeley: University of California Press, 1997.

Boone, Elizabeth Hill. *Aztec World.* Montreal, Canada, and Washington, DC: St. Remy Press and Smithsonian Institution, 1994.

Web Sites

"Aztec." *Ancient Scripts.com.* http://www.ancientscripts.com/aztec.html (accessed on November 22, 2004).

"Codex Mendoza." *Latino Studies Resources, Indiana University, Bloomington.* http://www.latinamericanstudies.org/codex-mendoza.htm (accessed on November 22, 2004).

"John Pohl's Mesoamerica: The Aztecs." *FAMSI: Foundation for the Advancement of Mesoamerican Studies.* http://www.famsi.org/research/pohl/pohl_aztec6.html (accessed on November 22, 2004).

"Realms of the Sacred in Daily Life: Early Written Records of Mesoamerica." *University of California, Irvine.* http://www.lib.uci.edu/libraries/exhibits/meso/sacred.html (accessed on November 22, 2004).

Nezahualcoyotl

Selected poems of Nezahualcoyotl
Reprinted from *Fifteen Poets of the Aztec World*.
Edited and translated by Miguel León-Portilla, 1992

Written in the fifteenth century; originally collected in *Romances de los señores de Nueva España*

The codices (singular: codex), or painted books, of the Aztec empire are renowned for providing historical and cultural facts. They were created to be "read" aloud by storytellers, or orators, who had memorized the stories and used the pictures and signs in the books to help their memory and to add details to their narrations (see ***Codex Borgia*** and ***Codex Mendoza*** entries). The books presented the key ideas and pictures that would help the reader, but they did not contain the narration itself because the Aztecs' writing system could not reproduce their full spoken language.

Some codices were actually meant to be sung or chanted. (To the Aztecs, singing meant chanting the words in a rhythmic manner—they did not add melody.) These were called *cuicamatl* (pronounced coo-ee-cah-MAH-tul), or "papers of songs." As the orators learned the songs, they looked at the corresponding pictures and signs in the codices. Then they used the books for all their "readings" or performances in which the songs were chanted before a live audience. Experienced storytellers and teachers in the *calmecacs*, or religious schools, taught students to memorize the songs as they were

> "Your heart is a book of paintings, you have come to sing, to make your drums resound, you are the singer."

set out in the books. Generation after generation of young orators became masters at "singing the books." Using both the books and their oral tradition of passing literature and history from generation to generation by the spoken word, the people of the Aztec empire developed a highly expressive literary tradition in the century before the Spanish conquest of Tenochtitlán (pronounced tay-notch-teet-LAHN) in 1521.

Most of the songs that passed through the generations were anonymous (no one knows who created them). Many were prayers or sacred hymns and other songs to be chanted by a group of people at ceremonies and festivals. Some songs, though, were the work of the *tlamatinime* (pronounced tlah-mah-TEE-nee-may; singular *tlamatini*)—men of words, or the poets and philosophers of the Aztec empire. These poems expressed the thoughts and feelings of their creators. The poems were highly philosophical, yet often personal, and they presented their ideas in beautiful or powerful images. The Aztecs called these poems "flower and songs," using the word "flower" as a metaphor (a word that is used to refer to something that it is being compared to) for art and poetry. The greatest of the *tlamatinime* was Nezahualcoyotl (pronounced nez-a-hwahl-coy-OH-tul, meaning "Hungry Coyote"; 1402–1473), the poet king of Texcoco.

The poet king

Nezahualcoyotl's city, Texcoco (also spelled Tezcoco), was settled by the Alcohuans, a Nahuatl-speaking (pronounced NAH-wah-tul) people who migrated into the Valley of Mexico in the early fourteenth century. The Alcohuans settled on the east side of Lake Texcoco around the same time the Aztecs settled on an island near the western side of the lake and began to build their city of Tenochtitlán. There were many other cities surrounding Lake Texcoco as well, including Chalco, Culhuacán (pronounced cool-whah-CAHN), Chapultepec (pronounced chah-pul-teh-PEC), and Tlacopán. Also on the shores of Lake Texcoco was Azcapotzalco (pronounced ahz-cah-poh-TZAHL-coe), the capital city of the powerful Tepanecs, who dominated the other cities of around the lake.

Nezahualcoyotl was born in Texcoco in 1402. His father was Ixtlilxochitl (pronounced eex-tleel-show-CHEE-tul), the highly respected king of Texcoco, and his mother was Matlalcihuatzin (pronounced math-lahl-chee-WHAHT-zeen), the daughter of a Tenochtitlán king. Though warfare was commonplace around the lake in the fourteenth century, Texcoco had grown and prospered. The people of the city, who called themselves Texcocans, had a reputation for their cultural refinement. They had significantly advanced the arts, law, education, and religion in their city.

In 1418, after many battles, the Tepanecs conquered Texcoco. As the Tepanecs bore down on the city, Ixtlilxochitl was forced to flee to the mountains with his fifteen-year-old son and heir to the throne, Nezahualcoyotl. They were unable to escape the pursuing Tepanecs, however. Nezahualcoyotl was hiding in a tree and watched in horror when a group of soldiers killed his father. Texcoco had fallen to the Tepanecs, so Nezahualcoyotl fled to some of the outlying cities. He made friends among the rulers of the cities around Lake Texcoco, hoping one day to have enough support to win his city back. Since his mother was from the Aztec royal family, he was well connected in Tenochtitlán.

Tezozómoc, the king of the Tepanecs, feared Nezahualcoyotl's claim to the throne in Texcoco and ordered him to be captured and killed. The Tepanecs eventually caught the young exile and put him in prison. Though the king ordered the guards to place Nezahualcoyotl in a cage and starve him to death, the guards secretly fed him. Later, when the order came to kill him, one of the guards helped Nezahualcoyotl to escape, even though doing so meant his own certain death. Nezahualcoyotl survived several other assassination attempts due to the loyalty of the people who served him. The people around him sensed his greatness and remembered better days in Texcoco when his father ruled. Many risked their lives, and several died, in their efforts to save him from the Tepanecs.

In 1425 Tezozómoc died. Shortly after the old Tepanec king's death, Nezahualcoyotl teamed up with the Aztec emperor Itzcoatl (pronounced eetz-coe-WHAH-tul; ruled c. 1427–1440). In 1428 an alliance of Nezahualcoyotl's friends and the Aztec army attacked Azcapotzalco and eventually destroyed the city. Afterwards, the Aztecs in Tenochtitlán rose to dominate the people in the Valley of Mexico. Nezahualcoyotl remained in Tenochtitlán for several years, even building a palace there, while planning his campaign to

Nezahualcoyotl surrounded by leaders from neighboring cities. *The Art Archive/National Archives Mexico/Mireille Vautier.*

regain the throne of Texcoco. Nezahualcoyotl realized that the cities around Lake Texcoco were too independent to unite in a single state ruled by a single king. Peace depended on the maintenance of a loose confederation. Thus in 1431 he created the Triple Alliance of Texcoco, Tenochtitlán, and the smaller city of Tlacopán and was crowned emperor of the three-city league. Within two years, he had regained the throne of Texcoco.

Nezahualcoyotl's reign

Under Nezahualcoyotl, Texcoco became the second most important city in the Aztec empire. Not long after he recovered the throne of his kingdom, Nezahualcoyotl created a code of laws that were so well regarded that they became the standard throughout the empire. During the ninety-one years in which Nezahualcoyotl and his son, Nezahualpilli (1460–1515) reigned, Texcoco was the center of legal scholarship for the entire empire. Nezahualcoyotl was also a great advocate of culture and education. Under his guidance, Texcoco drew great artists—poets, dancers, and musicians—and the top thinkers from all over Mesoamerica, quickly becoming the empire's center of learning. Nezahualcoyotl created the most extensive historical archives found in Mexico at the time of the conquest and many other educational institutions as well. Texcoco was considered the jewel of all cities in the Valley of Mexico, unsurpassed for its beauty and art.

Like many great thinkers, Nezahualcoyotl was gifted in many areas. He was a great ruler, poet, and promoter of culture and beauty, but he is also considered the greatest engineer of the Mesoamerican world before the conquest. In 1450 torrential rains raised the level of Lake Texcoco, flooding Tenochtitlán. Nezahualcoyotl proposed and designed a 9-mile (14-kilometer) dike (a barrier that controls the flow of water) running north to south down the lake. The dike protected Tenochtitlán from the flood waters and the salt waters the flooding brought in. The Aztec king, Montezuma I (c. 1397–1469), then asked Nezahualcoyotl to construct an aqueduct—a pipeline carrying fresh water—to run 3 miles (5 kilometers) from the shores of Lake Texcoco to the city of Tenochtitlán. These engineering feats were essential to the well-being of the Aztec capital.

During Nezahualcoyotl's long reign, the Aztec empire was consistently increasing its practice of human sacrifice (killing humans as offerings to the gods) until it reached massive proportions. With thousands of deaths every year, Tenochtitlán's practice developed into a widespread and powerful cult of human sacrifice that dominated daily life there. (A cult is a group that follows new religious doctrines and practices.) Nezahualcoyotl took an unpopular stand against human sacrifice. He stood for peace and kindness and participated in the cult of Tloque Nahuaque (pronounced tloe-kay nah-KWA-kay), the

"Lord of the Close and Near," a god who did not demand sacrifice. But the Aztecs demanded that all cities in their empire build temples to the primary Aztec god Huitzilopochtli (pronounced hweets-ee-loh-PAWCH-tlee), the god of war and sun, to whom constant sacrifices were offered. To avoid conflict, Nezahualcoyotl built the temple to Huitzilopochtli in Texcoco in 1467. Quietly following his own beliefs, that same year he completed a tower and a temple dedicated to Tloque Nahuaque.

The king's poetry

As a poet, Nezahualcoyotl took his place in a tradition of well-respected poets of the Aztec empire who created what is called lyric poetry (poetry that expresses intense personal feelings in the manner of a song). Many of the poets in this tradition were followers of Tloque Nahuaque, and they focused their songs on the ever-changing nature of human life. They believed that, because death could come swiftly and extinguish an existence in a moment, life was only a fleeting illusion. There seemed to be nothing permanent or solid. Their god, though greatly worshiped, was invisible to them. The poets found hope in their art. They believed that by being creative like their creator god, and in particular, by creating art, they could achieve immortality (never die). The lyric poems in this tradition, the "flower and songs," use flowers as symbols for art and also for life. Flowers grow and bloom, creating great beauty and joy, but they are fragile and quickly die. The goal of the artist is to create flowers, or poems, that will endure, continuing to bring beauty and joy to the world forever.

Scholars have identified about thirty poems that are attributed to Nezahualcoyotl. The poems focus on philosophical themes about the meaning of life, particularly its fleeting nature. Nezahualcoyotl seeks to understand the god he believes created the world, Tloque Nahuaque. This god is omnipresent (in all places at all times), yet completely invisible to human beings and impossible to understand. Yet in his poems Nezahualcoyotl strives for even a momentary understanding of his god; he also writes of the frustration of worshiping such a mysterious deity.

Many of the Spanish chroniclers at the time of the conquest and later historians have suggested that Nezahualcoyotl's poetry foreshadows the Christian religion. They propose that Nezahualcoyotl understood the Christian God without having been exposed to any Christian teachings. But, though Nezahualcoyotl does refer to Him as the "one and only God," most modern scholars do not believe his poetry expresses Christian beliefs. Rather, he was influenced by a more ancient Mesoamerican religion that had been passed down through the ages.

When they settled in Texcoco, Nezahualcoyotl's ancestors had brought with them the influences of Toltec culture (a society that had dominated the Valley of Mexico about 900–1200), which they had picked up in their travels through the Valley of Mexico. One of the Toltec institutions they adopted was the cult of Quetzalcoatl (pronounced kates-ahl-koh-AH-tul). The Toltecs viewed Quetzalcoatl as the creator of human life. He was also considered the god of rebirth after death, the arts, and peace. The Toltec king **Topiltzin-Quetzalcoatl** (see entry), a priest in the cult of Quetzalcoatl, reformed the Toltec religion to include holiness and morality. One of the king's reforms was the prohibition of human sacrifice.

Nezahualcoyotl and some of the other *tlamatinime* used the cult of Quetzalcoatl as a basis for their spiritual reflection. Quetzalcoatl was the inspiration for a kinder and more rational religion in which peace and order reigned. Over the years the god Tloque Nahuaque had become their deity as they searched for the truth about life, death, and the afterlife. In his poems, Nezahualcoyotl often comes close to giving up hope of ever being able to find the truth about God or the ever-changing human world. Like other lyric poets in his tradition, he finds hope in his art.

Things to remember while reading selected poems of Nezahualcoyotl:

- These poems were first created orally in the Nahuatl language. All punctuation and the lines of the poems are the work of someone who wrote them down long after Nezahualcoyotl's death. At best these written poems are probably an interpretation of the original formed by the many different people who recorded and translated them over hundreds of years.

- While reading, remember that these poems were called "flower and songs." "Flower" is often used as a metaphor for poetry and art.

- The first poem expresses the key problem at the heart of Nezahualcoyotl's spiritual search. Everything on Earth changes and disappears and human beings apparently have no control over their destiny.

- The second poem is a statement of Nezahualcoyotl's spiritual belief. The god that Nezahualcoyotl addresses in his second poem ("He Who invents Himself," probably referring to Tloque Nahuaque) is silent, invisible, and unknowable—a complete mystery to the humans who worship him. Nezahualcoyotl says, "No one is able to be intimate / with the Giver of Life," that is, no one can communicate with the god to find out what he is or how he works. Yet Nezahualcoyotl continues to believe the god is real and that he makes life possible: "at His side, near to Him / one can live on the earth."

- In the second poem, note the lines "Only as among the flowers, / we might seek someone, / thus we seek You." If being "among the flowers" is writing poetry, Nezahualcoyotl is describing how he seeks for his god—through his art.

- In the third poem Nezahualcoyotl discusses the artist as someone who sings, and who has "practiced" his art, and whose heart is a "book of paintings." These are possibly references to the art of "singing the book," or telling a poem by the use of a codex.

Selected poems of Nezahualcoyotl

Poem 1: untitled

I, Nezahualcoyotl, ask this:
Is it true one really lives on the earth?
Not forever on earth,
Only a little while here.

*Though it be **jade** it falls apart,*
Though it be gold it wears away,
*Though it be **quetzal plumage** it is torn **asunder**.*
Not forever on earth,
Only a little while here.

Poem 2: untitled

In no place can be the house of He Who invents Himself.
*But in all places He is **invoked**,*
*in all places He is **venerated**,*
His glory, His fame are sought on the earth.
It is He Who invents everything.
He is Who invents Himself: God.
In all places He is invoked,
in all places He is venerated,
His glory, His fame are sought on the earth.
No one here is able,
*no one is able to be **intimate***
with the Giver of Life;
only He is invoked,
at His side,
near to Him,
one can live on the earth.
He who finds Him,
Knows only one thing: He is invoked,
At His side, near to Him,
one can live on the earth.
In truth no one is intimate with You,
O Giver of Life!
Only as among the flowers,
we might seek someone,
thus we seek You,
we who live on the earth
while we are at Your side.
Our hearts will be troubled,
only for a short time,
we will be near You and at Your side.
The Giver of Life enrages us,
*He **intoxicates** us here.*
No one can be perhaps at His side,
be famous, rule on the earth.
Only You change things,

Jade: A green gemstone.

Quetzal plumage: The feathers of the quetzal, a bright green-feathered bird from Central America considered sacred in most Mesoamerican religions.

Asunder: Apart.

Invoked: Called forth.

Venerated: Profoundly respected.

Intimate: Familiar; in close contact.

Intoxicates: Stimulates or excites to a frenzy.

as our hearts know it:
No one can be perhaps at His side,
be famous, rule on the earth.

Poem 3: Song of Springtime

In the house of paintings
the singing begins,
song is practiced,
flowers are spread,
the song rejoices.
The song resounds,
little bells are heard,
to these answer
*our flowery **timbrels**.*
Flowers are spread,
the song rejoices.
Above the flowers is singing
the radiant pheasant;
his song unfolds
into the midst of the waters.
To him reply
all manner of red birds,
the dazzling red bird
beautifully sings.
Your heart is a book of paintings,
you have come to sing,
to make your drums resound,
you are the singer.
Within the house of springtime,
you make the people happy.
You alone bestow
flowers that intoxicate,
precious flowers.
You are the singer.
Within the house of springtime,
you make the people happy.

Timbrels: Drums or tambourines.

What happened next ...

Most of the codices that contained the sacred songs and the poems of the *tlamatinime* of the Aztec empire were destroyed by the Spanish soldiers and missionaries during the 1521 conquest; the Spanish thought the books might impede their efforts to convert the native people to Christianity. The missionaries also forbade the natives to sing their songs. As a result, numerous Aztec poems that had been passed down through many generations were lost.

Not all Spanish missionaries were insensitive to the Aztec and native traditions. In the second half of the sixteenth century, several missionaries realized that they had one last opportunity to counteract some of the destruction of the conquest. They set about to preserve some of the native culture. A few missionaries sought to save whatever songs remained in the memories of the Aztec elders (people who have authority because of their age and experience) by writing them down. They knew that it would not be long before the last elders died and the art form would vanish forever. A couple of prominent Texcocans, too, decided to record the songs before it was too late. Despite the restriction on singing the traditional songs, two different projects were undertaken to write down the poems of the native people of the Aztec empire.

The first project, which resulted in the collection *Romances de los señores de Nueva España* (Romances of the Lords of New Spain), is believed to have been initiated by a great-grandson of Nezahualcoyotl, Texcocan historian and writer Juan Bautista Pomar (c. 1535–1590). This collection, written in Nahuatl, contains ten poems attributed to Nezahualcoyotl. (The three poems reproduced here come from this collection.) The second collection, *Cantares mexicanos* (*Mexican Songs*), contains ninety-one songs. This collection was made possible by a Spanish missionary who gathered a group of *tlamatinime* between 1560 and 1580 to record (write down) the songs they had in their memories. Of the ninety-one songs, about twenty-five are attributed to Nezahualcoyotl. Two more of the poet-king's songs were recorded by his descendant, Texcocan historian Alva Ixtlilxochitl (1578–1650). Some of the songs recorded in the *Romances* are also recorded in *Cantares mexicanos*. Though different people orated them, the poems in the two collections are almost identical.

Did you know ...

- The tradition of chanting the ancient songs did not completely disappear after the 1521 Spanish conquest. Today some groups of people in Central Mexico continue to chant traditional poems, and scholars believe that some of their poems may be the words of the ancient *tlamatinime* that have been passed through the generations.

- It is likely that many native groups in Mesoamerica hid their codices when they realized the missionaries intended to destroy them. Some scholars believe the Aztec *tlamatinime* brought out their secret codices in order to perform their songs when they were recorded in the sixteenth century.

- Many scholars question how true to the original words spoken by Nezahualcoyotl these recorded poems of the Aztecs are. Being passed through the generations by spoken word—as remembered and interpreted by their orators—may have slowly changed them over the years before the conquest. Then, after the conquest, scholars question the interpretations of the Spanish missionaries who recorded the poems. It is quite difficult for people from one culture to understand the intricacies of poetry from another culture, even with the best of intentions. It is near impossible when the cultures are very different and do not have the same language. Another concern is that the act of writing down the poems changes them from what they were meant to be: oral performances in which the words were chanted to a live audience. Most scholars agree that the poems have been changed by these influences through the years. Yet extensive research has convinced many scholars that these poems do, in fact, represent a close version of the poems as they once were sung.

Consider the following ...

- Read the poem "Song of Springtime." Then consider the following passage of the poem:

      You alone bestow
      flowers that intoxicate,

precious flowers.
You are the singer.
Within the house of springtime,
you make the people happy.

1. Who is being addressed as "you?"

2. What does the poet mean by "flowers that intoxicate?"

3. What kinds of things happen in springtime? What might he be talking about as the "house of springtime?"

4. What is it that makes people happy?

- Write a report on Nezahualcoyotl's three poems. Describe what you think each poem expresses; then compare the poems to each other.

- In the classroom, have a group of students form a circle. Select someone to read the first poem aloud. Then discuss what the poet is saying in the poem and how he or she says it. Next have someone read the next poem, discuss its meaning and tone, and then do the same with the third poem. When you have read all three poems, discuss which poem you like the best and why you like it better than the others.

For More Information

Books

Fifteen Poets of the Aztec World. Edited and translated by Miguel León-Portilla. Norman: University of Oklahoma Press, 1992.

Thomas, Hugh. *Conquest: Montezuma, Cortés, and the Fall of Old Mexico.* New York: Simon and Schuster, 1993.

Web Sites

"Aztec Poetry." *Carnaval.com.* http://www.carnaval.com/dead/aztec_poetry.htm (accessed on November 24, 2004).

"The Flower Songs of the Hungry Coyote: Poet of Ancient Mexico." Edited and translated by John Curl. *Red Coral.* http://www.red-coral.net/Hungry.html (accessed on November 24, 2004).

Tuck, Jim. "Nezahualcoyotl Texcoco's Philosopher King." *Mexico Connect.* http://www.mexconnect.com/mex_/history/jtuck/jtnezahualcoyotl.html (accessed on November 24, 2004).

Montezuma II

Born 1466
Tenochtitlán, Valley of Mexico
Died 1520
Tenochtitlán

Aztec head of state

Among his own people, Montezuma II was called Montezuma Xocoyotzin, meaning Montezuma the Younger. His name is more correctly spelled Moctezuma or Motecuhzoma and is pronounced mohk-the-ZOO-mah show-coi-YO-tzeen. Montezuma II became the Aztec emperor, or *huey tlatoani* ("he who speaks for the people" or the "Great Speaker"), when the empire was at its peak. His armies had repeatedly proven their overwhelming power, and few cities in the Valley of Mexico could stand against them. The emperor had been a strong and respected ruler for many prosperous years in the Aztec capital, Tenochtitlán (pronounced tay-notch-teet-LAHN), before the Spanish first arrived in the area in 1518. It was Montezuma's great misfortune to have been in power at that time. Within three years of the arrival of the Spanish, the emperor was dead and dishonored, and his city and empire had fallen. And though the Aztec people fought long and bravely against the foreigners, Montezuma is doomed to be remembered as the emperor who did not fight back.

"There were four other great *Caciques* [leaders] who carried the canopy above their heads, and many more lords who walked before the great Montezuma, sweeping the ground on which he was to tread, and laying down cloaks so that his feet should not touch the earth. Not one of these chieftains dared to look him in the face."

Bernal Díaz, The Conquest of New Spain; *written in 1568.*

Montezuma II. *The Library of Congress.*

235

Growing up in the royal family

Montezuma was born into one of Tenochtitlán's leading royal families. In 1469 his father, Axayácatl (pronounced ash-eye-ah-KAY-tul; died 1481), was named the Aztec emperor, succeeding Montezuma I (c. 1397–1469), who had ruled since 1440. Like most children of Aztec nobles, Montezuma was taught from birth to be both a warrior and a priest. He attended the *calmecac,* or religious school, where he received strict discipline, rigorous military training, and instruction in the songs of the gods and other religious texts. He also was trained in astronomy and sacred calendars and other basic skills for becoming a priest. At the age of twelve Montezuma entered the "house of young men," a place of military training where he learned battle techniques and other skills necessary to an Aztec warrior.

When Axayácatl died in 1481, Montezuma's uncle, Tizoc, became the next *huey tlatoani.* By this time Montezuma had grown old enough to participate in raids into border towns. He quickly distinguished himself when he single-handedly captured three prisoners, a feat that enabled him to achieve the special rank of *tequihua,* or "master of cuts." Following the tradition of human sacrifice in the Aztec religion, Montezuma tied one of his prisoners to a stone, cut open his chest, and offered up his heart to the gods. Capturing and sacrificing prisoners brought great honor to the young prince. These achievements were significant because Montezuma was one of over a dozen potential successors to the throne of the empire. He had to distinguish himself as a warrior and leader to be in line for the position of *huey tlatoani* in the future.

Montezuma did not spend all his youth on the battlefield. For two or three years he studied in the temple, learning to become a priest. Montezuma was a good student in many areas: History and religion were his favorite subjects, and he was inclined to be philosophical or thoughtful at times. Some of his studies led him into the realm of magic. These studies seem to have made a lasting impression on him; many observers noted that Montezuma was highly superstitious (having an irrational belief in the powers of magic or fate over important events).

When Tizoc died in 1486, Montezuma's uncle, Ahuitzotl (pronounced ah-weet-ZOH-tul; ruled c. 1486–

1502), took over as *huey tlatoani*. Ahuitzotl was a fierce and warlike emperor and was responsible for doubling the size of the Aztec empire. He promoted Montezuma to a more prominent position in military affairs. The young prince shared his uncle's ambition and participated in several campaigns that greatly extended the borders of the Aztec empire.

Ahuitzotl undertook the rebuilding of Tenochtitlán, a tradition among Aztec emperors to demonstrate their power. His reconstruction included a tremendous addition to the Templo Mayor, a set of twin pyramids dedicated to the war god Huitzilopochtli (pronounced hweets-ee-loh-PAWCH-tlee) and the rain god Tlaloc (pronounced TLAH-lock). With the completion of the great temple in 1487, Ahuitzotl reportedly sacrificed some twenty thousand victims—nearly two complete tribes—to the gods. Many Aztecs rejoiced at this offering, because they believed the gods would look favorably on such a large sacrifice. However, the sacrificial killings angered other tribes, who feared they too would be subject to slaughter at the whim of the emperor.

The Aztec prince

Earning recognition for his skills as a warrior and for his learning, Montezuma quickly rose through the ranks of the Aztec military. Shortly after his thirtieth birthday, he was chosen to become the commander in chief of the Aztec army. This new position gave him overall control of the army; he was responsible for conquering new towns and punishing those who rebelled against the empire. While still in his early twenties, Montezuma married Tezalco, a beautiful young woman of the ruling class. When he became the head of the army, Montezuma was entitled to take a second wife. He chose the princess Acatlan, who was noted for her gentleness. Montezuma would have many more wives and father numerous children—estimates on his number of children range from 19 to 150—but Tezalco and Acatlan were his only principal wives, meaning that these marriages would last for the rest of their lives and the offspring from the unions were legitimate heirs. They had the honor of being "married on the mat," a distinction that gave them greater privileges in the emperor's household.

Illustration of Montezuma II's coronation as *huey tlatoani* **of the Aztecs.** *The Art Archive/Biblioteca Nacional Madrid/Dagli Orti.*

The new *huey tlatoani*

In 1502 Ahuitzotl died unexpectedly, and Montezuma was chosen to succeed him as *huey tlatoani*. Montezuma's reign began well. As a military leader, Montezuma conquered at least as many cities as Ahuitzotl had vanquished, expanding the empire out to the fertile coastal region near the present-day Mexican state of Veracruz. After his conquests, the Aztec empire encompassed all of central and southern Mexico, including the area that now forms the Mexican states of Puebla, Hidalgo, México, Morelos, Guerrero, and Oaxaca (pronounced wah-HAH-kah), as well as most of Veracruz and parts of Chiapas. The estimated population of the empire was about fifteen million people. Montezuma's armies were successful at keeping order in the conquered communities around the empire. They were also able to provide captives for sacrifice to the gods. During Ahuitzotl's reign the Aztecs had made thousands of human sacrifices, and the empire had grown considerably. Therefore, many Aztecs, including Montezuma, believed that the gods approved of such sacrifices and would award them more territory if they sacrificed more victims. Accordingly, Montezuma sacrificed huge numbers of people, including twelve thousand captives from a defeated rebel province.

Tribute (payments of goods or labor that conquered nations were required to contribute to the empire) flowed into Tenochtitlán, making it a place of incredible wealth, at least for some citizens. Products from all over Mesoamerica abounded in the city's huge markets, which swarmed with tens of thousands of people, both locals and traders from distant lands. Impressive pyramids graced the skies, echoing the shape of the mountains surrounding the city. Gold, silver, and jade objects lined the niches in every wall of the grand palaces and large homes of the nobility; attended by many servants, the nobles lived in luxury, enjoying fine food and clothing from faraway places in the empire. Everywhere the city was adorned with exquisite art. Fragrant flowers bloomed in its beautifully kept gardens. Bright-colored birds and exotic animals entertained the pedestrians passing by the perfectly maintained public grounds and palace courtyards.

In 1507 one of the key cycles of the Aztec calendar ended. Every fifty-two years the combined sacred and solar calendars finished their cycle, having used up all possible combinations of day names and numbers. The fifty-two-year period was called a "bundle of years." After the last day of the bundle, there was a twelve-day period before the next calendar cycle started, a time not recorded on any calendars. The Aztecs believed that in these twelve-day periods the world would be destroyed unless they performed the right sacrifices and ceremonies. As it turned out, the cycle that ended in 1507 was the last bundle the Aztecs would mark before their empire collapsed. Although Montezuma could not have known what was coming, many historians note that he exhibited a sense of pending disaster around that time. In 1509 he decided to give up leading his warriors in battle. According to accounts written by Spanish chroniclers (people who record historic events in writing), the emperor wished to devote himself to the worship of the gods.

News of foreigners

One day a messenger brought Montezuma a picture of a strange object spotted on the eastern coast. Drawn by an eyewitness, the picture showed three white "temples" atop three canoes that were floating on the ocean. It was probably the first report that Tenochtitlán received about the Spanish fleets that were sailing off the coast of Mexico. The Spanish had already discovered several Caribbean islands and were searching for new territory to conquer. More reports of the strangers in large ships continued to arrive over the next few years. Most historians estimate that Montezuma knew about the arrival of the Spanish in the Caribbean by at least 1513.

According to early Spanish accounts, the Aztecs reported that a series of bad omens (unusual events interpreted as signs of upcoming good or evil) occurred throughout the empire around this time. The omens heightened Montezuma's sense of doom as he pondered the meaning of the Spaniards' arrival. A temple burned with flames that were impervious to water; dreadful comets streaked through the sky; and two-headed men appeared before the emperor but refused to speak. Montezuma imprisoned his oracles (people, usually priests or priestesses, through whom the gods are said to speak), furious at their inability to predict better days. Though there were no women in sight, people heard voices of women wailing about imminent disaster. As workers dragged a massive stone to the capital city, intending for it to be used as a new sacrificial altar, the stone seemed to suddenly come to life, crying out in a loud voice that it did not want to enter the city. Then it shattered the bridge on which it rested, dragging the workers to their deaths. After enduring several years of these evil omens, the frustrated emperor had his oracles strangled.

One possible factor in Montezuma's sense of impending doom has been offered by history books since the Spanish conquest. Mesoamerican mythology (traditional, often imaginary stories dealing with ancestors, heroes, or supernatural beings) had long foretold that in the year 1 Reed, or 1519 by modern calendars, a bearded and fair-skinned Quetzalcoatl (pronounced kates-ahl-koh-AH-tul), the creator god of the ancient Toltecs, would return from the east to take over the Aztec world. Quetzalcoatl was a holy and benevolent (kind) god and, according to some of the ancient legends, one of the few gods that did not approve of human sacrifices. He was regarded as a father to humankind. In Toltec legend, Quetzal-coatl and the god of darkness, Tezcatlipoca (pronounced tez-caht-lee-POE-cah), were in an eternal battle for power. In the time of the Toltec civilization (900–1200), Tezcatlipoca had won the struggle. Quetzalcoatl is said to have sailed away from the Toltec city of Tula on a raft made of serpents after his defeat, promising to return in the year 1 Reed (see **Topiltzin-Quetzalcoatl** entry for more information). Historians have often explained Montezuma's behavior toward the Spanish by theorizing that he believed the fair-skinned, bearded Spaniards who arrived in Mexico in 1519 were Quetzalcoatl and his escorts coming in from the east, just as the god had promised. But many experts now believe that this theory was really only a tale told by Spanish soldiers who wanted to romanticize their conquest of the Aztecs.

The Spanish arrive

Two years after Montezuma II assumed the Aztec throne, Hernán Cortés (1485-1547), a young law student from a poor but noble Spanish family, gave up his studies and shipped out to the Caribbean islands. In 1518 Cortés was appointed to head an expedition to explore the newly discovered Mexican coast. Cortés had heard the stories of explorers who reported a magnificent and wealthy kingdom set on an island in a lake in Mexico. The ambitious young soldier wanted to conquer and rule the new territory, and he hoped to get rich in the process.

The Cortés expedition of eleven ships and about 550 soldiers set off for Mexico near the end of 1518. Months later, from Veracruz—one of many cities within the Aztec empire—Cortés sent word to Montezuma that he would like to meet with him in Tenochtitlán. Montezuma had by this time heard many reports of these strangers. He was especially disturbed to hear about their weapons, which according to the reports seemed to spew fire. Worse yet were the descriptions of their horses, which were bigger than any animal the Aztecs had ever seen.

Montezuma called together a council to decide how to proceed. Many of his advisers recommended gathering a full Aztec army to destroy the small Spanish force before they came to the city; others recommended treating Cortés as an honored ambassador from a great king. Montezuma seems to have been unable to decide what to do. As Cortés began to travel toward Tenochtitlán, the emperor repeatedly sent messengers with lavish gifts. By Aztec tradition, sending valuable gifts was an aggressive gesture, indicating the sender's power and dominance. The Spanish received the gifts and continued traveling toward Tenochtitlán. To the Aztecs, this response was highly inappropriate.

As the Spaniards traveled toward Tenochtitlán, they found unexpected friends among the Totonac people at Cempoala (pronounced sem-pwahl-AH) in central Veracruz. The Totonacs were tired of paying tribute to Tenochtitlán and were happy to tell Cortés the route to the city and to describe its great wealth. Cortés continued to gather support from other provinces of the empire as he continued in his travels.

The Spanish expedition arrived at the city of Tlaxcala (pronounced tla-SKA-lah) in south-central Mexico in September 1519. The Tlaxcalans were one of the only groups in the Valley of Mexico who had been able to withstand the power of the Aztec armies. They had been at war with the Aztecs for many years and were their bitter enemies. Still, they met the Spaniards in a fierce battle, perhaps believing the Spanish had allied themselves with Montezuma. After the battle, the Tlaxcalans had a change of heart and committed themselves to fighting with the Spanish against Tenochtitlán. This was a crucial factor in the Spanish conquest. When Cortés left Tlaxcala to continue his march to Tenochtitlán, a thousand Tlaxcalan allies were marching with him.

When Montezuma learned that the Spaniards were only 60 miles (97 kilometers) away, he finally decided to invite Cortés and his men to be his guests in Tenochtitlán. With his large armies and such a small force of Spaniards, he probably felt it was safe to do so. On November 8, 1519, Cortés marched along the longest causeway (a road built over the water; there were three causeways, each over a mile long, reaching from the shores of Lake Texcoco to the city) leading into Tenochtitlán. The people of Tenochtitlán and the other cities around Lake Texcoco watched anxiously as the strangers approached the city.

Montezuma was waiting for them in Tenochtitlán. According to Inga Clendinnen in *Aztecs: An Interpretation* (1991),

Montezuma had decided to allow the Spaniards into the city to impress upon them how powerful the Aztec emperor was. When they arrived, Montezuma entered the plaza, escorted in royal fashion by a small army of Aztec nobles who swept a path clear for him as he walked. He was dressed elegantly and covered by a large canopy carried by Aztec lords. The Spanish soldiers described him as a courteous and dignified man, of slender build and average height. He wore his dark hair long.

Cortés approached the Aztec emperor. Through interpreters he had acquired during his journey (see **Malinche** entry), he gave a speech on the virtues of the Christian religion and the king of Spain. Montezuma listened patiently to his words and offered to send tribute to the great king beyond the waters. Then the Aztecs showed the Spaniards their city and led them to the Templo Mayor, which had been built to

A feather headdress said to have belonged to Montezuma II. *The Art Archive/Museum fur Volkerkunde Vienna/Dagli Orti.*

honor the two principal Aztec gods, Tlaloc and Huitzilopochtli. Next to the temple was a *tzompantli* (pronounced zahm-PAHN-tli), a rack upon which the skulls of sacrifice victims had been hung. The Spaniards estimated that there were at least ten thousand skulls on the racks, and they withdrew from the temple area in horror. But Montezuma reportedly provided the soldiers with lodging in the city and treated them as his honored guests.

The capture and death of Montezuma

Although he and his men were treated well, Cortés disliked being surrounded by Aztec warriors. He came up with a plan to take the emperor captive, hoping that he could rule the people through Montezuma. Putting the plan into action, some of Cortés's men accused Montezuma of planning an attack on Spaniards stationed at Veracruz, and then they took him prisoner. Although Montezuma denied having any role in the attack, he agreed to accompany Cortés, asking only that he be allowed to take some of his family with him. As Montezuma was being led across town to his place of captivity, several Aztec warriors asked him if they should attack the Spaniards, but Montezuma insisted that he was only going to spend a few days with the Spaniards out of friendship. Despite being held prisoner, Montezuma continued to rule over his empire for several weeks, managing to persuade his people not to launch a major attack on the Spaniards. Thus, by most accounts, Montezuma submitted to the Spanish without a struggle. If this is true, his motivations remain a mystery.

Although Montezuma was in custody, he was allowed to go about his business more or less as usual for a couple of weeks. Cortés left the city for Veracruz to attend to urgent problems arising there. About 140 of Cortés's men remained in Tenochtitlán, attending the captive emperor. After Cortés had gone, the Aztecs began to celebrate a feast in honor of their god Huitzilopochtli. Perhaps the Spaniards panicked in response; for whatever reason, Cortés's lieutenant, Pedro de Alvarado (c. 1485–1541), ordered an attack on the Aztecs, and two hundred unarmed nobles were brutally murdered.

The Aztecs were furious, and they prepared to attack. Montezuma apparently saved the soldiers from immediate death by calling out to them from a rooftop, telling them to stop fighting. Most Aztecs regarded this as an act of cowardice. No longer willing to obey the emperor's commands, the Aztecs quickly decided to elect a new *huey tlatoani*. When Cortés returned, the Aztecs attacked.

Montezuma died during the struggle that followed Cortés's return, but no one knows for certain what happened to him. His death may have been an accident in the chaotic fighting, or he may have been murdered by one of Cortés's men. According to at least one Spanish report, Cortés asked Montezuma to go again to the rooftop to speak to his people. After first refusing, the emperor consented to make an appeal to the Aztecs to stop their attack. Some sources suggest that the Aztec warriors openly defied Montezuma's authority when he appeared on the roof. Cuauhtémoc (c. 1495–1522), Montezuma's nephew and son-in-law who would later become the last Aztec emperor, shouted to the crowd that Montezuma was no longer their *huey tlatoani* and should not be obeyed. According to this story, Montezuma was hit by a stone before he even had a chance to speak. A shower of stones followed, and the emperor was hit three times. On the morning of June 30, 1520, as the fighting continued, Montezuma died. Denied the traditional ceremonies of an emperor's funeral, Montezuma's body was dishonorably burned.

The fighting between the Aztecs and the Spanish continued for more than a year after Montezuma's death. The Spanish relied greatly on the aid of many cities within the Aztec empire to help crush Tenochtitlán. The Aztecs put up a fierce resistance before they were forced to surrender on August 13, 1521.

For More Information

Books

Burland, C. A. *Montezuma: Lord of the Aztecs.* New York: G. P. Putnam's Sons, 1973.

Clendinnen, Inga. *Aztecs: An Interpretation.* Cambridge, England: Cambridge University Press, 1991.

Díaz (del Castillo), Bernal. *The Conquest of New Spain.* Translated with an introduction by J. M. Cohen. London and New York: Penguin Books, 1963.

Thomas, Hugh. *Conquest: Montezuma, Cortés, and the Fall of Old Mexico.* New York: Simon and Schuster, 1993.

Web Sites

"Conquistadors: The Aztec Empire." *Oregon Public Broadcasting and PBS Online.* http://www.pbs.org/opb/conquistadors/mexico/adventure1/b3.htm (accessed on November 24, 2004).

"Montezuma II." *Civilizations in History.* http://home.echo-on.net/~smithda/montezuma2.html (accessed on November 24, 2004).

Malinche

Born c. 1501
Possibly in the village of Jaltipan, Isthmus
of Tehuantepec, Mexico
Died c. 1550
Mexico City, Mexico

Translator and interpreter

M alinche (pronounced mah-leen-CHAY; also known as Doña Marina; Malinalli; and Malintzin) was a young woman living as a slave or concubine (mistress; a woman who lives with and has a sexual relationship with a man but is not married to him) among the Mayas (pronounced MY-uhs) in 1519. She suddenly became a major player in the history of Mexico when she was awarded as a "gift" to a group of Spanish conquistadores (Spanish word for "conquerors"). Led by Hernán Cortés (1485-1547), the conquistadores were on a mission to conquer the Aztecs, and they brought Malinche along with them.

Malinche knew at least two native languages—Nahuatl (pronounced NAH-wah-tul), the language of the Aztecs, and one or more of the local Mayan languages—and her bilingual skills became invaluable to Cortés in his dealings with the indigenous, or native, people from Mesoamerica. Cortés's strategy for taking control of the region that is now called Mexico was based on his skills at talking: making deals, making friends, making promises, and generally stirring up trouble between the native groups surrounding the Aztec capital. To be effective, he needed to be able to speak directly and

"Though Malinche was there at all the great moments of the Conquest, although she spoke for Cortés, although the phrases she learned to utter on his behalf were carefully recorded, she left no one word of her own to tell us what she made of the apocalyptic [decisive and dramatic] events in which she participated."

Anna Lanyon, Malinche's Conquest.

Malinche, also known as Doña Marina. *The Art Archive/Mireille Vautier.*

clearly, even in the most dangerous circumstances. Malinche became his most valued assistant. She was brave and calm under pressure and had a keen intelligence and a quick wit. Without her interpreting skills and her knowledge of the dangers that lurked in every situation, it is possible that Cortés would have failed in his mission.

Background

Malinche was born sometime around the beginning of the sixteenth century in a community on the Isthmus of Tehuantepec in southern Mexico, probably in the village of Jaltipan. The village is in the area that was once the homeland of the Olmec people, who thrived from about 1200 to 400 B.C.E. along the southern gulf coast of Mexico. This region was not part of the Aztec empire, and the people who lived there had their own language. According to Anna Lanyon, author of *Malinche's Conquest* (1999), the Nahuatl speakers who had drifted into the area at the end of the fifteenth century called the language spoken there *Popoluca,* meaning "babble"; it is only spoken by a few of the old people of the region in the twenty-first century. No one knows if Malinche was a native Nahuatl speaker or if it was her second language.

Most of what is known about the life of Malinche was recorded by **Bernal Díaz** (1492–c. 1581; see entry), one of the Spanish conquistadores on the expedition with Cortés. In 1568 Díaz wrote down his vivid recollections of the expedition in *Historia verdadera de la conquista de Nueva España* (*The True History of the Conquest of New Spain*; also known as *The Conquest of New Spain*), a book that was first published in 1632. Díaz knew Malinche for four years; he was quite impressed with her and always spoke very highly of her.

Malinche told Díaz that she was born into a noble family. Her original name is thought to have been Malinalli (also spelled Malinali), the name of the twelfth day on the Mesoamerican calendar. (It was common for Mesoamericans to name their children for the day they were born.) When Malinche was a young girl, her father died and her mother remarried and had a son with her second husband. The mother evidently wanted her son to inherit the family's status, wealth, and leadership position—which was all part of Malinche's rightful inheritance. To make sure that her son received these benefits, Malinche's mother secretly sold Malinche to some traders from the market city of Xicalango (pronounced shee-cah-LAHN-go) and then told the people in her community that Malinche was dead.

Lanyon cites another possible reason behind Malinche's abandonment, noting that the day on which Malinche was born and for which she was named, Malinalli, was considered terribly unlucky. Mesoamericans firmly believed that their calendar systems could foretell the future, so it is possible that Malinche's mother believed her daughter was cursed and would bring trouble to the family.

Around the age of ten, Malinche was brought to Xicalango, where she was probably sold to a wealthy nobleman from the Maya town of Potonchan on the gulf coast of Mexico. In Potonchan, it is likely that Malinche lived in a household with other slaves and concubines. During her years there she learned to speak the local Mayan language in addition to whatever languages she had spoken before she arrived.

The Spanish arrive

At the time that Malinche was growing up, the Spanish conquistador Hernán Cortés (1485–1547) was taking part in the conquest of Cuba. In 1518 he left Cuba, setting off on an expedition to explore and conquer the Mexican territory. He had heard stories of a rich and powerful city on a lake island and was determined to find the island and take control of it. As the expedition traveled along Mexico's gulf coast, the Spaniards made contact with the Mayas of the region. Early in their travels, the Spanish had had the good fortune to encounter a fellow Spaniard, Jeronimo de Aguilar (c. 1489–c. 1531), who had washed up on the Mexican shore after a shipwreck in 1511. He had been living with the Mayas ever since, and he knew their language. Happily joining the expedition, Aguilar served as a translator.

In March 1518 the Spanish fleet arrived in the Maya village of Potonchan. The Mayas there decided to fight the intruders, and, soon after the Spaniards came ashore, a battle began. After a furious fight the Mayas were forced to withdraw. As gifts of surrender, they gave the Spanish expedition

Hernán Cortés, 1485-1547

Hernán Cortés was born to a poor but noble Spanish family in Medellín, Spain. He attended university but in 1504 decided to give up his studies to seek power and wealth in the Americas. Cortés settled initially on the island of Santo Domingo (Hispaniola); then in 1511 he joined an expedition to Cuba. There he worked as a notary (someone who is authorized to witness signatures and certify documents). In 1518 the governor of Cuba appointed Cortés to head an exploring expedition into the unknown territories of Mexico. However, before Cortés had even left Cuba, the governor ordered his arrest, realizing that Cortés sought to conquer Mexico, not merely explore it. Early in 1519 Cortés slipped away from Cuba with eleven ships and about 550 men from a variety of occupations. Cortés's route took him first to Yucatán and then up the Mexican coast to Veracruz, where he established a base for his operations.

For the next several months, Cortés gathered information, learning about the rich and powerful Aztec city of Tenochtitlán. Heading inland for the city, he sent a message to Aztec emperor Montezuma II (1466–1520), telling him he planned to visit Tenochtitlán. During his travels Cortés made contact with many of the indigenous, or native, groups along the way and made a strong alliance with the Tlaxcalans, enemies of the Aztecs. His expedition was also responsible for a massacre of thousands of people in the city of Cholula. Not long after arriving in Tenochtitlán, Cortés made a bold and rash move: He took Montezuma hostage and began an uneasy rule over the angry Aztecs in the city. However, soon after this Cortés learned that there was a Cuban commission in Veracruz with a warrant for his arrest, and he left Tenochtitlán to attend to the matter. After talking with some of the men who had come to arrest him, Cortés persuaded them to join him instead. They returned to Tenochtitlán and found the Aztecs preparing to attack the troops that Cortés had left in charge of the city. Montezuma was killed. No one knows for sure whether he was killed by the angry Aztecs or by the orders of Cortés. On the night of June 30, 1520, *la noche triste,* or the "sad night," the Spaniards were forced to flee. The Aztecs killed more than 860 Spaniards and a thousand Tlaxcalans that night.

Less than a year later, the determined Cortés returned to Tenochtitlán well equipped for battle. This time Cortés was joined by thousands of Amerindians (indigenous, or native people, from Mesoamerica) who saw an opportunity to overthrow Aztec rule. Fighting now proceeded from street to street and house to house, destroying the once proud city and its people. Finally, on August 13, 1521, the devastated Aztec people surrendered amid the ruins of their city.

The Spanish rebuilt Tenochtitlán and called it Mexico City. Cortés and his

Hernán Cortés.

interpreter Malinche settled there, and Malinche soon gave birth to Cortés's first son. Cortés had a wife in Cuba, but during his expedition in Mexico he had taken Malinche as a mistress. Three months after the conquest, Cortés's wife arrived and joined the household. Soon after her arrival, she died under mysterious circumstances; the cause of death appeared to be strangulation. Although there were investigations into the matter, Cortés was never formally accused of killing her.

In 1522 the Spanish king appointed Cortés the governor of New Spain. Cortés was less successful as a politician than he was as a conquistador, and trouble soon broke out on a variety of fronts. Cortés traveled to Honduras in 1524 to suppress a rebellion against his rule that had been initiated by one of his own lieutenants. Cortés had brought with him Cuauhtémoc (c. 1495–1522), the last emperor of the Aztecs, and other nobles of the Aztec empire. Much to the dismay of even his most loyal supporters, Cortés decided to execute the Aztec emperor and nobles, accusing them of treason. His reasons for this brutal act were not clear to others around him. He returned to Mexico City and found another revolt in progress, this one carried out by the conquistadores, who felt cheated at the distribution of the spoils of victory. An investigation of his term as governor led to his being removed from office, and he went to Spain in 1528 to try to clear his name. There he married a woman from a noble family; together they would have three daughters and a son. When Cortés returned to Mexico in 1530, he was able to enjoy his considerable wealth, but he was no longer entrusted with political power.

Cortés retired to Spain in 1540. He died in 1547, and, at his own request, was buried where he had first met Montezuma. During his life he had succeeded in his quest for power and gold. He had conquered the Aztec empire and paved the way for Spain's domination of the Americas. In fulfilling these goals, Cortés destroyed an advanced civilization and was responsible for the massacre and enslavement of tens of thousands of Mesoamericans.

food, some turquoise and jade objects, and twenty women, one of whom was Malinche. Cortés accepted the gifts. There were two priests along on the expedition, and they baptized the women and gave them Christian names. Cortés then divided the women up, giving one to each of the captains of the expedition. Malinche, who had been given the name Doña Marina, was given to one of Cortés's good friends, Alonso Hernández Portocarrero.

It was not unusual for sixteenth-century Spanish explorers and soldiers in Mesoamerica to receive women as peace offerings from Amerindian groups. The men who accepted these women as gifts did not usually write about it, and the women who were given away did not have the freedom or education to write for themselves, so there are few records of their experiences or even of their existence. These women were expected to provide whatever comforts these men desired. They hauled their firewood and water and cooked their food. They were also expected to act as concubines to the conquistadores. For Malinche, this was probably the second time she had been taken involuntarily as a concubine.

The interpreter

The Cortés expedition continued, sailing northwest along the Mexican gulf coast and stopping along the way to ask the local people about gold and the Aztec capital of Tenochtitlán (pronounced tay-notch-teet-LAHN). They eventually left Maya territory and entered the Aztec empire, where most people spoke the Nahuatl language. The interpreter, Aguilar, did not know this language, so he was no longer of any use. Cortés was discouraged. His strength lay in his ability to talk to the Amerindians—to make alliances and to cause frictions among them; without someone to translate, he was severely limited.

According to Díaz in *The Conquest of New Spain,* one day when Cortés and his crew were ashore on a fact-finding mission, some messengers of **Montezuma II** (see entry), the Aztec emperor, arrived in the town, seeking the fair-skinned man who had been asking about their city. The messengers spoke Nahuatl, and none of the Spaniards in the expedition understood what they were saying. Suddenly, Malinche stepped in, answering their questions by pointing to Cortés.

Cortés was surprised that she knew Nahuatl. Apparently, even though she had been away from her home for ten years, she had not forgotten the language.

Cortés quickly devised a system for conversing with Nahuatl-speaking people. He spoke in Spanish, and Aguilar translated his words into Mayan; then Malinche translated Aguilar's words into Nahuatl. When the Nahuatl speaker responded, the process was reversed. It could take a long time to have a conversation by this process and there were many chances of miscommunication, but the system worked and Cortés was able to converse with the many Amerindian groups he met on his way to Tenochtitlán. As they traveled, Malinche learned to ask the locals about gold and Tenochtitlán. Soon she was also preaching Christian ideas to the Amerindians they met. According to Díaz, she had taken her conversion to Christianity very seriously.

The trip to Tenochtitlán

Cortés sent word to Montezuma that he would like to meet with him in Tenochtitlán. The emperor sent gifts along with messages that it was not a good time for them to come. Cortés founded a settlement in the present-day Mexican state of Veracruz and then headed inland toward the Aztec capital.

In September 1519 the expedition arrived at the city-state (independent, self-governing community consisting of a single city and the surrounding area) of Tlaxcala in south-central Mexico. The Tlaxcalans had been one of the few groups who were able to hold out against the Aztec army. They had maintained their independence through brutal warfare, and they were bitter enemies of the Aztecs. Not knowing that the Spaniards were potential allies, they met the Cortés expedition in a fierce battle, and soon it was clear that the Spaniards were in terrible trouble. Malinche and Cortés went to the Tlaxcalans to try to make a deal. Somehow in the negotiations, the Tlaxcalans were persuaded not only to spare the Spaniards but to join them in fighting against the Aztecs at Tenochtitlán. This was an extremely important factor in the Spanish conquest. When Cortés left Tlaxcala to continue his march to Tenochtitlán, he had a thousand Tlaxcalan allies with him, and thousands more would join him later.

Malinche stepped forward to translate Cortés's formal and very polite announcement, stating that he was a messenger from a king who lived across the ocean. Montezuma responded, also very courteously. Necklaces were exchanged between the emperor and the explorer. Then Montezuma invited the Spaniards to follow him into his city (the Tlaxcala warriors were not invited inside).

For two weeks, Cortés and Montezuma engaged in many talks, with Malinche as their go-between. The other members of the expedition wandered freely through the city, admiring its beauty. In his firsthand account of the expedition, Díaz notes that the emperor and Cortés were deep in conversation, but there are many differing accounts of the words that passed between them, and nearly five centuries later there is still no agreement on what was actually said. Cortés wrote his own account of the conversation in a letter to the Spanish king. In the letter he states that Montezuma accepted him as a god returning to earth and declared himself to be a servant of the Spanish king; Cortés also claims in the letter that Montezuma agreed to let him immediately take power over Tenochtitlán. Historians agree that Cortés was a great liar and that he made up this report to justify his takeover of Tenochtitlán.

In all the meetings that occurred, Malinche was situated between Cortés and Montezuma. The Spanish and native writers who witnessed the meetings described Malinche as a very beautiful woman with a powerful presence. From a modern perspective, she is quite an interesting character because in her role as interpreter, she completely broke the standards of behavior for Mesoamerican women. According to Inga Clendinnen in *Aztecs: An Interpretation* (1991), women in the Aztec empire were prohibited from speaking in public places, particularly during public events. Yet, as the voice of Cortés, Malinche stepped up and addressed local lords and heads of state in a clear voice without fear or embarrassment. Díaz notes how impressed he was by her courage:

> Let me say that doña Marina, although a native woman, possessed such manly valour that though she heard every day that the Indians were going to kill us and eat our flesh with chillis, and though she had seen us surrounded in recent battles and knew that we were all wounded and sick, yet she betrayed no weakness but a courage greater than that of a woman.

In one excursion Cortés and Malinche went to view the Templo Mayor, the temple dedicated to the god Huitzilopochtli (pronounced hweets-ee-loh-PAWCH-tlee), where human sacrifices were carried out in massive numbers. Lanyon describes Malinche's experience:

> She saw the walls and floors caked with blood, and the hearts of that day's sacrificial victims still burning in the temple braziers [pans that hold burning coals].... To see what she did that day, and live, made her unique among Meso Americans, and she would have known it. In her world only priests and victims made the long and terrible journey up the hundreds of steps to the temple platform, and only the priests returned.

According to Díaz, Malinche fearlessly informed Montezuma that his gods were evil and told him that he should worship the Christian god instead. When Cortés decided to take Montezuma prisoner, it was Malinche who told the emperor that he was being taken into custody.

The fall of Tenochtitlán

Montezuma was a prisoner in his own land for about six months, and during that time the members of the Spanish expedition and the Aztec people who lived in the city grew less tolerant of each other. Then, while Cortés was away from the city, the Aztecs began to celebrate a feast in honor of their god Huitzilopochtli. Cortés's lieutenant, Pedro de Alvarado (c. 1485–1541), ordered an attack on them, and two hundred unarmed nobles were brutally murdered. The Aztecs were furious, and when Cortés returned, they began their attack on the Spaniards. In the ensuing battle, Montezuma was killed. No one knows how he actually died; some accounts say it was an accident, some say Cortés ordered the killing, and others claim that the Aztecs themselves killed their leader (see **Montezuma II** entry for more information).

Shortly after the death of Montezuma, on the night of June 30, 1520, the Spaniards decided to flee from the increasing attacks of the Aztecs, but a full force of Aztec warriors attacked them as they raced across the causeways leading out of Tenochtitlán. Hundreds of Spaniards and even more Tlaxcalans were killed that night, a night the Spanish called *la noche triste,* meaning "the sad night." Malinche managed to escape and hid under one of the bridges of the causeway until it was safe to flee.

Nearly a year later and after much preparation, Cortés mounted a larger and more brutal attack on Tenochtitlán. Many sources say that Malinche was with Cortés and the Spanish throughout the terrible battle. After three months of combat the sick and starving Aztecs who had survived in the ruined city were unable to fight anymore. They surrendered on August 13, 1521. Malinche was at the side of Cortés to translate the formal arrangements for surrender.

The mother of Mexico

After the surrender, Malinche lived with Cortés in Mexico City, a new city built upon the ruins of Tenochtitlán. About a year later, in May 1522, she gave birth to Cortés's first son. Cortés named the boy Martín, after his own father. Spanish soldiers fathered many children by Amerindian women, but the son of Cortés and Malinche was the first publicly acknowledged *mestizo* (person of mixed European and Amerindian ancestry) in Mexico. Because of this, people often refer to him as the first Mexican, and to Malinche as the symbolic "mother of Mexico."

Malinche took one more journey with Cortés, to interpret for him while he was on another exploring mission in Honduras. During this trip in 1524, she married one of his officers, a Spanish man named Juan Xaramillo de Salvatierra. No one knows the circumstances of this arrangement. During their travels, the expedition stopped in the town where Malinche's mother and brother still lived. Díaz reports that there was a tender scene among the family members and that Malinche was forgiving and kind to her mother, the woman who had sold her to strangers. But Malinche did not choose to stay in her first home; instead she continued on the journey with the Spaniards. After returning to Mexico City, she gave birth to a girl, the daughter of her new husband. Cortés went back to Spain, and Malinche was no longer an object of public interest. There are no records of the rest of her life.

No one will ever know what Malinche thought or felt as she participated in the Spaniards' brutal defeat of the Aztecs. Malinche has long been reviled for helping the foreigners overthrow the native people of Mexico. In fact, modern Mexicans use the word *malinchista* as an insult, meaning traitor, or someone who loves foreigners. Feelings about Malinche run deep in Mexico even today. Her struggles as a twice-sold woman falling involuntarily into the power of the conquistadores can elicit contempt or sympathy, but her place in Mexico's history is never forgotten.

For More Information

Books

Clendinnen, Inga. *Aztecs: An Interpretation.* Cambridge, England: Cambridge University Press, 1991.

Díaz (del Castillo), Bernal. *The Conquest of New Spain.* Translated with an introduction by J. M. Cohen. London and New York: Penguin Books, 1963.

Lanyon, Anna. *Malinche's Conquest.* Crows Nest, Australia: Allen and Unwin, 1999.

Thomas, Hugh. *Conquest: Montezuma, Cortés, and the Fall of Old Mexico.* New York: Simon and Schuster, 1993.

Periodicals

Krauss, Clifford. "A Historic Figure Is Still Hated by Many in Mexico." *New York Times* (March 26, 1997). This article is also available online at http://www.emayzine.com/lectures/la.htm (accessed on November 19, 2004).

Lenchek, Shep. "La Malinche: Harlot or Heroine?" *Guadalajara-Lakeside* (December 1997). This article is also available online at http://www.mexconnect.com/mex_/history/malinche.html (accessed on November 19, 2004).

Web Sites

"The Conquest of Mexico: Cortés and La Malinche." *Pyramid Press.* http://thedagger.com/archive/conquest/malinche.html (accessed on November 19, 2004).

Bernal Díaz

Excerpt from The Conquest of New Spain

Translated with an introduction by J. M. Cohen, 1963; originally published as *Historia verdadera de la conquista de Nueva España* (*The True History of the Conquest of New Spain*)

Written in 1568; published in 1632

Of the many Spanish accounts of the fall of the Aztec capital of Tenochtitlán (pronounced tay-notch-teet-LAHN) in 1521, the one that is most often quoted in history books is *Historia verdadera de la conquista de Nueva España* (*The True History of the Conquest of New Spain*) written by Bernal Díaz del Castillo (1492–c. 1581) in 1568. Díaz, a member of the Spanish expedition that conquered the Aztec empire, was blessed with a healthy curiosity, an eye for detail, a remarkable memory, and a clear and conversational way of relating what he saw. His book, though not elegantly written, is full of historic and dramatic details that cannot be found elsewhere.

Díaz was born around 1496 in Medina del Campo, Spain. His family was respectable but poor, and Díaz had little education. As a young man, he was lured by the tales of fortunes waiting to be made in the newly discovered Americas. In 1514 he set out for the New World, settling first in the area of present-day Panama and then moving to Cuba. While he was based in Cuba, he participated in two expeditions that explored the coasts of the Gulf of Mexico in 1517 and 1518, respectively.

"We were scarcely four hundred strong, and we well remembered the words and warnings … we had received to beware of entering the city of Mexico, since they would kill us as soon as they had us inside…. What men in all the world have shown such daring?"

In 1519 Díaz joined a third expedition, this one organized by its Spanish captain, Hernán Cortés (1485–1547). Díaz, with more honesty than most of the Spanish chroniclers of the history of the conquest, noted that the purpose of those who joined the Cortés expedition was to "serve God and His Majesty, to give light to those in darkness, and to grow the rich." Díaz was an eyewitness to most of the important events leading up to the conquest of Mexico and he participated in the campaigns leading to the fall of Tenochtitlán. His exact involvement, however, is not clear. His chronicles suggest that he exercised some authority and enjoyed the confidence of Cortés, but he may have exaggerated his own position. The evidence indicates that he was little more than a common foot soldier.

After the conquest of the Aztecs, Díaz settled in the province of Coatzacoalcos (pronounced koe-aht-sah-koe-AHL-kos; sometimes spelled Quetzalcoalco), southeast of Veracruz, where he had been awarded grants of land and native labor in the *encomienda* system. This system gave Díaz and the other Spanish conquistadores (Spanish word for "conquerors") who conquered Tenochtitlán and other parts of the Americas a grant that gave them the right to demand labor or payment from the Amerindians living in a particular expanse of territory. Strictly speaking, it was not slavery, but it came close. These properties, however, provided Díaz with only a modest livelihood, so in 1540 he went to Spain to plead for more substantial recognition of his merits and services. He was rewarded by a somewhat better *encomienda* in the province of Guatemala. There he settled, becoming a respected citizen, a local judge, and the father of several children.

Writing a history

Díaz began to record his memories of the conquest in the early 1550s but the work initially went slowly. Writing was not a familiar pastime for an old soldier. Then, in the 1560s, he read a book titled *The History of the Conquest of Mexico* (1552), written by Francisco López de Gómara (1510–1564), a former chaplain of the Cortés family who had never been to the New World and could only base his account of the conquest on what Cortés had told him. Gómara's account irritated Díaz, who felt that it glorified Cortés's role at the expense of the expedition's common soldiers. This injustice provided him the motivation to complete his own account, which he titled *The True History of the Conquest of New Spain* (also called *The Conquest of New Spain*).

Most of Díaz's history is focused on the years of the Spanish conquest of Tenochtitlán (1519–21), but he also wrote about his experiences on the first two expeditions to Mexico in 1517 and 1518, and about events later in his life up until 1568. Díaz's writing style in the book is rough and unpolished. The narrative is long, wordy, and full of unsophisticated comments and digressions. Yet he wrote with simple honesty. Unlike other accounts from the era, his chronicle is not designed to justify his trips or to make his leader appear heroic. The book is engaging because Díaz was a natural storyteller with a deep sense of personal involvement and excitement. *The True History of the Conquest of New Spain* is a major historical document and also one of the great adventure stories of the Americas.

Things to remember while reading the excerpt from *The Conquest of New Spain*

- As this excerpt begins, Díaz is describing the scene as the Cortés expedition makes its way into Tenochtitlán from the shores of Lake Texcoco after the difficult journey over the mountains. The people who live in the various cities around the lake are looking upon the expedition in astonishment and the Spanish soldiers are equally amazed by what they see.

- To get to the city of Tenochtitlán, built on an island in the middle of the lake, the expedition had to cross one of three large causeways (roads built over the water) that connected the island to the shore at various points. Each one of these causeways was several miles long and about 25 to 30 feet (8 to 9 meters) wide. The causeways were constructed of wooden beams that fit together like a jigsaw puzzle and could be taken apart quickly if an enemy approached. Until the Spanish arrived, no one ever attacked the city.

- Díaz comments on the abundance of canoe traffic he and the rest of the expedition come across as they head into Tenochti-

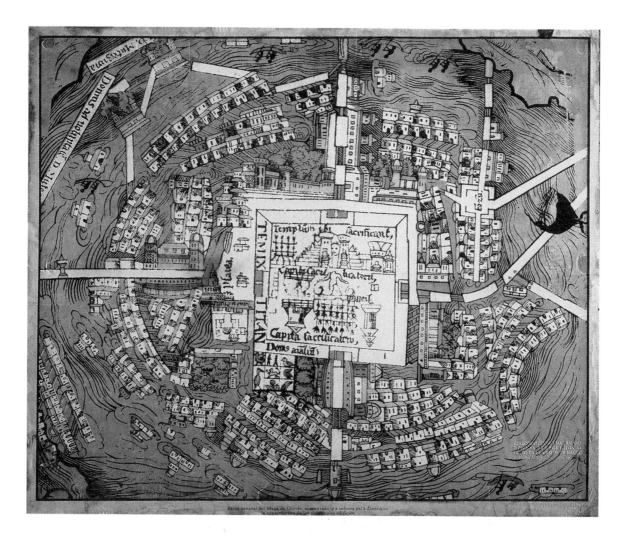

Parte central del Mapa de Cortés, aumentado y a colores para distinguir
la arquitectura de los principales edificios.

A map of Tenochtitlán, attributed to Hernán Cortés, showing the causeways connecting the island city to the mainland. *The Art Archive/Museo Ciudad Mexico/Dagli Orti.*

tlán. The city of Tenochtitlán had an estimated 150,000 to 200,000 people at that time, and, with all the other cities around the lake, it was an area of dense population.

- Díaz calls the Aztec capital Mexico, or the city of Mexico, rather than Tenochtitlán.

- Iztapalapa (pronounced ees-tah-pah-LAH-pah), Texcoco, Tacuba, and Coyoacan (pronounced coi-yo-AH-cahn) were cities surrounding Lake Texcoco and part of the Aztec confederation.

- Huexotzinco (pronounced whay-showt-SING-koe), Tlascala (also Tlaxcala), and Tlamanalco were cities the

Cortés expedition had encountered on its journey to Tenochtitlán. The people of these cities considered the Aztecs their enemies and had entered into an alliance with the Spaniards.

- Although Díaz exclaims in this excerpt "as I write, it all comes before my eyes as if it had happened only yesterday," remember that he wrote his book forty years after the events he was recording.

Excerpt from The Conquest of New Spain

The Entrance into Mexico

Early next day we left Iztapalapa with a large escort of these great Caciques, and followed the causeway, which is eight yards wide and goes so straight to the city of Mexico that I do not think it curves at all. Wide though it was, it was so crowded with people that there was hardly room for them all. Some were going to Mexico and others coming away, besides those who had come out to see us, and we could hardly get through the crowds that were there. For the towers ... were full, and they came in canoes from all parts of the lake. No wonder, since they had never seen horses or men like us before!

With such wonderful sights to gaze on we did not know what to say, or if this was real that we saw before our eyes. On the land side there were great cities, and on the lake many more. The lake was crowded with canoes. At intervals along the causeway there were many bridges, and before us was the great city of Mexico. As for us, we were scarcely four hundred strong, and we well remembered the words and warnings of the people of Huexotzinco and Tlascala and Tlamanalco, and the many other warnings we had received to beware of entering the city of Mexico, since they would kill us as soon as they had us inside. Let the interested reader consider whether there is not much to ponder in this narrative of mine. What men in all the world have shown such daring? But let us go on.

We marched along our causeway to a point where another small causeway branches off to another city called Coyoacan, and there, beside some towerlike buildings, which were their shrines, we were

Caciques: Local rulers of communities within the empire.

Causeway: A road built over a body of water.

Daring: Bravery.

Dignitaries: People with important ranks or positions.

Cloaks: Clothing.

Chieftains: Leaders.

Liveries: Special clothing worn by servants or other people who attend a noble or king.

Montezuma: Montezuma II; Aztec ruler and emperor of Mexico, 1502–20.

Litter: A couch attached to a frame and surrounded by curtains, used to transport one person.

Feudal: Relating to a system in which a lord or nobleman owns land and has special rights to the loyalty, work, and produce of the people who live on and farm his land as well as obligations to protect them.

Vassals: People in a feudal system who live on and farm the lord's land and live under his protection.

Chalchihuites: (pronounced chahl-chee-WHEE-tays) Precious ornaments.

Doña Marina: Aztec princess; interpreter for Hernán Cortés.

Musk: A substance taken from the skin of a male musk deer with a very strong odor that is used as a perfume.

Indignity: Insult.

met by many more Caciques *and* **dignitaries** *in very rich* **cloaks.** *The different* **chieftains** *wore different brilliant* **liveries,** *and the causeways were full of them.* **Montezuma** *had sent these great* Caciques *in advance to receive us, and as soon as they came before Cortes they told him in their language that we were welcome, and as sign of peace they touched the ground with their hands and kissed it.*

There we halted for some time while Cacamatzin, the lord of Texcoco, and the lords of Iztapalapa, Tacuba, and Coyoacan went ahead to meet the great Montezuma, who approached in a rich **litter,** *accompanied by other great lords and* **feudal** Caciques *who owned* **vassals.** *When we came near to Mexico, at a place where there were some other small towers, the great Montezuma descended from his litter, and those other great* Caciques *supported him beneath a marvelously rich canopy of green feathers, decorated with gold work, silver, pearls, and* **chalchihuites,** *which hung from a sort of border. It was a marvelous sight. The great Montezuma was magnificently clad, in their fashion, and wore sandals of a kind for which their name is* cactli, *the soles of which are gold and the upper parts ornamented with precious stones. And the four lords who supported him were richly clad also in garments that seem to have been kept ready for them on the road so that they could accompany their master. For they had not worn clothes like this when they came out to receive us. There were four other great* Caciques *who carried the canopy above their heads, many more lords who walked before the great Montezuma, sweeping the ground on which he was to tread, and laying down cloaks so that his feet should not touch the earth. Not one of these chieftains dared to look him in the face. All kept their eyes lowered most reverently except those four lords, his nephews, who were supporting him.*

When Cortes saw, heard, and was told that the great Montezuma was approaching, he dismounted from his horse, and when he came near to Montezuma each bowed deeply to the other. Montezuma welcomed our Captain, and Cortes, speaking through **Doña Marina,** *answered by wishing him very good health. Cortes, I think, offered Montezuma his right hand, but Montezuma refused it and extended his own. Then Cortes brought out a necklace which he had been holding. It was made of those elaborately worked and coloured glass beads called* margaritas, *of which I have spoken, and was strung on a gold cord and dipped in* **musk** *to give it a good odour. This he hung round the great Montezuma's neck, and as he did so attempted to embrace him. But the great princes who stood round Montezuma grasped Cortes' arm to prevent him, for they considered this an* **indignity.**

Montezuma II welcomes Hernán Cortés to Tenochtitlán.
© Bettmann/Corbis.

Then Cortes told Montezuma that it rejoiced his heart to have seen such a great prince, and that he took his coming in person to receive him and the repeated favours he had done him as a high honour. After this Montezuma made him another complimentary speech, and ordered two of his nephews who were supporting him, the lords of Texcoco and Coyoacan, to go with us and show us our quarters. Montezuma returned to the city with the other two kinsmen of his escort, the lords of Cuitláhuac and Tacuba; and all those grand companies of Caciques and dignitaries who had come with him returned also in his **train.** And as they accompanied their lord we observed them marching with their eyes downcast so that they should not see him, and keeping close to the wall as they followed him with great **reverence.** Thus space was made for us to enter the streets of Mexico without being pressed by the crowd.

Who could now count the multitude of men, women, and boys in the streets, on the roof-tops and in canoes on the water-ways, who had come out to see us? It was a wonderful sight and, as I write, it all comes before my eyes as if it had happened only yesterday.

Train: Procession of people.

Reverence: Profound honor and respect.

Primary Source: Bernal Díaz

*They led us to our quarters, which were in some large houses capable of accommodating us all and had formerly belonged to the great Montezuma's father, who was called Axayácatl. Here Montezuma now kept the great shrines of his gods, and a secret chamber containing gold bars and jewels. This was the treasure he had inherited from his father, which he never touched. Perhaps their reason for lodging us here was that, since they called us **Teules** and considered us as such, they wished to have us near their **idols.** In any case they took us to this place, where there were many great halls, and a **dais** hung with the cloth of their country for our Captain, and matting beds with canopies over them for each of us.*

On our arrival we entered the large court, where the great Montezuma was awaiting our Captain. Taking him by the hand, the prince led him to his apartment in the hall where he was to lodge, which was very richly furnished in their manner. Montezuma had ready for him a very rich necklace, made of golden crabs, a marvelous piece of work, which he hung round Cortes' neck. His captains were greatly astonished at this sign of honour.

After this ceremony, for which Cortes thanked him through our interpreters, Montezuma said: "Malinche [referring to Cortes' interpreter], you and your brothers are in your own house. Rest awhile." He then returned to his palace, which was not far off.

*We divided our lodgings by companies, and placed our **artillery** in a convenient spot. Then the order we were to keep was clearly explained to us, and we were warned to be very much on the alert, both the horsemen and the rest of us soldiers. We then ate a **sumptuous** dinner which they had prepared for us in their native style.*

So, with luck on our side, we boldly entered the city of Tenochtitlán or Mexico on 8 November in the year of our Lord 1519.

What happened next ...

Díaz sent his manuscript to Spain for publication in the 1570s, but his book was not published in his lifetime.

Díaz died c. 1581. Throughout his last years, he complained of poverty and lamented the inadequacy of the re-

Teules: An altered version of the Nahuatl word *teotl,* meaning semidivine persons or supernatural beings.

Idols: Symbols of an object of worship, such as small statues of a god.

Dais: A raised platform.

Artillery: Weapons.

Sumptuous: Extravagant.

wards he had received for his services to the king during the Spanish conquest.

The True History of the Conquest of New Spain did not appear in print until 1632 and then only after the editor, a Spanish priest, had considerably altered the text. It was not until 1904–5 that a true edition appeared, prepared by a Mexican historian from the original manuscript, which had survived in Guatemala.

Did you know …

- Díaz and the other Spanish conquistadores who conquered Tenochtitlán expected to be rewarded for their efforts by the *encomienda* system. The king of Spain gave the *encomenderos* of New Spain, the Spanish people receiving the grants, the right to demand payment and the labor of the people of a specified district. These districts could be large. Cortés had an *encomienda* made up of twenty-three thousand heads of Amerindian households, but most *encomiendas* were smaller than two thousand households. *Encomenderos* did not live on the land and they mostly left the working of the land to the Amerindians. In most cases, an *encomendero* demanded from the headman of his district as much payment as he felt the grant could produce, and left it to the headman to collect the payment in whatever way he saw fit. In return for the payment, the *encomendero* was obliged to protect the Amerindians, to appoint and pay for priests for the district, and to contribute to the military defense of the district.

Consider the following …

- Díaz's story of his first sight of Tenochtitlán is very dramatic; in fact, it is easy to imagine the scene as a movie or a play. With your classmates, create a short play from the scene presented earlier. Assign a different task to each classmate: one or two people should direct the play, a small group should write it together (there are not too many lines and it is fine to create your own), and there should be actors to play Montezuma, Cortés, Díaz, and Malinche, and anyone else in the script. Another small group should be in charge of scenery; everyone not acting in a role should be "extras" in the play's crowd scene.

- Imagine you are a soldier in Cortés's unit entering Tenochtitlán. After reviewing Díaz's description of entering the city for the first time, describe what you might be thinking and feeling in his circumstances.

- Many of the Spanish writers who recorded their version of the events during and after the conquest of Mexico were not very fair in their portraits of the Amerindians, either minimizing their achievements or depicting them as savages. Looking at Díaz's descriptions of the people of Tenochtitlán, do you think he is being fair in his portraits? Do you notice any peculiarities in the way he speaks about the Aztec people?

For More Information

Books

Cerwin, Herbert. *Bernal Díaz: Historian of the Conquest.* Norman: University of Oklahoma, 1963.

Clendinnen, Inga. *Aztecs: An Interpretation.* New York: Cambridge University Press, 1991.

Díaz (del Castillo), Bernal. *The Conquest of New Spain.* Translated with an introduction by J. M. Cohen. London and New York: Penguin Books, 1963.

Thomas, Hugh. *Montezuma, Cortés, and the Fall of Mexico.* New York: Simon and Schuster, 1993.

Web Sites

"Bernal Díaz del Castillo." *The Latino/A History Project.* http://www.latinohistory.com/people.php?id=96&print=1 (accessed on November 22, 2004).

Rashkin, Peter. "The Conquest of Mexico." *The Full Deck: A Webzine.* http://thedagger.com/archive/conquest/conquest1.html (accessed on November 22, 2004).

"Travel Narrative Resources." *World History Sources.* http://chnm.gmu.edu/worldhistorysources/unpacking/travelanalysis.html (accessed on November 22, 2004).

Aztec Poetry

"Elegies on the Fall of the City"

Three Aztec poems reprinted from *The Broken Spears: The Aztec Account of the Conquest of Mexico*. Edited and with an introduction by Miguel León-Portilla. Translated from Nahuatl into Spanish by Angel Maria Garibay K. English translation by Lysander Kemp, 1992

Created c. 1521

"How can we save our homes, my people / The Aztecs are deserting the city: / the city is in flames, and all / is darkness and destruction."

Unknown Aztec poet, "The Fall of Tenochtitlan"

The three poems featured in this entry were created by Aztecs who were in Tenochtitlán (pronounced tay-notch-teet-LAHN) at the time of the Spanish conquest of 1521 and survived to tell about it. Two of the three poems were found in a song collection called *Cantares mexicanos* (*Mexican Songs*). This collection was made possible by a Spanish missionary, who worked with a group of *tlamatinime* (pronounced tlah-mah-TEE-nee-may; singular: *tlamatini*), the poets and philosophers of the Aztec empire, between 1560 and 1580 to write down the songs of the Mesoamericans. Most experts believe the collection is the work of the renowned Spanish missionary Bernardino de Sahagún (1499–1590) and some of his native assistants, men who were well versed in Nahuatl (pronounced NAH-wah-tul) and trained by Sahagún in Spanish and Latin as well. This team collected ninety-one songs over a period of many years. It took many more years before their collection attracted the interest it deserves. The songs, or poems, in the collection provide modern readers with a window into the Mesoamerican experience.

The Broken Spears

When Mexican scholar and writer Miguel León-Portilla (1926–) first published *Visión de los vencidos* in 1959, his work introduced a new approach in the study of ancient civilizations of the Americas. For his book, León-Portilla gathered sources that had been written by Nahuatl-speaking people around the time of the Spanish conquest. He then had his book translated into English—in 1962 it published as *The Broken Spears: The Aztec Account of the Conquest of Mexico*—to reach an even wider audience. Unlike most of the scholars who preceded him, León-Portilla believes the history of the Aztecs should be learned through texts written by the Aztecs themselves.

The last two chapters of León-Portilla's book provide a native account of the final battle between the Spanish and the Aztecs in Tenochtitlán, the Aztec capital. In the final chapter, León-Portilla presents three *icnocuicatl* (pronounced eek-no-kwee-CAH-tul), or "songs of sorrow," poems expressing the utter despair of the Aztec people after their city is conquered. León-Portilla notes in his introduction to the poems that "they reveal, with greater eloquence than other texts, the deep emotional wound inflicted on the Indians by defeat."

The fall of Tenochtitlán

The end of the Aztec empire did not come swiftly or quietly. It was the result of a violent battle that took place in Tenochtitlán between April and August 1521. There were two hundred thousand men, women, and children living in the beautiful and prosperous island city when the Spanish conquistadores (Spanish word for "conquerors") mounted their last attack. By moderate estimates, about one hundred thousand Aztecs, or half the city's population, died during the siege. Everything in the city—markets, temples, palaces, and homes—was completely destroyed. An overview of the fall of Tenochtitlán is presented in this entry as a background to the poems that follow.

The Aztec emperor Montezuma II (1466–1520) died in Tenochtitlán during the first battle between the Aztecs and a group of Spanish conquistadores led by Hernán Cortés (1485–1547). In this first battle, the Aztecs soundly defeated the Spaniards, forcing them to retreat from the city. Afterward, the Aztecs celebrated their victory and elected a new emperor, Montezuma's brother Cuitláhuac (pronounced kweet-LAH-whahk; d. 1520). They had been so successful in their attack on the Spaniards that they felt sure there would be no more trouble. Nonetheless, they prepared for further war, determined to answer another Spanish assault with full force.

In the midst of these war preparations, an epidemic of smallpox struck. Smallpox and other contagious diseases carried by the Spanish were new to the Americas, and the Aztecs had no resistance to the germs. When the epidemic struck, thousands of people in Tenochtitlán became ill and then died of the disease. The emperor Cuitláhuac ruled for only eighty days before he succumbed to smallpox. He was replaced by the last Aztec emperor, Cuauhtémoc (pronounced koo-ow-TAY-mawk; c. 1495–1522).

In the meantime, after their retreat from Tenochtitlán, Cortés and his troops had taken refuge with their allies, the Tlaxcalans, who were bitter enemies of the Aztecs. The Tlaxcalans were not part of the Aztec empire; they had managed to remain independent only because they were fierce and powerful warriors. During his stay with them, Cortés was preparing for another attack on Tenochtitlán. He traveled through the Valley of Mexico, making allies of many other Amerindian groups (indigenous, or native Mesoamericans). Cortés used persuasion, promises of riches, and sometimes force to convince them to join his cause. The fierce Tlaxcalans could be very persuasive, often scaring other groups into joining the Spaniards. One by one, Mesoamerican communities that had

A map of the route taken by Hernán Cortés from the east coast to the Aztec capital of Tenochtitlán. *The Art Archive/Museo Ciudad Mexico/Dagli Orti.*

long been subjects of the Aztec empire stopped paying tribute (payments of goods or labor that conquered nations were required to contribute to the empire) to Tenochtitlán. When Cortés was ready to make a renewed attack on Tenochtitlán, his small army of Spaniards had the support of about 150,000 Amerindian warriors.

Tenochtitlán was located on an island in Lake Texcoco, so it had natural protection on all sides. Unfortunately for the Aztecs, Cortés had crafted a new battle strategy that took this into account. First he had his men build thirteen boats, and then he moved his large army to the shores of the lake. On April 28, 1521, Cortés began the seventy-five-day siege of Tenochtitlán. He started by placing his fleet of ships in the waters surrounding the city and his troops at the shore end of each of the causeways (roads built over the water) that led into the city. Tenochtitlán had three causeways: each one was several miles long and 20 to 30 feet (6 to 9 meters) wide. With this strategy, he was able to establish a blockade, ensuring that no food or water could reach the island from the mainland. Then the Spanish attacked, charging into the city from every entry. The Aztecs resisted the invasion fiercely, initially giving up little ground. After a time, though, the blockade and smallpox had ravaged the population of Tenochtitlán. The Aztec people were dying of starvation or dysentery (disease causing severe diarrhea), and the warriors had grown weak. But still the warriors fought on, showing remarkable bravery.

Slowly the Spanish forces worked their way through the city, killing the people and destroying the buildings as they went. The Spanish soldiers used their cannons to break down walls and level the buildings of Tenochtitlán, reducing them to rubble. Then they set the remaining buildings on fire. Meantime, the residents of the city found themselves cornered, forced to retreat but with almost nowhere to go. As the summer progressed, tens of thousands of men, women, and children crowded into the last stronghold against Spanish forces: the market area of Tlatelolco, the northern district of Tenochtitlán.

By August the situation in Tenochtitlán had grown hopeless for the Aztecs, and on August 13, 1521, they surrendered. Cuauhtémoc either gave himself up or was captured by the Spanish. The twenty-five-year-old emperor had proved a

LICA·ASI·COMO·DE·LOS·EDIFICIOS·RELIGIOSOS·Y·CIVILES·Y·REUNION·DE·LOS·CUATRO·GRANDES·SEÑORES

brave leader during the siege, and in present-day Mexico he remains a symbol of the strength of the besieged people. In some accounts of his surrender, he is said to have grabbed Cortés's dagger and pleaded to be killed since he could no longer defend his city or his people. (Cortés spared him at that time but later had him tortured and killed.) After the surrender, the Tlaxcalans, longtime enemies of the Aztecs, mercilessly slaughtered many defenseless people.

Mural depicting a busy Aztec market in Tlaxcala before the Spanish conquest. *The Art Archive/Mireille Vautier.*

After the surrender there was nothing left of the once magnificent city. Spanish soldiers reported that there were dead bodies everywhere. In his book *Historia verdadera de la conquista de Nueva España* (*The True History of the Conquest of New Spain*; also known as *The Conquest of New Spain*) Spanish conquistador **Bernal Díaz** (1492–c. 1581; see entry) described what the soldiers saw as they walked through the defeated city: "I solemnly swear that all the houses and stockades in the lake were full of heads and corpses. It was the same in the streets and courts … we could not walk without treading on the bodies and heads of dead Indians. Indeed, the stench was so bad that no one could endure it." The surviving Aztecs were sick, starved, and ragged. They tried to escape the ruins of their city, jumping into canoes or fleeing across the causeways by foot, but the Spaniards blocked the exits. Spanish troops kidnapped many of the women to keep as their concubines (women who are not wives, but live with and have sexual relations with a married man). They branded a good number of Aztec men and then forced them to work under slave-like circumstances. The Spaniards also captured the Aztec rulers, crushing any hope that the Aztecs might reclaim power. For the Aztec people who survived the siege of Tenochtitlán, there was no possibility of recovering the life and the civilization they had known.

Things to remember while reading "Elegies on the Fall of the City":

- The first poem was written soon after the fall of Tenochtitlán, around 1523. Its writers were from Tlatelolco, a district within Tenochtitlán. Tlatelolcans were citizens of Tenochtitlán, but from the founding of Tlatelolco in 1358 until 1473, they had had their own government and royalty. As you can see in this poem, the Tlatelolcans clearly felt distinct from other residents of the city.

- In the first poem, the narrator calls on Motelchiuhtzin the Huiznahuacatl, Tlacotzin the Tlailotlacatl, and Oquitzin the Tlacatecuhtli. These were the princes from the royal families of the Triple Alliance of Aztecs, Texcocans, and Tlacopáns, the confederacy of powers that ruled over the entire empire.

- The second poem addresses the capture of Cuauhtémoc, the last Aztec emperor. After conquering Tenochtitlán, Cortés took him to his base in a section of Mexico City called Coyoacan. Imprisoned in Coyoacan with Cuauhtémoc were Coanacoch (pronounced coe-AH-nah-coach), the king of Texcoco, and Tetlepanquetzal (tet-lay-pahn-KAYT-sal), the king of Tlacopán. These were the three kings of the Triple Alliance.

- The second poem refers to Doña Isabel, a daughter of Montezuma II. After the conquest, Cortés (referred to as the "Captain-General" in the poem) set up a house in Coyoacan and brought his interpreter and mistress, **Malinche** (c. 1501–c. 1550; see entry), to live with him. Then, as was customary for a victor in battle, he brought the daughters of the fallen Aztec ruler into his own household. Montezuma's daughters were Doña Isabel, Doña Maria, Doña Ana, and Doña Marina. Doña Isabel would later become pregnant with Cortés's baby.

- The third poem is written in the tradition the Aztecs called *xochicuicatl* (pronounced show-chee-kwee-CAH-tul), or "flowers and songs." Poems of this kind were created by elite poet-philosophers called *tlamatinime*. The poems were highly philosophical, yet often personal, and the poets presented their ideas in beautiful or powerful images. The word "flower" in these poems is used as a metaphor (a word that is used to refer to something that it is being compared to) for art and poetry. Traditionally, the creators of "flowers and songs" found hope and comfort in art, but this poem is also an *icnocuicatl,* or "song of sorrow."

"Elegies on the Fall of the City"

"The Fall of Tenochtitlan"

Our cries of grief rise up
and our tears rain down,
for Tlatelolco is lost.
The Aztecs are fleeing across the lake;

Illustration of the bloody battle for Tenochtitlán between the Spaniards and the Aztecs. *The Art Archive/Antochiw Collection of Mexico/Mireille Vautier.*

Tlacatecuhtli: "Chief of men," the top person in the city-state who presided over both religious and military matters.

they are running away like women.
How can we save our homes, my people?
The Aztecs are deserting the city:
the city is in flames, and all
is darkness and destruction.
Motelchiuhtzin the Huiznahuacatl,
Tlacotzin the Tlailotlacatl,
Oquitzin the **Tlacatecuhtli**
are greeted with tears.
Weep, my people:
know that with these disasters

we have lost the Mexican nation.
The water has turned bitter,
our food is bitter!
These are the acts of the **Giver of Life**....

"The Imprisonment of Cuauhtemoc"

The Aztecs are **besieged** in the city;
the Tlatelolcas are besieged in the city!
The walls are black,
the air is black with smoke,
the guns flash in the darkness.
They have captured Cuauhtemoc;
they have captured the princes of Mexico.
The Aztecs are besieged in the city;
the Tlatelolcas are besieged in the city!
After nine days, they were taken to Coyoacan:
Cuauhtemoc, **Coanacoch, Tetlepanquetzaltzin.**
The kings are prisoners now.
Tlacotzin consoled them:
"Oh my nephews, take heart!
The kings are prisoners now;
they are bound with chains."
The king Cuauhtemoc replied:
"Oh my nephew, you are a prisoner;
they have bound you in irons.
"But who is that at the side of the **Captain-General**?
Ah, it is Dona Isabel, my little niece!
Ah, it is true: the kings are prisoners now!
"You will be a slave and belong to another:
the collar will be fashioned in Coyoacan,
where the **quetzal** feathers will be woven.
"Who is that at the side of the Captain-General?
Ah, it is Dona Isabel, my little niece!
Ah, it is true: the kings are prisoners now!"

"Flowers and Songs of Sorrow"

Nothing but flowers and songs of sorrow
are left in Mexico and Tlatelolco,
where once we saw warriors and wise men.
We know it is true
that we must **perish**,
for we are **mortal** men.

Giver of Life: A form of address to a god who has created or sustains human life.

Besieged: Surrounded with armed forces.

Coanacoch: The king of Texcoco; one of the three kings in the Triple Alliance.

Tetlepanquetzaltzin: Tetlepanquetzal, the king of Tlacopán; one of the three kings in the Triple Alliance.

Captain-General: Hernán Cortés.

Quetzal: A bright green-feathered bird from Central America considered sacred in most Mesoamerican religions.

Perish: Die.

Mortal: Subject to death; human.

You, the Giver of Life,
you have ordained it.
We wander here and there
*in our **desolate** poverty.*
We are mortal men.
We have seen bloodshed and pain
*where once we saw beauty and **valor**.*
We are crushed to the ground;
we lie in ruins.
There is nothing but grief and suffering
in Mexico and Tlatelolco,
where once we saw beauty and valor.
Have you grown weary of your servants?
Are you angry with your servants,
O Giver of Life?

Desolate: Miserable.

Valor: Bravery.

What happened next ...

Cortés promised Cuauhtémoc that the Spanish would treat him with dignity after his surrender. While Cuauhtémoc was in captivity, however, Cortés's soldiers began to revolt because they felt they had not received enough rewards for their efforts in conquering Tenochtitlán. Cortés allowed his men to torture Cuauhtémoc, hoping he might reveal the location of more gold or treasure. Cuauhtémoc told them nothing. In 1522 (some sources say 1523 or 1525) Cortés made a vague accusation of "conspiracy" against Cuauhtémoc and the two other Triple Alliance kings, Coanacoch and Tetlepanquetzal. As a result, he had all three kings hanged.

The Spanish extended their rule outside the city of Tenochtitlán until most of the people of the vast former empire fell under their power. Over the next century the populations of these native peoples dwindled. The Spanish were ruthless in killing the Aztec priests, whom they considered agents of the devil, especially after hearing reports from Spanish soldiers who had witnessed their comrades being sacrificed. In Tenochtitlán, the Spanish missionaries began their work immediately, converting the people to Christianity.

Soon most of the Nahuatl-speaking people in the empire had adopted the Roman Catholic religion; some accepted it only to avoid death or punishment, but others embraced it sincerely. In their efforts to convert the population, the missionaries burned all the codices (Aztec painted books) they could find and eliminated many other cultural artifacts of the Aztecs in their efforts to convert the population. Some Aztecs clung to their own gods, worshiping in private. These people kept the native religion alive, and some present-day groups continue to worship the traditional Aztec gods.

After the conquistadores had defeated the Aztecs at Tenochtitlán, they felt they deserved rewards. The Spanish government reluctantly agreed to an *encomienda* system, giving the conquistadores land grants that allowed them to use all the Amerindians in a particular region as unpaid laborers. Under this system, the *encomendero,* or grant holder, was supposed to give the Amerindians training in Christianity and the Spanish language and to protect them from invasion. The Amerindians, in turn, were to pay tribute to the conquistador. Conditions for the various Amerindian groups differed: some suffered and even died while working under conditions similar to slavery; others simply began paying tribute to the Spaniards, just as they had previously done with the Aztec rulers.

Did you know ...

- Miguel León-Portilla took most of the text for his book *The Broken Spears* from the *Florentine Codex* (more properly called the *General History of Things in New Spain*), a twelve-volume book compiled by Bernardino de Sahagún and his talented group of native assistants. Sahagún arrived in Mexico in 1529, just eight years after the conquest, to teach at a missionary school near Tenochtitlán. While he was teaching his young native students religion and the arts in Spanish and Latin, Sahagún took it upon himself to learn about Aztec culture and the Nahuatl language, beginning a lifetime of research.

- In the 1540s he conducted a series of interviews with Aztec elders (older people in a community who understand its history and traditions). Bit by bit, the elders described to him the history and traditions of the Aztec people. With the help of Nahuatl-speaking assistants, Sahagún recorded the words of the elders in their own language. By about 1580 the manuscript of his book, the *Florentine Codex*, was complete. The *Florentine Codex* is organized by subject, with volumes dedicated to such topics as history, the gods, the calendar, Aztec society, and the Aztec perception of the natural world. Its pages present a column of Nahuatl text on the right, comments in Spanish in a column on the left, and illustrations in between. The book is considered the most comprehensive resource about the native people of Mesoamerica.

Consider the following ...

- Form a small group with your classmates. Read the poems out loud and then discuss them.

- Compare the poem "Flowers and Songs of Sorrow" with the poem called "Song of Springtime" (see **Nezahualcoyotl** entry). Note the differences and the similarities between the two poems.

For More Information

Books

The Broken Spears: The Aztec Account of the Conquest of Mexico. Edited by Miguel León-Portilla. Translated by Angel Maria Garibay K. and Lysander Kemp. Boston: Beacon Press, 1992.

Clendinnen, Inga. *Aztecs: An Interpretation*. Cambridge, England: Cambridge University Press, 1991.

Díaz (del Castillo), Bernal. *The Conquest of New Spain*. Translated with an introduction by J. M. Cohen. London and New York: Penguin Books, 1963.

Fifteen Poets of the Aztec World. Edited and translated by Miguel León-Portilla. Norman: University of Oklahoma Press, 1992.

Lanyon, Anna. *Malinche's Conquest*. Crows Nest, Australia: Allen and Unwin, 1999.

Thomas, Hugh. *Conquest: Montezuma, Cortés, and the Fall of Old Mexico*. New York: Simon and Schuster, 1993.

Periodicals

Wyss, Hilary E. "Missionaries in the Classroom: Bernardino de Sahagun, John Eliot, and the Teaching of Colonial Indigenous Texts from New Spain and New England." *Early American Literature* (fall 2003): p. 505.

Web Sites

"Aztecs: Conquest." *Empires Past: Thinkquest.* http://library.thinkquest. org/16325/y-conq.html (accessed on November 22, 2004).

León-Portilla, Miguel. "Bernardino de Sahagun and the Codex Florentine." *Codex Florentine.* http://codiceflorentino.tripod.com/english.htm (accessed on November 21, 2004).

Where to Learn More

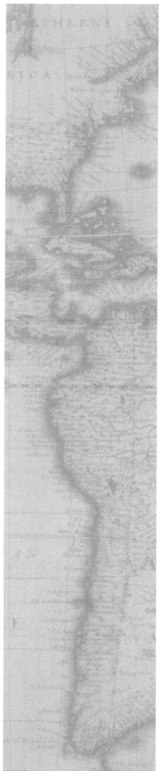

Books

Adorno, Rolena. *Guaman Poma: Writing and Resistance in Colonial Peru.* Austin: University of Texas Press, 1994.

Ascher, Marcia, and Robert Ascher. *Code of the Quipu: Databook.* I & II. Ann Arbor: University of Michigan Press, 1978 and 1988.

Ascher, Marcia, and Robert Ascher. *Code of the Quipu: A Study in Media, Mathematics, and Culture.* New York: Dover Publications, 1997.

Berdan, Frances, and Patricia Rieff Anawalt. *The Essential Codex Mendoza.* Berkeley: University of California Press, 1997.

Betanzos, Juan de. *Narrative of the Incas.* Translated and edited by Roland Hamilton and Dana Buchanan from the Palma de Mallorca manuscript. Austin: University of Texas Press, 1996.

Boone, Elizabeth Hill. *Aztec World.* Montreal, Canada, and Washington, DC: St. Remy Press and Smithsonian Institution, 1994.

The Broken Spears: The Aztec Account of the Conquest of Mexico. Miguel León-Portilla, ed. Translated from Nahuatl to Spanish by Angel Maria Garibay K. English Translation by Lysander Kemp. Boston: Beacon Press, 1992.

Burland, C. A. *Montezuma: Lord of the Aztecs.* New York: G. P. Putnam's Sons, 1973.

Byland, Bruce E. "Introduction and Commentary." In *The Codex Borgia: A Full-Color Restoration of the Ancient Mexican Manuscript.* New York: Dover Publications, 1993.

Cerwin, Herbert. *Bernal Díaz: Historian of the Conquest.* Norman: University of Oklahoma, 1963.

Clendinnen, Inga. *Aztecs: An Interpretation.* Cambridge, England: Cambridge University Press, 1991.

Coe, Michael D. *Mexico: From the Olmecs to the Aztecs.* 4th ed. London and New York: Thames and Hudson, 1994.

Coe, Michael D., and Mark Van Stone. *Reading the Maya Glyphs.* London and New York: Thames and Hudson, 2001.

Davies, Nigel. *The Ancient Kingdoms of Peru.* London and New York: Penguin Books, 1997.

Díaz, Bernal. *The Conquest of New Spain.* Translated by J. M. Cohen. London and New York: Penguin Books, 1963.

Díaz, Gisele, and Alan Rodgers. *The Codex Borgia: A Full–Color Restoration of the Ancient Mexican Manuscript.* New York: Dover Publications, 1993.

Duran, Diego. *Book of the Gods and Rites and the Ancient Calendar.* Norman: University of Oklahoma Press, 1971.

Fagan, Brian. *Kingdoms of Gold, Kingdoms of Jade: The Americas before Columbus.* London and New York: Thames and Hudson, 1991.

Galvin, Irene Flum. *The Ancient Maya.* New York: Benchmark Books, 1997.

Garcilaso de la Vega, El Inca. *Royal Commentaries of the Incas and General History of Peru: Part One.* Translated by Harold V. Livermore. Austin & London: University of Texas Press, 1966.

Henderson, John S. *The World of the Ancient Maya.* 2nd ed. Ithaca, NY, and London: Cornell University Press, 1977.

Kandell, Jonathan. *La Capital: The Biography of Mexico City.* New York: Random House, 1988.

Lanyon, Anna. *Malinche's Conquest.* Crows Nest, NSW, Australia: Allen and Unwin, 1999.

León-Portilla, Miguel. *Fifteen Poets of the Aztec World.* Norman: University of Oklahoma Press, 1992.

Malpass, Michael A. *Daily Life in the Inca Empire.* Westport, CT: Greenwood Press, 1996.

Meyer, Michael C., and William L. Sherman. *The Course of Mexican History.* 5th ed. New York and Oxford: Oxford University Press, 1995.

Newsome, Elizabeth A. *Trees of Paradise and Pillars of the World: The Serial Stela Cycle of "18-Rabbit-God K," King of Copan.* Austin: University of Texas Press, 2001.

Nicholson, H. B. *Topiltzin Quetzalcoatl: The Once and Future Lord of the Toltecs.* Boulder: University of Colorado Press, 1999.

Sarmiento de Gamboa, Pedro. *History of the Incas.* Translated by Clements Markham. Cambridge, England: The Hakluyt Society, 1907.

Thomas, Hugh. *Conquest: Montezuma, Corés, and the Fall of Old Mexico.* New York: Simon & Schuster, 1993.

Time-Life Books. *Incas: Lords of Gold and Glory.* Alexandria, VA: Time-Life Books, 1992.

Townsend, Richard F. *The Aztecs.* London and New York: Thames and Hudson, 2000.

Urton, Gary. *Signs of the Inka Khipu: Binary Coding in the Andean Knotted-String Records.* Austin: University of Texas Press, 2003.

Von Hagen, Adriana, and Craig Morris. *The Cities of the Ancient Andes.* London and New York: Thames and Hudson, 1998.

Web Sites

Adorno, Rolena. "Early Peruvian Recorded Daily Life Under the Rule of Spanish Conquistadors." *The New World,* Spring 1990. http://muweb.millersville.edu/~columbus/data/art/ADORNO01.ART (accessed on December 8, 2004).

"The Ancient Aztecs. Technology: Calendars." *Oracle Think Quest.* http://library.thinkquest.org/27981/calendar.html (accessed on December 8, 2004).

"Aztec." *Ancient Scripts.com.* http://www.ancientscripts.com/aztec.html (accessed on December 8, 2004).

"Aztec Calendar." *Artcamp.* http://www.artcamp.com.mx/AZ/4.html (accessed on December 8, 2004).

"Aztec Poetry." http://www.carnaval.com/dead/aztec_poetry.htm (accessed on December 8, 2004).

"Bernal Díaz: Travel Narrative Resources." *World History Sources.* http://chnm.gmu.edu/worldhistorysources/unpacking/travelanalysis.html (accessed on December 8, 2004).

"Calendars and the Long Count System." *Tikal Park.* http://www.tikalpark.com/calendar.htm (accessed on December 8, 2004).

Cámara Riess, Francisco. "Pacal's Tomb." *Mundo Maya Online.* http://www.mayadiscovery.com/ing/archaeology/default.htm (accessed on December 8, 2004).

"Codex Mendoza." *Latino Studies Resources, Indiana University, Bloomington.* http://www.latinamericanstudies.org/codex-mendoza.htm (accessed on December 8, 2004).

"The Conquest of the Inca Empire: Francisco Pizarro." *The Applied History Research Group/The University of Calgary.* http://www.acs.ucalgary.ca/applied_history/tutor/eurvoya/inca.html (accessed on December 8, 2004).

"Conquistadors: The Aztec Empire." *Oregon Public Broadcasting and PBS Online.* http://www.pbs.org/opb/conquistadors/mexico/adventure1/b3.htm (accessed on December 8, 2004).

Criscenzo, Jeeni. "Temple of the Inscriptions." *Jaguar Sun.* http://www.jaguar-sun.com/temple.html (accessed on December 8, 2004).

Curl, John. "The Flower Songs of the Hungry Coyote: Poet of Ancient Mexico." Translated by John Curl. *Red Coral.* http://www.red-coral.net/Hungry.html (accessed on December 8, 2004).

"Felipe Guaman Poma de Ayala: El primer nueva corónica y buen gobierno (1615/1616)." *The Guaman Poma Website: A Digital Research Center of the Royal Library, Copenhagen, Denmark.* Department of Manuscripts and Rare Books, Det Kongelige Bibliotek. http://www.kb.dk/elib/mss/poma/ (accessed on December 8, 2004).

Fought, Steven. "Maya Arithmetic." *The Math Forum.* http://mathforum.org/k12/mayan.math/ (accessed on December 8, 2004).

"Garcilaso Inca de la Vega." *Selections from the Library of José Durand: University of Notre Dame Rare Books and Special Collections.* http://www.rarebooks.nd.edu/exhibits/durand/biographies/garcilaso.html (accessed on December 8, 2004).

"John Pohl's Mesoamerica: Ancient Books: Highlands México Codices." *FAMSI: Foundation for the Advancement of Mesoamerican Studies.* http://www.famsi.org/research/pohl/jpcodices/index.html (accessed on December 8, 2004).

León-Portilla, Miguel. "Bernadino de Sahagun and the Codex Florentine." http://codiceflorentino.tripod.com/english.htm (accessed on December 8, 2004).

"Letter from Hernando Pizarro to the Royal Audience of Santo Domingo," in *Reports on the Discovery of Peru,* 1872. http://www.shsu.edu/~his_ncp/Pizarro.html (accessed on December 8, 2004).

"Lost King of the Maya" (transcript: PBS airdate February 13, 2001). *Nova Science Programming On Air and Online.* http://www.pbs.org/wgbh/nova/transcripts/2804maya.html (accessed on December 8, 2004).

Mann, Charles C. "Anthropology: Cracking the Khipu Code." *Science Magazine,* June 13, 2003. http://209.157.64.200/focus/f-news/928058/posts (accessed on December 8, 2004).

"The Maya Calendar." *Maya World Studies Center.* http://www.mayacalendar.com/f-cuenta.html (accessed on December 8, 2004).

"Maya Mathematics." *Maya Astronomy Page.* http://www.michielb.nl/maya/math.html (accessed on December 8, 2004).

"The Maya Number System." *Oracle Think Quest Education Foundation.* http://library.thinkquest.org/J0112511/mayan_number.htm (accessed on December 8, 2004).

"The Mayan Calendar." *Calendars Through the Ages.* http://webexhibits.org/calendars/calendar-mayan.html (accessed on December 8, 2004).

McNally, Shelagh. "City of Kings." *Mundo Maya Online.* http://www.mayadiscovery.com/ing/archaeology/default.htm (accessed on December 8, 2004).

Meyer, Peter. "The Maya Calendar." *Hermetic Systems.* http://www.her metic.ch/cal_stud/maya/chap1.htm#5 (accessed on December 8, 2004).

Murphy, Vincent. "Copan: In the Valley of the Kings." *Mundo Maya.* http://www.mayadiscovery.com/ing/archaeology/default.htm (accessed on December 8, 2004).

Pohl, Mary E., Kevin O. Pope, and Christopher von Nagy. "Olmec Origins of Mesoamerican Writing." http://www.anthro.fsu.edu/re search/meso/Pohltext.doc (accessed on December 8, 2004).

Poma de Ayala, Felipe Huaman. "Extracts from *The First New Chronicle and Good Government.* Translated by David Frye. http://www-personal. umich.edu/~dfrye/guaman.htm (accessed on December 8, 2004).

"Popol Vuh: The Mayan Book of the Dawn of Life." Translated, and with commentary, by Dennis Tedlock, 1985. *University of Wisconsin, Eau Claire.* http://www.uwec.edu/greider/Indigenous/Popol_Vuh/Popol %20Vuh.htm (accessed on December 8, 2004).

Popson, Colleen P. "Earliest Mesoamerican Writing?" *Archaeology,* March/April 2003. http://www.archaeology.org/0303/newsbriefs/ olmec.html (accessed on December 8, 2004).

Potier, Beth. "String Theorist: Anthropologist Gary Urton Untangles the Mystery of Inkan Khipus." *Harvard University Gazette,* May 22, 2003. http://www.news.harvard.edu/gazette/2003/05.22/03-urton.html (accessed on December 8, 2004).

"Realms of the Sacred in Daily Life: Early Written Records of Mesoamerica." *University of California, Irvine.* http://www.lib.uci.edu/libraries/ exhibits/meso/sacred.html (accessed on December 8, 2004).

Rojas, Sal. "The Great Aztec Sun Stone." *BrownPride.com.* http://www. brownpride.com/history/history.asp?a=aztecs/sunstonehistory (accessed on December 8, 2004).

Senior, Meghan. *Time and the Aztec Mind: The Aztec Calendar Sun Stone in Context.* http://rubens.anu.edu.au/student.projects97/aztec/ACal Stone.html/ACAL.html (accessed on December 8, 2004.)

Stuart, David. "Hieroglyphs and History at Copán." *Altar Q and Copán.* Peabody Museum, Harvard University. http://www.peabody.harvard. edu/Copan/text.html (accessed on December 8, 2004).

Stuart, George E. "City of Kings and Commoners: Copán." *National Geographic,* October 1989. http://muweb.millersville.edu/~columbus/ data/art/STUART01.ART (accessed on December 8, 2004).

"Tour Copán with David Stuart." *Nova Science Programming On Air and Online.* http://www.pbs.org/wgbh/nova/maya/copa_transcript.html (accessed on December 8, 2004).

"Who Is Buried in Pakal's Tomb?" *Mesoweb.* http://www.mesoweb. com/palenque/features/sarcophagus/pakals_tomb.html (accessed on December 8, 2004).

Wilford, John Noble. "The Khipu: String, and Knot, Theory of Inca Writing." *New York Times,* August 12, 2003. http://www.ee.ryerson.ca:8080/ ~elf/abacus/inca-khipu.html (accessed on December 8, 2004).

Index

clothing of, 266
Cortés and, 168, 189, 241–45,
    250, 254–57, 266–68, 267
    (ill.)
death of, 245, 250, 257, 272
Díaz on, 266–68
headdress of, 243 (ill.)
life of, 236–37
rule of, 158, 238–40
Spanish conquest and, 154–55,
    240–45
Montezuma Ikhuicamina. *See*
    Montezuma I
Montezuma Xocoyotzin. *See*
    Montezuma II
Months, patron, 104
Moon Jaguar, 113, 114
Mortality, 279
Motecuhzoma Xocoyótzin. *See*
    Montezuma II
Motelchiuhtzin the Huiznahua-
    catl, 276
Mother of Mexico, 258–59
Mummies, 18–19
Musk, 266
Myths. *See* Creation myths

N

Nahuatl language, 211, 227,
    247–48, 252–53
Narrative of the Incas (Betanzos),
    3, 9, 21–31, 57, 58
Nemontemi, 182
New Fire Ceremony, 182–83, 218
Newborn Thunderbolt, 141
Newsome, Elizabeth, 117
Nezahualcoyotl, 154, 158,
    221–33, 224 (ill.)
laws of, 225
life of, 222–26
Montezuma I and, 173, 176–77
Poem 1, 228–29
Poem 2, 229–30
Poem 3, 230–31
poetry of, 221, 226–30
rule of, 225–26
"Song of Springtime," 232–33
Nezahualpilli, 225
Ninancuyoci, 53
Nobles
    Aztec, 179

Inca, 24, 25, 26, 27–29, 64
Nomadic life, 7
Number systems
    Arabic, 91, 95
    bar and dot, 84, 87–92, 89
        (ill.), 90 (ill.), 103, 118
    decimal, 35, 88, 90
    Inca, 33, 35, 37–38
    Maya, 73, 87–92
    Olmec, 82, 87
    Roman, 91
    vigesimal, 88, 90, 91, 102
    Zapotec, 87
Nurturers, 145

O

Oaxaca Valley, Mexico, 74, 77, 84
Obeisance, gestures of, 29
Obsidian blade, 185
Obsidian Serpent. *See* Itzcoatl
Obsidian Snake. *See* Itzcoatl
Olmec
    calendars, 82, 84, 93
    history of, 74, 77, 78, 82
    Long Count, 101–2
    Maya and, 73
    number systems, 82, 87
    writing systems, 81–86
Olmec Stone Roller Stamp, 76,
    77, 81–86, 83 (ill.), 84 (ill.)
Omens, 240
Oquitzin the Tlacatecuhtli, 276
Oral tradition
    Aztec, 161–62, 174, 178–79,
        221–22
    Quiché Maya, 139, 142
    quipu and, 34–35
    Toltec, 168–69
Orejones, 24, 28
Oxford University, 217

P

Pacal, 76, 78, **127–36,** 127 (ill.)
Pachacutec, 11–19, 11 (ill.)
    Betanzos on, 2–3, 24, 25–29
    Chancas and, 8, 12–13
    rule of, 1–3, 23–24
Pachacuti. *See* Pachacutec

Palenque, Mexico
  abandonment of, 135
  architecture, 73, 78, 128,
    129–35, 130 (ill.)
  rulers of, 78, 127, 131, 132
  stelae, 111
  Temple of Inscriptions,
    130–34, 130 (ill.)
Panuco, 178
Paris Codex, 149, 197
Patron months, 104
Peasants. *See* Working class
Perish, defined, 279
Perpetual, defined, 26, 45
Philip III (King), 65, 69
Pierno, 47
Pizarro, Francisco
  Atahuallpa and, 4, 9, 55–56,
    60, 66–67, 67 (ill.)
  Doña Angelina Yupanqui and,
    3
  Poma de Ayala on, 69
Pizarro, Hernando, 44, 56
Place of Reeds. *See* Tula, Mexico
Plague. *See* Epidemics
Plumed Serpent. *See* Sovereign
  Plumed Serpent
Poetry
  Aztec, 154, 155, 221–33,
    271–83
  Inca, 23
  interpretation of, 227, 232
  of Nezahualcoyotl, 221–33
  quipu and, 34–35
Pohl, Mary, 81–82, 84, 85
Poma de Ayala, Felipe Huaman,
    9, **63–71**. *See also La primer
    nueva corónica y buen gobierno*
  on Atahuallpa, 61 (ill.), 66–69,
    67 (ill.), 68 (ill.)
  illustrations of, 61 (ill.), 63,
    66–69, 70
  life of, 63–65
  on *quipu*, 38 (ill.)
  Spanish conquest and, 64–65,
    66, 69
Pomar, Juan Bautista, 231
Pope, Kevin, 85
Popol Vuh, 76, 79, **137–50**
  background of, 137–38
  Part One, 142–47
  replacement of, 139–40
  text of, 140–49

Popoluca language, 248
Porters, 46
Portocarrero, Alonso Hernándex,
    252, 254
Portresses, 46
Post-Classic era, 74, 75, 138
Potonchan, Mexico, 249
Pottery, Maya, 146 (ill.)
Pre-Classic era, 74
Pre-Columbian civilizations, 73
Pre-Hispanic codices, 196–99
Priest-rulers, Toltec, 166
Priests
  Aztec, 181, 195–96, 280
  Maya, 93–94
  Mesoamerican, 205–6
  *La primer nueva corónica y buen go-
    bierno* (Poma de Ayala), 4, 9,
    38 (ill.), 61 (ill.), 63, 65–70
Principal wives, 29, 52, 237
Prisoners of war, 238–39
Proskouriakoff, Tatiana, 107
Puberty ceremony, 52
Pulque, 164
Puma, 145
Pyramids, 130–34, 177–78. *See
  also* Architecture

Q

Quarters, 45
Quechua language, 2, 17, 21, 23,
    64, 65–66, 69
Quetzal bird, 144, 144 (ill.), 165,
    279
Quetzal bird snake. *See* Quetzal-
  coatl
Quetzal plumage, 229
Quetzalcoatl, 161 (ill.), 168 (ill.)
  Codex Borgia on, 200
  cult of, 164
  Kukulcán and, 141
  Nezahualcoyotl and, 227
  Spanish conquest and, 167–68,
    240–41
  Topiltzin-Quetzalcoatl and,
    162, 163
  worship of, 165
Quiché Maya
  history of, 75, 137–38, 148
  modern, 149
  Popol Vuh and, 76, 79, 137